P9-APT-347

People of the Mandate

About the author:

Canadian author **W. Harold Fuller** is Vice-Chairman of the International Council of World Evangelical Fellowship. He is also a member of the executive of the Evangelical Fellowship of Canada and of the North America Council of WEF. He was a founding member of the Association of Evangelicals in Africa and of the Nigerian Evangelical Fellowship.

An editor for over 40 years, Fuller is the author of nine books and numerous articles. He and his wife, Lorna, continue their ministry based in Canada, where he was born of British missionary parents. The Fullers themselves served in Africa for 26 years with SIM (founded as Sudan Interior Mission, now Society for International Ministries) and have ministered for the gospel in six continents. During their travels they have had personal contact with many of their contemporaries named in this book.

WITHDRAWN

WORLD EVANGELICAL FELLOWSHIP PUBLICATIONS

Outreach and Identity Series

The Biblical Doctrine of Regeneration
Contextualization: A Theology of Gospel and Culture
Evangelicals and Social Ethics
The Unique Christ in our Pluralistic World
An Evangelical Response to Confessing the One Faith
Evangelical Christianity and the Environment
Pornography: A Christian Critique
Karl Barth's Theology of Mission
Theology and the Third World Church
Sharing Good News with the Poor
Theology of Theological Education

BR
1640
.A2
F85
1996

People of the Mandate

The story of the World Evangelical Fellowship

Harold Fuller

Foreword by Luis Palau

WEF

GOSHEN COLLEGE LIBRARY
GOSHEN, INDIANA

BAKER BOOK HOUSE
Grand Rapids, Michigan

Copyright © W. Harold Fuller, World Evangelical Fellowship 1996

First published 1996 jointly by WEF in association with Paternoster
Publishing, P.O. Box 300, Carlisle, Cumbria, CA3 OQS, U.K and Baker
Book House, Box 6287, Grand Rapids, MI 49516–6287, USA.

02 01 00 99 98 97 96   7 6 5 4 3 2 1

Scripture quotations taken from the HOLY BIBLE,
Copyright 1973, 1978, 1984 by International Bible Society.
Used by permission of Hodder & Stoughton Limited.
All rights reserved.

'NIV' is a registered trademark of International Bible Society.
UK trademark number 1448790

Unless otherwise stated, demographic and religious statistics are quoted
from Patrick Johnstone, *Operation World*
(Carlisle, OM Publishing, 1993).

The right of W. Harold Fuller to be identified as the Author of this Work
has been asserted by him in accordance with the Copyright, Designs and
Patents Act 1988.

*All rights reserved. No part of this publication may be reproduced, stored
in a retrieval system, or transmitted in any form or by any means,
electronic, mechanical, photocopying, recording or otherwise, without the
prior permission of the publisher or a license permitting restricted
copying. In the U.K. such licenses are issued by the Copyright Licensing
Agency, 90 Tottenham Court Road, London W1P 9HE.*

British Library Cataloguing in Publication Data

A catalogue record for this book is available from the British Library.

ISBN 1-900890-00-3
(WEF)
Library of Congress Cataloging-in-Publication Data

A catalogue record for this book is available from the Library of Congress

ISBN 0-8010-2134-0
(Baker Book House)

Printed and bound in Great Britain

DEDICATED TO
the memory of
the People of the Mandate who,
in the unity of the Spirit,
established the Evangelical Alliance in 1846,

and with thanksgiving
for all who continue to fulfil that vision
through the World Evangelical Fellowship.

COMMENTS ON THE WORLD EVANGELICAL FELLOWSHIP

WEF is the whole church reaching the whole world with the whole Gospel. In WEF we learn from one another and provide strength of genuine oneness in Christ.

Tokunboh Adeyemo, Africa

WEF has helped us to understand what it means to function as an evangelical fellowship, to grow into an effective organization for the work of the gospel.

John Champion, South Pacific

Since its beginning, the World Evangelical Fellowship has been a major force in uniting evangelicals throughout the world. I have been deeply interested in its work and I rejoice in the unique ministry God has given it. My earnest hope is that it will be used in an even greater way in the future to draw evangelical Christians together as we seek to proclaim Christ in these ominous and exciting times.

Billy Graham

WEF provides us with a model and ideas, enabling us in Europe to interact with Christians around the world and gain a perspective in what God is saying to the Body of Christ, the church. Through WEF, we gain practical help in matters such as religious liberty and thinking through theology – both important in the stressful circumstances Europe is going through.

Stuart McAllister, Europe

WEF's vision is extraordinary – in its mission outreach, its unity, and its integrity. It provides us in Latin America with a framework and connects us to churches worldwide. That is very important to us.

Reuben Proietti, Latin America

WEF is the structure through which evangelicals in the Caribbean can link with other evangelicals around the world in proclaiming a wholistic Gospel to the ends of the earth.

Gerry Seale, Caribbean

WEF provides an effective forum which enables national and regional fellowships to join in prayer and fellowship. We can share our concerns and our experiences. It also enables us to make a biblical response to international issues that affect Asia.

Francis Sunderaraj, India

There are many fine programs and organizations helping the church, but WEF represents and helps the Body of Christ worldwide in a special, wholistic way.

Joshua Tsutada, Japan

Contents

Foreword

By Luis Palau

Fulfilling the Great Commission in every generation is possible only through the co-operation of the entire Body of Christ – men and women 'from every tribe and language and people and nation' whom Christ has purchased with his blood (Rev. 5:9).

The World Evangelical Fellowship has encouraged this unity among evangelicals, reminding us we are part of a church worldwide and keeping the apostle Paul's vision before us:

> Make every effort to keep the unity of the Spirit through the bond of peace. There is one body and one Spirit—just as you were called to one hope when you were called—one Lord, one faith, one baptism; one God and Father of all, who is over all and through all and in all (Ephesians 4:3–6).

Christians throughout church history have believed that the church worldwide is expected to be one because of the prayer of Jesus Christ in John 17.[1]

Despite denominational differences in forms of worship and organization, despite cultural diversity and regional variations, despite economic turmoil through the centuries, Christians have desired to work together, embrace one another, encourage one another, and represent the Body of Christ to the world in a measure of unity.

In its present form, the World Evangelical Fellowship came into being as a response in the last 150 years to that deep longing

---

[1]'My prayer is not for them alone. I pray also for those who will believe in me through their message, that all of them may be one, Father, just as you are in me and I am in you. May they also be in us so that the world may believe that you have sent me. I have given them the glory that you gave me, that they may be one as we are one: I in them and you in me. May they be brought to complete unity to let the world know that you sent me and have loved them even as you have loved me' (vv 20–23).

nourished by a shared belief in the death and resurrection of Jesus
Christ and his return in power and great glory.

PROMOTING UNITY

WEF promotes unity primarily through its national fellowships. I
well remember taking part in the 1980 Consultation on World
Evangelization in Pattaya, Thailand. Forty of us Latin American
representatives gathered spontaneously to study the creation of an
entity that could open communication channels between leaders,
churches and service organizations across Latin America. We
formed an *ad hoc* committee under the name CONELA – the
Consultation of Evangelicals in Latin America – with a mandate to
call a continent-wide meeting by early 1982. Some 200 distinguished
Latin American evangelical leaders met in Panama that April, and
CONELA was officially launched.[2]

At the time, it was hard to overemphasize the importance of
CONELA's task. Leftist ideologies were penetrating the Latin
American church, and there was no united defence of the biblical
gospel, nor offensive as to how Christians should apply biblical
principles in their churches.

Numbering some twenty million Christians scattered among
Latin America's 300 million people, the evangelical church was at
a crossroads. Would it move ahead in evangelism and biblical
penetration of society, or turn to the left for spurious options that
would rob the church of its revolutionary stance on spiritual and
moral issues?

CONELA played a significant role in shepherding the shepherds
who led the flock of God through this rocky political and
socio-economic moment. The vision for CONELA, however, is
much broader and all-embracing. The founders of CONELA moved
to inspire thousands of Latin American young people to think
worldwide missions. This has come about. The leaders desired to
link arms with those of like-minded faith around the world who
have not given up on basic Christian truth and doctrine, whose
theological stand left no doubt it was orthodox, historical, revealed
Christianity as expressed in Scripture, distilled in the Apostles'
Creed, and expanded for the twentieth century in the Lausanne
Covenant.

[2]See chapter 4.

WORLDWIDE HORIZON

In recent years, the World Evangelical Fellowship has helped CON-ELA to flourish. Like any organization, CONELA ran the risk of becoming stale, but when it joined the WEF family, it was injected with new vision, new life, new expectations, and a broad worldwide horizon.

The strength of WEF is its roots in tens of thousands of local churches, which in turn gather through their national fellowships to study world trends, reaffirm basic doctrines, face together changing conditions as the decades go by, and reinforce convictions. As well, WEF can be a clearing-house in defence of oppressed, persecuted, and unjustly imprisoned Christians in various places of the world. The Evangelical Alliance of Great Britain, for instance, has been outstanding in its defence before embassies of the trampled rights of Christians. Over the next decades WEF could strengthen this role if more personnel and financial support could be garnered.

Naturally one of the risks of any organization is that it can become a bureaucracy, that its leaders perpetuate themselves over decades and begin to lose touch with grass roots realities around the world. Another risk is doctrinal deviation, which seems to affect many Christian institutions after one or two generations. WEF has been able to avoid both. On the one hand, the financial restraint of a lean budget has called for only devoted believers. The unity of the church worldwide is strong on the foundation of a biblical faith, so that neither doctrinal corruption nor institutional lethargy has set in.

New generations should embrace WEF because the vision of the Lord Jesus Christ is that we should 'make disciples of all nations' (Matt. 28:19). Christians who love the church worldwide, who love missionary work and the spread of the good news of Jesus Christ, must stimulate and motivate support for this worldwide network. May all who have the means encourage WEF's leadership so that they may fulfil their role at this critical hour of history.

Dr. Fuller's book is an historical landmark in telling WEF's story. Well-informed Christians and serious historians must read it to understand evangelicalism's great advance across the nations in the last fifty years of the twentieth century.

– Luis Palau[3]

---

[3]Evangelist Luis Palau began preaching as a teenager in his native Argentina. Today his ministry extends to six continents through public evangelistic crusades, radio, television, and books, all sponsored by the Luis Palau Evangelistic Association.

Preface

People of the Mandate?

MANDATE TO DO WHAT?

Simply put, the mandate for Christ's followers is to live his life and do his will in this troubled world. Expressed in another way, it is to serve our generation according to the will of God, as David of Israel did in his (Acts 13:36a).

That is a challenge. A challenge to demonstrate love, peace, joy – and all the other aspects of the fruit of the Spirit in a hostile world. A challenge to cry out, like the prophet Amos, for righteousness and truth in a society sold into unrighteousness. A challenge to call upon men and women to be reconciled to God, and then to one another. A challenge to ensure that no man, woman, or child, will be able to accuse us of not having done our utmost to share the Good News, the 'evangel'.

That is quite a mandate. In this book I want you to meet men and women who have accepted this mandate. They will explain why they felt compelled to accept it and how they are fulfilling it. The People of The Mandate, those who try to live by the 'evangel' and share it, are called evangelicals. They are active around the world in every race, every nation, and thousands of distinct cultures. One hundred and fifty million of them are embraced by the World Evangelical Fellowship.

Fellowship is a pleasant word. The psalmist extolled unity, and Jesus prayed that his disciples would practise it. Yet unity as an end in itself is sterile. Or it can be sought for the wrong purpose, as the story of the Tower of Babel warns us. It can lead to compromise in trying to achieve artificial oneness. A cemetery has unity, of a sort; it has harmony, in a sense. But it is dead.

When Jesus spoke of unity, he used the example of a living organism – his body. That kind of unity comes from life within, the unity of the Spirit of God. The Body of Jesus Christ on this earth is not unified for hedonistic purposes – to admire its oneness and enjoy its ease. It is a Body that has purpose, a mission – the Mandate given by God himself. The Mandate changes 'fellowship' from passive unity into dynamic partnership in the gospel (Phil. 1:5). Moreover, the Mandate is mandatory, not optional. It demands obedience. Yet fulfilling it is not just a duty; it is a joy – the life of Christ flowing through his people.

The World Evangelical Fellowship is the result of vision – a dream, if you like. Without men and women of vision and faith, WEF would not be where it is today. But worldwide, evangelicals have moved beyond the visionary stage to the reality of the market square, of advance into the front lines, of engagement in the arena.

This book explores the response of the People of the Mandate.

– WHF

Introduction

Meet the people of the mandate

The passenger beside me on the flight from Nairobi to London was a businessman returning from a holiday safari. When he learned that I worked with the church, he told me how surprised he had been to see large numbers of Kenyans going to church on Sunday.

'We have outgrown religion in Britain, I am afraid', he commented. Whatever he meant by that, I sensed that he found it difficult to explain the baffling phenomenon he had seen: crowded churches.

I was returning from a meeting of the Executive of the World Evangelical Fellowship (WEF) in Nairobi. The four of us who met were from the four quarters of the world, and were very much aware that Christianity around the globe is vibrant.

My fellow passenger was surprised to hear that whereas nominal Christianity is shrinking, evangelical Christians are growing in number, even in his own nation. He listened with interest as I explained the difference between 'religion' as a human system, and the personal experience of faith in Jesus Christ as Saviour. I also told him that evangelicals feel they have a mandate – to share the good news of the gospel with the rest of the world.

This book tells the story of the People of the Mandate, and the oneness they experience in the World Evangelical Fellowship. My fellow passenger may have been surprised to hear about evangelicals, but I have many friends who have been surprised to learn about WEF itself. Most people know about 'Amsterdam 1948 and the World Council of Churches', but 'Woudschoten 1951 and the World Evangelical Fellowship' usually does not ring a bell. Is this the world's best-kept secret?

And yet it is a truly amazing story. As I researched it, I was gripped by the lives of men and women in many cultures, in many diverse circumstances, but all experiencing the power of the living Christ in daily life.

In their diversity they find oneness in the Holy Spirit, centred around Christ as revealed in the Bible. One hundred and fifty years ago, in 1846, their predecessors proposed that they express that oneness in a global fellowship. This is the story of how that concept survived and grew into the World Evangelical Fellowship. It is the story of 150 million evangelicals helping each other to witness and worship in a changing world. (Appendix A provides a diagram showing how this co-operation functions organizationally.)

As I sat down to write, I faced a problem: how to introduce the reader to all the wonderful people of WEF and their challenging circumstances – and do it within some 250 pages. I have had to select representative stories and case studies illustrating what WEF is and what it does. I regret I have not been able to include the names of many more people and their organizations. However, I know they will understand, for the desire of us all is that Jesus Christ alone will receive the honour and glory.

In Appendix B, I do include a list of countries in which there are WEF member bodies.[1] As I interviewed many of their leaders and the WEF leadership itself, the one common comment was their awe that God had given them the privilege of being part of this worldwide ministry – part of what he is doing around the globe. I had the same feeling for myself.

On that flight from East Africa, I had some surprises for my fellow passenger. I know you also will find some happy surprises in this amazing story of the *People of the Mandate*.

W. Harold Fuller

---

[1] *WEF's structure*: Churches, para-church agencies, and individuals may become members of the National Evangelical Fellowship (sometimes called Alliance or Association) in their own nation. These NEFs become members of their Regional Evangelical Fellowship, and together they become members of the worldwide body: the World Evangelical Fellowship. WEF is administered by the International Director, who is assisted by International Staff (Commissions and Departments). He is responsible to an elected International Council.

CHAPTER 1

Putting Hands and Feet to the Vision

A runaway village boy eventually finds a worldwide family of 150 million.

'I saw a man in white standing beside you as you preached!' the Bulgarian said to Jun Vencer after the service.

A few hours earlier, Agustin 'Jun'[1] Vencer had flown in to Sofia, the capital of Bulgaria. As International Director of the World Evangelical Fellowship, he had been invited by evangelical leaders to discuss their newly-formed national fellowship, which was facing serious harassment.

'There is a prayer meeting this afternoon, and we would like you to lead us in a Bible study,' his host had told him at the airport. Vencer was suffering from jet lag and gastric flu, but he reasoned that he could muster up enough energy to give a brief Bible study to a small group of elderly men and women. At least, that is how he envisaged the group, bearing in mind the repressive Communist era just ended.

Vencer was amazed to find the church crammed with young and old. They overflowed into the aisles and filled the balcony. Vencer's weary mind tried to recall outlines he had used as a pastor in the Philippines, but nothing seemed to fit this vibrant crowd. With a quick prayer, Vencer launched into a Bible exposition.

Afterwards at the door of the church, Vencer asked the pastor what the member meant by his description of a man in white.

'He means that he saw an angel standing beside you', the pastor explained.

Vencer recalled the record of angelic manifestations in the book of Acts, but he had never expected to be part of one himself. What he did know was that God had come to his rescue in that meeting.

---

[1] In the Philippines, Vencer's homeland, 'Jun' is a common nickname, short for 'Junior'.

God gave him not only physical strength but also a powerful message that obviously met the need.

A CONFRONTATION

The next day Vencer with his travel-colleague, Dwight Gibson, met with the Bulgarian Evangelical Fellowship leaders. They were having problems gaining government approval — required by law before the Fellowship could own property, perform marriages, and conduct other legalities. They wanted the visitors to accompany them to meet the personal adviser to the President of Bulgaria. But as Vencer read a translated copy of the petition they planned to present, he became concerned. It was a very confrontational charge of discrimination against evangelicals.

'How can I get out of this?' Vencer wondered. 'I'm a guest in this country, and the hotel has already kept my passport for security reasons. Now these brothers are asking me to accompany them to deliver their list of hostile accusations. The government will be sure that I'm a rabblerouser!'

Vencer suggested that the evangelical leaders pray more about the petition, and meanwhile he prayed too. But their minds were made up, and God showed Vencer that if they wanted him to accompany them, he must be supportive.

'Lord, if it's true that you sent your angel yesterday to strengthen me, please be sure he goes ahead of me now!' Vencer prayed as the group set off for the formidable State building. They were in Sofia, the city named 'Wisdom'. They would need divine wisdom.

There was not one but a trio of presidential advisers awaiting the evangelicals. Scowling across a long table at the pastors, they had their own accusations. Ever since freedom had come in 1989, exotic cults had invaded the nation: Hare Krishnas, Mormons, Children of God, apocalyptic sects, Buddhist-type mystics, Jehovah's Witnesses. Parliament was considering a law that would recognize only three religions: Orthodox Christianity, Judaism, and Islam.

'You evangelicals open the way for these cults to enter!' the presidential advisers charged, echoing verbally the attacks made in the nation's newspapers.

Vencer's Bulgarian friends looked across at him, waiting for his input. With another prayer for wisdom, he spoke up.

'We understand your need to protect the nation from harmful groups', he told the officials. 'But may I explain what evangelicals are? They are not a cult but part of a worldwide family numbering 150 million believers. Bulgaria is one of 110 fellowships worldwide. Here in Bulgaria evangelicals may be a small minority, but they have a long history and heritage. To deny them recognition is to marginalize a vital force in nation-building, and to ignore the fundamental right of religious liberty.'

Immediately the atmosphere changed. The three presidential advisers listened intently as Vencer explained that evangelicals are not a cult but are responsible Christians seeking to maintain the historic faith of the apostles and the early church.

'Our vision goes back two thousand years, to the commands of Jesus Christ,' he declared.

'We will see that this document gets to the President!' they promised. With or without angels, God was answering prayer.

RUNAWAY BOY

Years before, the proverbial guardian angel must have been watching over the 12-year-old Jun Vencer when he ran away from school and his uncle's home. He was angry – angry with his surgeon father who had dumped the family, moving away to the southern island of Mindanao in the Philippines. Angry that his uneducated mother apparently was not good enough for his father, a professional. Angry at the rain that dripped through the rural bamboo shack his family called home, while wealthy kids slept in dry, concrete houses. Angry that he had to attend school while staying with an uncle in the city. He would show his family and the world that he could make it on his own!

But a couple of weeks in the tough world of street kids only increased his hostilities — and landed him in the local police station. News of the runaway episode reached his father. Conscience-stricken, the man sent for the boy.

Jun Vencer had never learned to love his father, but suddenly life took on new possibilities, living with a man who not only ran a medical clinic but was also joint owner of a print shop and a weekly newspaper.

Young Jun thought much about the advice his grandfather had once given him, 'Poverty is no excuse for not doing your best.' Handling odd jobs at the print shop, he learned the value of the printed word, reading anything he could find. He absorbed some basic principles of running a business and developed early signs of entrepreneurship. At thirteen he produced leaflets for his father's campaign for councillor and later became his electoral agent.

Between print jobs he spent time as a handyman at his father's private clinic. Once when his father was away on a call, he prepared to sew up a patient's leg wound. It was only when the patient turned out to be a Protestant pastor that Jun dropped the idea. Brought up a Catholic, Jun recoiled from the thought of experimenting on a 'priest', even if he were a Protestant.

Jun's father was able to get his teenage son back into secondary school, where he finished top of his class. What next? Studying medicine was his natural inclination, but when his father had a bout of illness, Jun missed the enrolment deadline. Intrigued by his uncle's law practice and aware of the injustices he saw all around him, young Jun enrolled in Law courses, and eventually gained his Law degree.

While his academic life was improving, his spiritual life was in chaos. The more he learned, the more life seemed meaningless. At college, radical nationalism was appealing, but Marxism also seemed empty. Perhaps the answer lay in existential philosophy? Or one of the many cults? Certainly Catholic saints and ritual did not bring him any peace of spirit.

LINKS IN A CHAIN

God put together the links in a chain that led to salvation: an evangelical Catholic teacher, a born-again nurse, a caring Baptist church, personal Bible reading, and then a Christian and Missionary Alliance church (CMA). When he finally submitted to Jesus Christ as Saviour and Lord, the wandering boy had found his way home, spiritually.[2]

At the CMA church, the young lawyer met his sweetheart, Annabella, and the two married. Vencer launched into a string of jobs that not only used but also developed his gifts, preparing him for the worldwide ministry that God had in mind.

In the 70s and 80s Vencer held, at different times, administrative positions with a number of organizations, including the CMA national office, the Philippine Bible Society, the Billy Graham Evangelistic Association, World Vision, World Relief, and the Philippine Council of Evangelical Churches (PCEC). Along the way, CMA ordained him as a pastor, as a result of his personal theological studies and leadership in church ministries.

As Executive Director of PCEC, Vencer soon found that the organization existed chiefly on paper. His office was in a church basement. PCEC was looked down upon as an irrelevant and reactionary group. Churches were struggling to support themselves; why should they contribute to the nationwide Philippine Council of Evangelical Churches? What good did it do, anyway? There was no

[2]For the full story, see *Poor Is No Excuse*, by John Allan, (Paternoster Press, Carlisle, and Baker Book House, Grand Rapids, 1989).

vision of the impact that an evangelical fellowship could have upon the nation. Moreover, the nation faced a lot of unrest, with the Communist New People's Army gaining strength and Muslims threatening secession in the South.

Vencer looked for models in other parts of the world. Through being on the International Council of World Vision, he had come into contact with other national evangelical fellowships, and had learned of their common ties in the World Evangelical Fellowship. In 1979 WEF invited Vencer to become a member of its International Council. From that vantage point he was able to see how evangelicals in other countries were grappling with the same issues he faced in his own nation.

'The Philippine Council of Evangelical Churches affiliated with WEF because of its focus on the centrality of the local church to reach out and accomplish the mandate God has given it', Vencer states. 'It provides the networking to enrich the Body of Christ. It enables us to become effective evangelists and church-planters, to disciple our own nation.'

HOW TO MOVE A HOUSE

'We have a Filipino tradition called bayanihan', Vencer explains. 'That is the community spirit that gets the job done – as when a bamboo house needs moving from a flooded area to higher ground. Everyone gets involved: men hoist the hut on their shoulders; women make food for everyone. Children clap their hands and sing.'

Vencer preached bayanihan to evangelicals all over the Philippines. But it took more than preaching to turn PCEC into the effective body it is today. Surveys showed that most Bible schools and seminaries were not preparing pastors to meet the 'whole-person' needs of communities. Few pastors had any concept of management: defining their purpose, identifying God-given goals, and developing people and resources to meet those goals. Pastors were not developing the spiritual gifts of the members to minister. Evangelicals were not being the 'salt and light' God intended them to be.

As Vencer challenged the churches to rectify this situation, their vision and motivation grew. When WEF's World Relief provided PCEC with resources for relief and community development, evangelical churches began to see one way in which they could make a combined impact on the nation. PCEC was actually doing something, serving the church, serving the community, serving the nation. It was worth supporting!

However, when Vencer proposed setting up an indigenous

organization, Philippine Relief and Development Service (PHILRADS), some leaders balked. 'We are too poor,' they protested. 'Churches can hardly pay their pastors.'

'Poverty is no excuse', Vencer told them, remembering his grandfather's advice. PCEC formed PHILRADS, and Filipino churches along with overseas aid agencies have turned it into an effective agency to assist communities ravaged by tropical hurricanes, floods, and erupting volcanoes. PHILRADS also attacks the chronic poverty that plagues the country. Local churches help care for an average of 40,000 families a year, as well as handling community projects.

AMAZING TRANSFORMATION

Meanwhile, PCEC offices have moved out of the church basement into a three-storey headquarters with an office staff of 35, with 50 others located throughout the nation. The budget has increased from $5,000 to $2 million. Five thousand churches provide volunteer help.

'The Philippines used to be known as "The Sodom and Gomorrah of the Pacific", a symbol of social unrest, oppression, and poverty', comments Vencer. 'When evangelicals started working together, they not only changed their own image but also made an impact on the nation. Now we have a new credibility, and even government officials consult us on the best way to handle community problems.'

Nationwide programmes are commendable, but what about the spiritual and physical results in individuals? Vencer saw the answer when he went back to the village where his grandfather had challenged him not to give up because of poverty. Vencer had nearly forgotten how tragically depressed the village was. He challenged the community elders to do something themselves to overcome the desperate poverty and inertia. He got them some financial help to start, but they had to do the work themselves.

BIGGEST SURPRISE

Eight months later the elders asked him to come and see the results. He was amazed at the transformation in progress. But what delighted him most was to be asked to baptize 32 new converts.

Then the biggest surprise came. In the middle of the baptismal line-up was his own mother, who had sacrificed so much for her family. Through the years she had superstitiously clung to her crucifix and a ritualistic Christianity. But now she was eager to confess her faith in the Saviour, who had transformed her runaway boy.

Vencer's vision was to see the gospel, that had proved so effective in changing a rural village, do the same throughout his nation. Under his leadership, PCEC adopted a nation-wide programme: Discipling A Whole Nation (DAWN). Its goal is to plant an evangelical church in every community in the Philippine islands.

Initial surveys revealed that fewer than 10% of Filipino villages had an evangelical church. Through working together, evangelicals pushed that figure up to 33%. In the mid-80s there was a total of 10,000 churches throughout the islands. The DAWN goal is to increase that to 50,000 churches by the end of the century.

'WEF was instrumental in helping us develop these goals', says Vencer. 'Through WEF Commissions and networking with other national evangelical fellowships, we have found advice, encouragement, and tools. Other agencies have helped us greatly too.'

GOING GLOBAL

Vencer became increasingly involved with WEF. Besides his membership on the International Council of WEF, he became a member of the International Relief and Development Alliance, a consortium encouraged by WEF to increase co-operation between relief and development agencies. He became founding chairman of the Evangelical Fellowship of Asia.

But Vencer really went global in 1992, when he was installed as International Director for WEF. All that had gone into developing him thus far – his personal walk with God, his organizational experience, his gifts of leadership, his background in Law, his concern over injustice and poverty, his theological studies, and his pastoring – all came together to equip him to work with the Church of Jesus Christ worldwide.

'The size of Jun Vencer's heart is about the size of his fist – as with all of us', stated Joshua Tsutada, Chair of the Evangelical Fellowship of Asia, in giving the Charge at Vencer's installation service during the Ninth General Assembly, held in Manila in June 1992. 'But the real size of his heart is like that of Jesus: he loves the world.'

'We pray for him in the spirit of 2 Chronicles 1:10: "Now give him wisdom and knowledge, that he may lead this people, for who is able to govern this great people of yours?".'

THE CHURCH HELPING ITSELF

'WEF is church-based, with the concept of the church helping itself to grow and reach out', Vencer commented as he took on the wider responsibilities. 'WEF is our own grass roots world fellowship, where we can talk to each other and strengthen each other.'

In some countries, Vencer noted that evangelicals had a long history of working together. In others, evangelical co-operation was fairly recent. During his 1993 visit to Bulgaria, for instance, he had seen how strategically important it was to that tiny group of evangelicals to be part of the worldwide body.

'I did not know if the Bulgarian evangelicals would get government registration', he said later; 'but I knew that being part of WEF could help them at least to survive – to encourage them to proclaim the gospel in their own land. That's when I realized afresh why WEF has a unique role in the world. God is using its constituency – those 150 million believers around the world in 110 fellowships – to make governments sit up and pay attention to evangelicals. "Constituency" is the only word some governments understand. They ask, "How many people do you represent?".'

When Vencer returned to the Philippines, he decided to do something more. He had been stressing the concept of networking – one national fellowship helping another. Now he challenged businessmen in Manila to help establish an office for the Bulgarian Evangelical Fellowship. In a short time, Vencer was able to send a cheque off to Sofia.

'What we want to see is partnership around the world, with one country helping another according to their ability', says Vencer. 'Financial aid does not come just from the West—although the West continues to make a lot happen through its generous giving. In WEF we see a symbiotic relationship developing—Filipinos helping Bulgarians; Japanese and Koreans and Singaporeans helping other nations. That is a beautiful thing. The Body of Christ, whether in affluent or poverty-stricken areas, is contributing in some way to the discipling and transforming of the nations.'

REVERSING INDIVIDUALISM

Vencer sees the partnering network of WEF as an antidote to the individualism that unfortunately accompanied the work of some missionaries from the West.

'I can only give thanks to God for what Western missionaries have done over the past 200 years,' comments Vencer. 'They were pioneers. They bore the brunt of the task at the time. But because of their own individualistic cultures, they often gave visible unity a low priority. Missionaries should understand and practise the unity of the Spirit in their own lands – then when they go to another culture, they will be able to replicate that unity.

'Most para-church agencies today work with and through national churches. But there are a few that do not. I wonder if some independent movements are a means to avoid accountability to the churches.

'Through its national fellowships, WEF is reversing the process of individualism and lack of accountability. WEF helps restore unity among evangelicals. We provide a vision of the inter-connection of the church worldwide. At the same time, WEF helps consolidate the fruit of the sacrificial work that missions and other agencies have accomplished.'

FRANCHISING THE VISION

'God's people need to have a clear vision', Vencer stresses. 'Often they do not take action because they do not have a vision of what God can do. They are in survival mode, a crisis mentality. By working through national fellowships, WEF helps them see what God can do through them in their nations.

'But the next problem is that they get busy with many pro-grammes that sap their strength without most effectively fulfilling the vision. We do not go in to impose programmes on churches. That is the beauty of WEF and the national fellowships – we help the churches utilize the systems and structures and (in many cases) the programmes already there. But they need to align all these towards the goal of winning and discipling their nations for Christ.'

WEF does this mainly through the Commissions it has developed over the years: Missions, Religious Liberty, Theological, Women's Concerns, and Youth. These are aided by Departments that focus on Communications, Evangelism and Church Planting, Leadership Development, Pastoral Training, Publications, Resource Develop-ment, and Church and Society.

When Vencer meets secular business people in his travels, they often ask, 'What's your business?'

'I am franchising', Vencer begins with an inward chuckle.

'What are you franchising?'

'I am franchising national fellowships to develop their churches to reach their nations', he explains. Having captured his questioners' attention, he tells them how Christ can change a life and a nation.

'WEF's strategy is to franchise its ministries within the national fellowships, which in turn will franchise those ministries within the denominations and churches', he explains. 'To do this, WEF itself needs to know exactly what must be done and exactly how it can happen. Then we help the national fellowships do the same.

'My vision for WEF is the same one given to the church two thousand years ago – that the nations of the world should be discipled. National fellowships are the most viable structure to mobilize and equip all evangelicals in their countries to handle the task. We'd like to see six hundred thousand churches around the world mobilized to evangelize the nations and disciple believers.'

Vencer and his colleagues in WEF know that to fulfil that vision, God has not chosen angels with wings, but rather men and women with hands and feet.

To facilitate the franchising process, Vencer has developed the Leadership Development Institute, complete with a management manual[3] and a team of volunteers who donate their time to lead seminars for the national fellowships.

Since taking office in December 1992, Vencer has contacted leaders from each national fellowship or regional association through leadership seminars. After developing the programme, Vencer turned it over to the leadership of an experienced management executive, Rafael G. Navarro.

'Seventy per cent of the national fellowships need assistance in leadership training', estimates Navarro.

'This is what our people need', enthused Aisake Kunanitu, President of the Evangelical Fellowship of Fiji. 'Word has got around, and those who missed the seminar are asking for a repeat.'

'I'M TIRED OF WAITING'

If people think Vencer is impatient, they are probably right, in some respects. 'I'm tired of waiting!' he exclaims as he travels the globe and realizes what evangelicals could do.

He is impatient with petty squabbles that keep some evangelicals from working together. He is impatient with the apathy of many Christians to the needs of the world – the need of those who have not heard the gospel, the need of suffering people, the need of oppressed communities. He is impatient with lack of resources, when he knows so much could be done to equip believers to evangelize and disciple their nations, if the funds for leadership development were available.

---

[3] Agustin 'Jun' Vencer, Jr., *The World for Jesus Christ: A Primer for Leaders of National Evangelical Fellowships.* (Singapore: WEF, 1994).

Vencer is even impatient with himself, when he is weary from criss–crossing the globe as he shares the vision of WEF. 'God has not always come to my rescue just when I wanted,' he once told friends. 'But he has always come in time!'

'Don't bite off more than you can chew!' advised Kenneth Hansen, an American business executive who contributed generously to WEF right up to the time of his death. Vencer had sought his counsel on how to handle his gigantic task. 'You are working in many cultures; give time for people to catch the vision', Hansen urged.

'Slow down and don't carry such heavy baggage!' a medical doctor told the slightly-built Filipino, when Vencer complained of chest pains. 'Your heart is strong, but it is showing the same strain as a weight-lifter's.'

Vencer then realized that his suitcases were usually weighed down with his laptop computer, portable printer, batteries, video and still cameras to document ministries, an iron to save laundry/pressing costs, resource books, and working files—before he added personal clothing and toiletries!

Jetting around the globe puts its own strain on Vencer's body, as he finds himself in a variety of situations. For instance, one seminar was at a mountain campsite. The pastors who trekked in over the hills insisted that he and another speaker sleep on the only bed, while they slept on the floor. Vencer appreciated their thoughtfulness, but knew that sleep would still elude him in a shared bed. He helped build a makeshift bunk above the first bed. In the night, he had to step over sleeping bodies and find his way down a dark trail to the toilet facilities.

At his next seminar in another country, the accommodation was quite a contrast. It was in a major Asian city, where his hosts paid for a room in a five-star hotel. 'But I gave thanks for the blessings of the campsite as well as for the hotel!' Vencer commented.

MUSLIM REPORTER'S INTERVIEW

Vencer realizes the importance of communicating cross-culturally. 'Our team is truly international,' he says. 'Since taking up this appointment, I have been reading a lot on corporate culture and international management. Also, the national culture varies with each country. As I travel, I have to ask the Lord to guide me in what I say in public.'

That was true not only in a country like Bulgaria, but also on the other side of the world, in Papua New Guinea. There, a Muslim was among reporters from three newspapers that interviewed him after a Leadership Development seminar was officially launched by the Prime Minister. The Chief Justice also attended the opening session.

'You stated that the church must re-engage with society', the Muslim reminded him. 'Are you saying that more Christians should be placed in government?'

'Any Christian government official must first of all be fair to all sections of the nation', Vencer replied.

'What about those who oppose you?' the reporter pressed.

'A Christian must love those who oppose him, as well as those who support him', stated Vencer. Of the three published interviews, the Muslim's was the most fair and understanding.

A BIGGER JOB THAN CONGRESS

At one stage, some evangelical Filipinos had urged Vencer to run for the Senate. They had already printed election banners. But Vencer declined. He did not feel personally called to the political arena. However, he strongly urges evangelicals not to abdicate their critical role in transforming society and helping to shape a nation's destiny.

Vencer helped form a group of religious leaders who meet quarterly with the nation's President and Cabinet members. Evangelicals put forward their biblical views during these meetings. Vencer has had the opportunity to urge national leaders to follow the example of Jesus Christ in servant-leadership.

Family values are also high on Vencer's agenda. As with most people in leadership, however, he worries over the need to find more family time with his wife Ann and their three children. Once when he was packing for yet another trip, he was touched to discover that his daughter, then a young child, had removed the kit containing his razor and toothbrush from his suitcase and hidden them – so her daddy would not be able to travel.

His son John had begun to resent the ministry that took his father away so often. Then, thanks to a supporter's gift, John was able to accompany his father on a WEF trip to Europe.

'Now I understand what my Dad does, and why he needs to travel', John said when he returned home. 'I would like to work with WEF when I graduate!'

Vencer's children are not the only ones who find it difficult to understand what is involved in the work of WEF. Many Christians have never heard of it, let alone how and why it started and what it does. Perhaps one reason is that WEF is not another mission or another church. To WEF leaders, what counts is the success of the church and its mission agencies; so apart from promoting them, WEF publicity has been low-key.

Nevertheless, people are asking, 'What is WEF? And how did the vision for the World Evangelical Fellowship get started in the first place?'

In the words of a brochure published by the Evangelical Alliance of Britain, *Who Do Evangelicals Think They Are?*

CHAPTER 2

Keeping Faith

A remarkable conference in 1846 started a movement that is still making a strategic impact today.

Clive Calver was addressing a council meeting when his personal assistant entered the room and whispered in his ear.

'Sorry friends', Calver announced, standing up and donning his coat. 'The BBC[1] wants me for a live debate. My assistant will take over.' And Clive Calver, Director General of the Evangelical Alliance of the United Kingdom, was out of the door and into a taxi. On the way through London's winding streets, he telephoned his staff to explain. 'The BBC has just asked me to give the evangelical view on a statement made by David Jenkins. He claims that the biblical story of the Magi and the star is fiction. Please FAX me evidence by the time I reach Broadcasting House.'

The EA researchers swung into action. They knew that David Jenkins was a liberal bishop who denied the virgin birth, the resurrection, and Christ's second coming. They also knew that Broadcasting House was the headquarters of the prestigious British Broadcasting Corporation. And they were used to getting sudden requests like this from the EA Director when the media called him.

They checked Chinese astronomical tables and consulted a Cambridge University professor whose research had confirmed the phenomenon of the star, and had the information ready for Calver to go on the air. That evening a significant percentage of Britain's population heard him defend the Scriptures.

At least it was not a call at midnight – as sometimes happened – asking him for the evangelical view on euthanasia or some other controversial topic. But whatever the hour or topic, Calver seizes the opportunity to comment from the word of God.

[1]BBC: the British Broadcasting Corporation, Britain's major radio and television broadcaster, enjoying great credibility in the UK and around the world.

'Ten years ago, the BBC and most of the UK hardly knew we existed', says Calver. 'Or if they knew about us, they thought we were a crazy fringe element not worth considering in society. We are glad that has changed.

'There are other people who think we are some kind of new cult', Calver continues. 'Actually, what we believe and what we do goes right back to Jesus and his disciples—back to the apostles. We believe what they taught about the death and resurrection of Jesus, about the way of salvation, and about holy living. They made an impact on every aspect of their society. That is what we are trying to do today.'

SURVIVING CAESAR AND MARX

Calver traces evangelical roots through the intervening centuries, in the basic biblical stand taken by the early church fathers, such as Polycarp, Tertullian, Justin Martyr, and Augustine; the English Bible translators, Wycliffe and Tyndale; the Reformers, such as Luther, Calvin, and Zwingli; the evangelists of the 18th century, Wesley and Whitefield; and the 19th century preachers, Spurgeon and Moody.

In different parts of Europe, people's movements, such as the Waldensians, Moravians, Puritans, Huguenots, and Mennonites, protested[2] against the perceived degeneration of the institutional church and the oppression of a state religion that denied them freedom of faith and worship. Thousands were tortured and killed for their faith.

Once he has his critics' attention, Calver likes to tell them about the spiritual revivals of the 19th century, and the call for Christian unity that brought about the birth of the Evangelical Alliance in 1846. Three years before, in 1843, an *ad hoc* committee, composed of members from a wide cross-section of churches, convened a meeting to discuss Christian unity. Enthusiastic response outstripped the organizational planning, for 11,000 tickets were issued for a hall that could seat fewer than 400 people, and the overflow crowd had to leave in disappointment.

It was a time not only of spiritual awakening but also of social and religious uncertainty. Industrial cities were hit by strikes and riots. The effects of the French Revolution, half a century earlier,

---

[2] The term 'Protestant' that eventually came into use derived from the 'protestation' of Lutheran and Reformed minorities at Speyer in 1529, against the political and religious repression of spiritual renewal. The term was not just negative in connotation but included affirmation and resolute confession.

were still sending ripples across the English Channel; the humanist philosophy of the Enlightenment was challenging biblical belief; and Charles Darwin was developing his evolutionary theory, to be published in the next decade.[3]

In London, Karl Marx and Friedrich Engels were publicly debating their ideology and preparing to publish their *Communist Manifesto* (1848).[4] Political ferment was building in France, Germany, and Italy, which would each be riven by revolution in 1848.

VOLATILE CHURCH SCENE

The church scene was changing too. Three centuries earlier, the Protestant Reformation had freed most of Northern Europe from domination by a corrupt and superstitious form of Roman Catholicism. As a substitute, many people turned to the liturgy of the Protestant state church or to sects.

By the 18th century, evangelists John Wesley and George Whitefield met a spiritual hunger through their preaching of the gospel.[5] Their goal was not to start a new denomination but to bring men and women to personal saving faith in Jesus Christ. However, even though Wesley, in his own thinking, remained an Anglican, many converts no longer felt at home in the established church. Wesley's systematic biblical teaching, which became known as Methodism, made a profound impact on Britain. Some believers formed independent Bible study groups, trying to establish an identity.

In the 19th century the Brethren movement, led by one-time Anglican J.N. Darby of Ireland, produced outstanding Bible teachers and spontaneous worship. Its strong anti-clerical, anti-denominational viewpoint was a reaction to the stifling effects of nominal 'churchianity'. Although much good has come from the movement, there have been splinter leaders who have gone to the other extreme of fragmentation and separatism among true believers.

Wary of attempts to reunite, several of the new Protestant groups avoided interdenominational conferences entirely. Some evangelicals

---

[3]Charles Darwin, *On the Origin of Species by Natural Selection.*

[4]John W. Sigsworth compares the radical influence of both Karl Marx and John Wesley on society, one from an atheistic standpoint and the other from a spiritual standpoint, in *World-Changers* (Stirling, ON: Easingwold Publications, 1982). Written before the collapse of Soviet Communism, this study is even more significant today.

[5]Two secular analysts, Ronald Wraith and Edgar Simpkins (an economist and a sociologist) attribute the radical moral change (and resultant economic progress) of British society to the Wesleyan revival, in *Corruption in Developing Countries* (London: George Allen and Unwin, 1963).

were convinced they should not even pray together, lest they dishonour the Holy Spirit.[6]

In 1843, the Scottish Disruption saw a substantial proportion of ministers withdraw from the Church of Scotland to form the Free Church, a movement generally denounced in the British Isles, although seen by some clergy as an opportunity for renewal. On the other hand, in 1845, a prominent Anglican, John Henry Newman, caused a sensation by switching to the Roman Catholic Church. Over the next twenty years, a significant number of Anglican priests, theologians, and church members followed his lead, but their departure in some ways strengthened the evangelical movement within the Anglican Church.[7]

In Europe, the history of the cruel Spanish Inquisition of the previous three-and-a-half centuries (officially terminated in 1834) had left evangelicals fearful of any hint of resurgent Roman Catholic power.[8] Evangelicals felt squeezed between an ecclesiastical backlash on the one hand, and atheistic rationalism on the other.

UNITY OUT OF CHAOS

Against this background of reaction, fragmentation, and suspicion, many evangelical Christians longed to rediscover biblical unity. They felt the need to stand together for mutual strengthening, even survival. The Second Great Awakening, a spiritual revival lasting 50 years (1791–1842 approximately), had created a desire for closer fellowship.

In the 1830s and 1840s several books on the topic of Christian unity were published in Europe and America. In Switzerland in the 1830s, the church historian Merle D'Aubigne, proposed a 'fraternal confederation'. In 1842 Dean Kniewel of Danzig toured Belgium, England, France, Germany, and Switzerland to promote friendship

[6]Ruth Rouse, and Stephen Neill, eds., *A History of the Ecumenical Movement* (Geneva: World Council of Churches, 1954).

[7]For an excellent summary and analysis of these and other events surrounding the formation of the Evangelical Alliance, see John Wolffe, 'The Evangelical Alliance in the 1840s: An Attempt to Institutionalize Christian Unity,' in *Voluntary Religion*, (London: The Ecclesiastical History Society, 1986), pp. 333–346.

[8]Although perhaps difficult to understand in today's tolerant climate, this concern was not unfounded. The Vatican was drafting dogmas and decrees to counter the spread of Protestant concepts. In the next decade (1854) the Vatican declared the dogma of the Immaculate Conception of Mary, in 1864 published the *Syllabus of Errors* (proscribing many Protestant concepts, including democracy), and in 1870 promulgated the dogma of Papal Infallibility.

among Christians of all denominations. In 1843, a meeting in Scotland commemorating the 200th anniversary of the historic Westminster Assembly,[9] sent out a plea for closer unity.

Across the Atlantic, American churches had been revitalized by the Second Great Awakening. In 1843, Presbyterian William Patton of New York wrote to British Congregationalist John Angell James, recommending an inter-church conference to outline the truths on which churches agreed. Patton's letter from across the Atlantic confirmed James' own call a year earlier, for biblical unity.

This widespread desire for closer fellowship led to a series of discussions about forming an 'Evangelical Alliance.' This resulted in a General Conference from August 19 to September 2, 1846, in Freemasons' Hall, London.

HISTORIC SPIRITUAL CONFEDERATION

It was an historic gathering, with more than 800 leaders from 52 'bodies of Christians' meeting for 13 days. Canada, England, France, Germany, Holland, Ireland, Scotland, Sweden, Switzerland, the United States of America, and Wales were all represented.

Before they departed, delegates decided to form a 'confederation' under the name, 'The Evangelical Alliance'. They agreed upon a doctrinal statement that defined basic evangelical views. Emphasizing that they were not forming 'a new ecclesiastical organization', they also stated that their signatures did not compromise the personal convictions of any member.

Their purpose was to promote the Christian unity that already existed among 'all who, loving the Lord Jesus Christ, are bound to love one another'.[10] The conference emphasized 'that the church of the living God, while it admits of growth, is one church, never having lost, and being incapable of losing, its essential unity. Not, therefore, to create this unity, but to confess it, is the design of their assembling together.'[11]

---

[9]In 1643 the English Parliament convened an assembly of religious leaders and parliamentarians at Westminster to advise in restructuring the Church of England along Puritan lines. The resultant Westminster Confession of Faith, completed in 1647, has become the most influential doctrinal statement in the English-speaking world, forming the basis for the doctrinal statements of most Protestant churches. Source: Walter A. Elwell, ed, *Evangelical Dictionary of Theology*, (Carlisle, UK: Paternoster Press, Grand Rapids: Baker Book House, 1984), p. 1168.

[10] J.W. Ewing, *Goodly Fellowship*, (London: Marshall, Morgan, and Scott, 1946).

[11]Minutes of the Proceedings of the Conference held at Freemasons' Hall in London, August 19-September 2, 1846.

That seminal concept not only characterized the Alliance formed in 1846, but also its subsequent history in every land and every era. It was to stand the test of every imaginable assault, internal and external. In fact, its premise proved true during the conference, when the question of slave ownership arose. Although slavery (not only of Africans but of other races) was common around the world at the time, evangelicals in Britain had just pressured Parliament into abolishing slavery throughout the Empire (1833). In their view an owner of slaves should not be a member of the Alliance.

The American delegates personally opposed slavery, but their nation was rife with tensions that would result in a murderous civil war (1861–65) over the issue. The problems were so complex, they felt any statement made by an external body would only 'strengthen our enemies, weaken our friends', and hinder 'the progress of emancipation in the United States'.[12] Reluctantly, the conference did not make any resolution on the subject, agreeing not to interfere in each other's internal affairs. (After the Civil War, the Americans did abolish slavery, and evangelicals there reconstructed their national alliance.)

The heated argument over membership was followed by forgiveness. The 'essential unity' of believers stood the test. However, the debate slowed down the global development of the new Alliance.

Although there would be no central office or co-ordinating staff for another century, the original vision of a loose confederation was kept alive by national bodies: Britain, Canada, and Switzerland in 1846; France, Germany, Sweden, the United States of America in 1847[13] and India in 1849. Turkey, Spain, Portugal, and others followed. The process has continued.

In place of a co-ordinating office, periodic General Conferences (11 between 1851 and 1907) kept these national fellowships in touch with each other. From January 1861 a Universal Week of Prayer also helped to fulfil the global vision of 1846.

Delegates to the historic 1846 Conference parted with the sense that some kind of miracle had taken place. In spite of the factious furore of the times, God had enabled them to establish the Evangelical Alliance. Psalm 133 was one of the Scriptures read at the opening of the conference, and delegates left with its initial words ringing in their minds: 'How good and pleasant it is when brothers live together in unity!'

---

[12] S.S. Cox, American delegate, speaking at the eleventh day morning session of the 1846 Conference. Ibid. p. 411.

[13] A committee was formed in USA May 1847 (Ewing:1946, p. 23), but the American Civil War prevented any national follow-up. A national fellowship was finally formed in 1867. (See Chapter 3.)

THE EVANGELICAL CENTURY

In Britain, the 19th century (1800s) came to be dubbed 'The Evangelical Century' by church historians, as evangelicals worked together and made an impact on their nation. Many leaders in the 1846 Conference had been involved in earlier spiritual awakenings throughout Britain and in the USA, and were active in the spiritual awakening of 1859. Evangelicals in government applied biblical principles to the law of the land. Early in the century, statesman William Wilberforce crusaded against slavery and, later, social reformer Anthony Ashley-Cooper (Lord Shaftesbury) campaigned for better working conditions for the disadvantaged, including children, women, and the poor.

In the heart of London, Charles Spurgeon called men and women to repentance, and J. Hudson Taylor helped broaden the stream of missionaries taking the gospel to other lands. The 20th century began with a major international missions conference held in New York City (1900). In 1910, the World Missionary Conference held in Edinburgh, Scotland, planned strategy for 'the evangelization of the world in our time'.[14]

DECAY SETS IN

It would have been easy for evangelicals to feel triumphant, but in fact, decay had already set in. Before the end of the 19th century, the ecumenical German philosopher, Friedrich Nietzsche, would announce, 'God is dead!' The so-called 'Higher Criticism' of liberal theology was permeating university theological departments and many denominational seminaries. While the 1910 Edinburgh Conference was the greatest international missions conference up to that time, several members voiced inclusivist concepts that later characterized the theological compromise of the ecumenical movement.

At the World Missionary Conference held in Jerusalem in 1928, the Secretary of the International Missionary Council circulated a book, *Reality*, that questioned the deity of Jesus.[15] In the first half of the 20th century, liberal theology increasingly affected mainline denominations. Although there were strong voices calling for a return to conservative biblical teaching, theological accommodation

---

[14]The slogan of the American Methodist, John R. Mott, who chaired the Continuation Committee and became chairman of the International Missionary Council formed in 1921. IMC was later absorbed into the World Council of Churches.

[15]W. Harold Fuller, *Mission-Church Dynamics* (Pasadena: William Carey Library, 1980).

became an inevitable *modus operandi* in the formation of the World Council of Churches in 1948.

Meanwhile, back in Britain, church attendance was diminishing, and by the 70s the number of evangelicals had dropped to 2% of the population. Since 1900, the number of full-time Anglican clergy had been reduced by half. Methodist missiologist Elliott Kendall argued that the era of taking the gospel to others was over because the British Empire (which he mistakenly assumed was the motivation for missionary outreach) was defunct.[16] An Anglican Bishop, John Robinson recommended changing the gospel to make it more relevant.[17] Little wonder that the Evangelical Alliance declared England itself to be a mission field.[18]

In the midst of these attacks on the evangel, it was regrettable that many who did believe God was alive and that the Bible was relevant, were not on speaking terms with each other.

THE TURNING POINT

That was the fragmented, discouraging scene 34-year-old Clive Calver found when Britain's Evangelical Alliance asked him to become Director General in 1983. The Council had just met to consider whether the EA should be allowed to die without artificial life support.

Calver, a student demonstrator before his conversion, had been a member of the EA Council and Director of British Youth for Christ. He also had been growing spiritually as a result of discipling by men such as former WEF International Director Gilbert Kirby (whose daughter he married), and three busy American evangelists: Billy Graham, Luis Palau, and Leighton Ford. On different occasions, they took time to coach the upstart 'Brit'.

'For one hundred years, evangelicals had been on the decline', says Calver. 'The first thing we had to do was define "evangelicals". Then we looked at the basis of our unity. It did not depend on our agreeing with each other on secondary matters, but rather on our oneness in Christ.'

Calver challenged British evangelicals to act like the Body of Christ: 'When Jesus comes back, he is not coming for a separate arm and a separate leg, or for fingers and toes. He is coming back for a complete, living Bride!'

---

[16]Elliott Kendall, *The End of an Era* (London: SPCK, 1978).

[17]John A.T. Robinson, *Christian Freedom in a Permissive Society* (London: SCM Press, 1970).

[18] John L. Bird, *England a Mission Field* (London: Evangelical Alliance, 1963).

Calver believes that a turning point resulted from a very unlikely event the following year, in 1984. David Jenkins, Bishop of Durham, the fourth-ranking bishop in the Church of England, publicly declared that the body of Jesus was still in the grave. 'Now, that was not surprising, coming from Bishop Jenkins', Calver explains. 'He and I had been publicly debating his denial of such basics as the virgin birth, the authority of Scripture, and the uniqueness of Christ. The secular media loved the debate. It also put Christianity on the front pages!'

But when Jenkins announced that the body of Jesus was still in the grave, Britain's evangelicals asked themselves what really was important to their faith. 'They realized that it did not matter whether they worshipped with their hands in the air or in their pockets', says Calver. 'But, as the apostle Paul had written, if Christ did not rise from the dead, that really mattered! They needed to get together to defend the truth of the gospel. So the varied tribes of evangelicals in Britain began to come together, not on the basis of forms of worship, but on the basis of the historic creeds of the church: the authority of the Scriptures, the deity of Christ, his death and resurrection, and salvation by faith in his redemption alone.'

'TRIBAL HEADS' WORK TOGETHER

Calver says that little would have happened without getting 'the Tribal Heads of Evangelicalism', as he calls them, working together in the common cause of a biblical witness to the nation. Leaders and members of evangelical groups not only serve on the 80-member EA Council but also (in the case of the Executive) give a day a week on average, actively working for the Alliance. The current President of the EA is Sir Fred Catherwood, former Vice-President of the European Parliament, and son-in-law of the noted Bible expositor, the late Martin Lloyd-Jones.

Another strength in the mix of the 'United Kingdom' is the development of National Alliances in England, Scotland, Wales, and Northern Ireland, along with the African-Caribbean Alliance.

Setting targets, the EA has seen the evangelical population percentage increase from 2% to 3% of Britain's population. Now nearly half of all Protestant churchgoers are evangelical, and young evangelicals are becoming the majority among students in many mainline theological colleges. In the 90s, membership of the EA has been growing by up to 25% a year. A cross-section of evangelicals meets at two locations in an annual 'Spring Harvest' of witness, worship, and learning, attended by 80,000.

Evangelicals also remembered the mandate of the 1846 Conference. That included addressing public ills. They realized that, like their forebears, they could actually do something to change society. The EA now publishes a journal and periodic literature, and has 20 commissions dealing with evangelical concerns in British church life as well as in society. These include drugs, poverty, unemployment, racism, homelessness, prostitution, abuse of women, AIDS, and homosexuality. In the EA offices across from the park in which Whitefield used to preach, EA press staff now receive up to 70 calls a week from the secular media requesting the evangelical viewpoint on public issues.

'We could not handle this kind of growth without the commitment of my staff colleagues,' says Calver. 'There are 45 of us at HQ now. Although we may represent a cross-section of views on secondary matters – that really enriches our lives and ministry – we all recognize Jesus as Lord.'

RIGHT OR LEFT?

'I don't understand you', Britain's Chancellor of the Exchequer (Treasury Board Secretary) once told the EA Director. 'One minute you are talking about social issues, and the next about moral issues! What are you evangelicals—left-wing or right-wing?' Calver told the Chancellor that evangelicals were both, because they served a calling higher than politics. And they were concerned about problems on earth as well as the promise of heaven.

For instance, The Evangelical Alliance Relief (TEAR) Fund has established great credibility in assisting relief and development projects worldwide. EA's Religious Liberty Commission not only keeps an eye on political abuses in Britain, but also plays its part as a member of the European Evangelical Alliance (EEA). When the Turkish government, which was applying for membership of the European Economic Community, arrested an entire church congregation during a wedding, EA sent over its International Secretary, Mike Morris. Morris let Turkish officials know that he was alerting evangelicals in the European Economic Community. Christians in Turkey began to note some improvements in their situation.

'We are not just interested in getting a handful of people to relate to one another', sums up Calver. 'We're interested in taking back our country for Jesus. We want to take the Scriptures into the whole of society and say, "This is what God has to say about how you should live.".'

LOOKING FOR TRUTH, NOT DOUBTS

All of which explains why Clive Calver does not object to being awakened by calls from the BBC for an interview. In a nation with very little Christian television and radio, evangelicals take every opportunity available on secular stations. Half the national viewing public have been tuned in to some of Calver's statements on behalf of evangelicals.

In one televised debate between Calver and a leading liberal theologian, the host asked the liberal, 'Paul, why are your churches empty and Clive's full?'

'Well, Jesus was left with only a handful of followers at the cross', the liberal answered. 'Numbers don't matter!'

'That may be right,' countered Calver, 'but when the Holy Spirit got hold of that handful, they soon became a multitude!'

The former leader of the British Labour Party, Neil Kinnock, once asked Calver, 'Why are your churches growing?'

'Because people are looking for the truth—not for doubts', replied Calver. 'The EA is committed to personal conversion, biblical truth, justice, and the cross of Jesus Christ.'

Which means that evangelicals in Britain, from whichever church or community, are seeking only to fulfil the mandate given by Jesus to his disciples. And they are doing it in public![19]

---

[19] At the author's request, Clive Calver was checking the facts in this chapter, when his Personal Assistant had to FAX apologies for missing the deadline. A serious sex scandal in an 'alternative youth service' of a mainline church had hit the headlines, and Calver, as EA spokesman, was asked to give the views of evangelicals. 'Clive has been on TV, radio, and in the press—and was invited to contribute the guest editorial in a national newspaper (a first in EA history). His schedule has gone completely "out of the window!" ', staff explained. (See Appendix E for the editorial, which we include as an example of evangelical 'salt and light' in today's society.—WHF)

CHAPTER 3

Reviving the Mandate

'Impossible' some said, but in 1951 a world body was born.

If you asked David M. Howard to tell you his most memorable experience, he would have to think for a moment.

Was it the joy of re-visiting Victor Landero in South America?

While Howard was Latin America Mission Field Director in Colombia, he was impressed by this remarkable evangelist. They prayed and planned together. Although Landero, middle-aged at the time, was winning hundreds of Colombians to Christ on the edge of the rainforest, he had a burden to tell unreached tribespeople about his Saviour. In 1990, Howard went back to Colombia and found his friend, now aged seventy, pressing farther into the jungle with the gospel.

'I haven't seen much response in 15 years,' Landero confided. 'The Chocos are so nomadic and resistant! But I keep going because you told me about your missionary brother Phil in Northern Canada. You said it was 16 years before he saw his first convert among the Athabaskans!' Howard will never forget the warm 'abrazo' hug the Colombian gave him.

Or was it on the snow-swept prairie plains of Urbana, Illinois, in the United States?

Howard can still hear the excited chatter of 17,000 college-age students crowding into the vast Assembly Hall of the University of Illinois, Urbana, to learn about God's will for their lives. As Missions Director for InterVarsity Christian Fellowship, USA, in the 70s, Howard had directed IVCF's international missions conferences. Missionaries all over the world have since told him, 'We made our commitment at "Urbana".'

Perhaps Howard would cite a different kind of conference he directed, overlooking the azure Gulf of Siam.

Leighton Ford of the Lausanne Committee for World Evangelization had asked David Howard to organize and direct the Consultation on World Evangelization held in Pattaya, Thailand (1980). It was an unforgettable experience to be involved with 850 key evangelists and leaders from 87 countries, gathered to pray and to plan strategy for world evangelization. Many had been struggling against great odds; all were learning from one another. Since then Howard has met them in many lands, spreading the gospel.

How about his visit to Romania just after the Berlin Wall crumbled?

Howard still calls it 'absolutely amazing!' The wall and Communist domination were broken in 1989. In 1990, Howard was taking part in the inaugural conference of the just-formed Evangelical Alliance of Romania. The venue itself was symbolic: the Palace Hall in Bucharest, built by Communist Iliescu Ceausescu. In that hall, less than a year before, the ruthless dictator had boasted that the changes sweeping the rest of Eastern Europe would never affect Romania. A month later, the people executed him. Now the name of Jesus Christ was being praised from that very platform.

Most amazing was the number of evangelicals crammed into the Palace Hall: 4,000 – and the Evangelical Alliance was only a couple of months old!

Or does 'most memorable' describe the visit David and his wife Phyllis made to Chinese pastor Samuel Lamb's house church?

That was in 1992, on their way from Singapore to the USA, after handing over the torch of WEF leadership to Jun Vencer. The Howards had heard of Pastor Lamb, but meeting him in his home in Guangzho was the experience of a lifetime. They found the Pastor's apartment above a police station in a four-storey building.

'We hope the police will not make a problem for you because of our visit', the Howards said.

'No problem!' replied Lamb, sprightly at 70, in spite of having been imprisoned for 20 years. 'The police know everything I do anyway. I have nothing to hide!'

Pastor Lamb explained that the police regularly called him in for interrogation, especially after meetings of his 'house church'. Up to one thousand people worship together on Sundays in rooms throughout the building, linked by closed-circuit TV monitors.

As the Howards were talking with the pastor and his wife, David noticed several elderly women sewing in a corner of the room. The pastor explained that the police had confiscated the church hymn books, so the women were stitching together pages of newly-copied hymns.[1] This pastor and congregation knew what it meant to follow Christ.

* * * * *

[1] For the full story of Pastor Lamb, see Ken Anderson's *Bold as a Lamb* (Grand Rapids, MI: Zondervan, 1991).

Understandably, David Howard finds it difficult to single out the most memorable occasion from the thousands he has experienced in more than 40 years of ministry with different organizations. But of one thing he is certain: his ten years as International Director of the World Evangelical Fellowship (1982–1992) have been the most fulfilling of his life.

And that is saying a lot!

David, the third in a family of six children, was brought up in an atmosphere of missions. His parents served with the Belgian Gospel Mission and on several mission boards. When his father, Philip, became editor of the influential *Sunday School Times* in Philadelphia, USA, the family found itself at the heart of American evangelicalism. David remembers a stream of mission and church leaders visiting his parents' home. Little wonder that the six children grew up to become involved in Christian ministry – one a pastor, one a seminary professor, and four as missionaries. One of David's sisters, Elisabeth, married Jim Elliot, who became one of the 'Auca Martyrs' in 1956.

REFOCUSSING THE VISION

WEF, which David Howard came to find so challenging, was the result of a dream that first came into focus in 1846: a global association of evangelicals. Some critics called it impossible, but the subsequent history of the Evangelical Alliance proved it was not so impossible. Individual national fellowships kept the vision alive. The major lack was a global structure.

Then came the two World Wars of this century. They threatened worldwide co-operation on any basis – secular or religious. However, following the end of World War II in 1945, the nations picked themselves up, licked their wounds, and dusted off their national dreams. Both victor and vanquished hoped for a new era. On June 26, 1945, 51 nations confidently put their signatures to the United Nations Charter.

Meanwhile, Christians of all stripes prayed for the rebuilding of church relations worldwide. True, that meant different things to different churches. The main established denominations sought conciliar union, and in 1948 the World Council of Churches was established at an ecumenical gathering in Amsterdam, Holland. It brought together more than 160 Protestant and Eastern church denominations in at least 48 countries.

Evangelicals felt the need to witness to their oneness, not in organizational union, but in the unity of the Holy Spirit. They realized they could accomplish more together than they could individually. And in the post-war pluralistic atmosphere, they needed to strengthen one another.

That is what led to the International Convention of Evangelicals August 5–11, 1951. It did not take place in a splendid hall or a famous city. Instead, it was held at a Dutch student retreat bearing the name Woudschoten, near Zeist in Holland. It turned out to be one of the most significant international evangelical conclaves since 1846.

The spirit of 1846 had been kept alive by national fellowships, periodic international conferences, and annual weeks of prayer. The 91 men and women from 21 countries who gathered at Woudschoten in 1951 took the step that had had to be postponed in 1846: they actually established a global administrative body – a worldwide fellowship to provide the 'umbrella' that national fellowships had lacked for over a century.

That inaugural meeting of WEF did not happen on the spur of the moment. The vision came into focus through a series of consultations on both sides of the Atlantic, and the felt need of national fellowships around the world.

NEW THRUST FROM THE NEW WORLD

One of the key people God used to make it happen was a dynamic preacher's son from New England, USA. If ever there was an entrepreneur for the Kingdom of God, it was J. Elwin Wright. He opened conference grounds in Rumney, New Hampshire, that soon became an evangelical centre for all of New England. In 1929 Wright founded the New England Fellowship. In the years to come, conference guests gathered in the big tent to hear up-and-coming speakers. These included Harold Ockenga, Charles Fuller, Walter Maier, Carl Henry, and, in 1948, Billy Graham. A year later, the whole nation took notice of the youthful Graham, after his first Los Angeles crusade.

Before there was a national Youth For Christ, Wright started a regional programme called Youth for Christ. He encouraged the opening of Christian elementary schools. In New Hampshire, he operated an orphanage and pushed through child welfare legislation; in Florida he organized missions for migrant workers' children. He opened Christian bookshops and lobbied successfully on behalf of Christian radio broadcasting. Yet somehow he also found time to crisscross the continent, preaching Christ and pleading for unity among believers.

All this interdenominational activity brought people and ideas together not only in New England but across the nation. Evangelicals started thinking it was high time to have an association on a nationwide scale.

'Evangelicals are a very large majority of Christians,' asserted Harold Ockenga. 'But we are discriminated against because of the folly of our divided condition.'

After several consultations, 150 delegates gathered in St. Louis, Missouri, for the National Conference for United Action Among Evangelicals, April 7, 1942. There they formed the National Association of Evangelicals.

As membership grew, the fledgling association showed that it was meeting an important need. NAE published *United Evangelical Action* and spawned special interest associates, including National Religious Broadcasters (1944), World Relief (1944), and Evangelical Foreign Missions Association[2] (1945). [EFMA's non-denominational counterpart, Interdenominational Foreign Missions Association, had already been founded in 1917.[3] The two associations continue to work together, sharing some of the same constituencies.] Today, counting all agencies, the USA provides 52% of the world's Protestant missionaries.

NAE soon earned the recognition of State and Federal governments. By the 90s, NAE listed 50 denominations, over 400 congregations, and 120 Christian organizations, representing a combined membership of four-and-a-half million people. The U.S. now accounts for 24% of the world's evangelicals.[4]

WITHERED SPIRITUAL ROOTS

The spiritual foundations of the nation can be documented as far back as 1620 when the Pilgrim Fathers signed the Mayflower Compact. America's most prestigious universities – Princeton, Yale, and Harvard – were originally founded to educate men and women in Christian values.[5] However, the nation founded in 1776 experienced the same ebb and flow of faith and faithlessness that Britain and Europe passed through. Early in this century, the debate

---

[2] In 1991 the name was changed to Evangelical Fellowship of Mission Agencies (EFMA).

[3] For the definitive history and study of IFMA, see *75 Years of IFMA*, by Edwin L. Frizen, Jr. (Pasadena: William Carey Library, 1992).

[4] Patrick Johnstone, *Operation World* (Grand Rapids: Zondervan, 1993). As Johnstone explains, figures are difficult to compare worldwide, because of different categories used by different sources, including 'membership' and 'affiliated' totals. *OW* gives total of U.S. evangelicals as 49 million members or 74 million affiliated.

[5] Howard F. Dowdell, 'The Faith of Early American Universities.' Unpublished paper, 1964.

between biblical orthodoxy and liberal theology split the ranks of many a church.

At the same time, the term 'fundamentalism' went through a transition. A series of booklets named *The Fundamentals* was published in the 20s and widely distributed. These well-reasoned apologetics for the historic, biblical faith were written by a roster of respected conservative scholars.[6]

However, by the 1920s, the label 'Fundamentalist' was often used to describe mindless, reactionary elements. The 'Monkey Trial' in Dayton Tennessee became a stereotype.[7] A cynical press used it to try to make monkeys out of all evangelicals.

Since then, theologian Carl Henry, evangelist Billy Graham, and a host of others have graciously and effectively won back public credibility for evangelicals, through intellectual integrity coupled with uncompromising faith. Graham, known for his public gospel campaigns, initiated the influential magazine, *Christianity Today*, first edited by Henry.[8]

From its start in 1942, the NAE rejected negative reaction in favour of positive defence of biblical faith and the rights of evangelicals to promulgate it. Its effectiveness in protesting about discrimination against evangelicals soon earned it a reputation outside the US. Christians in other nations saw the advantage of 'standing up, standing together,' as the official NAE history is titled.[9] They began writing to NAE for membership.

THE GLOBAL VISION

NAE realized it was a national body, and that the enquiring fellowships needed to belong to a wider, international body. Off to

---

[6]Mark Ellingsen, *The Evangelical Movement*, (Minneapolis: Augsburg. 1988).

[7]This was the trial of John T. Scopes, charged with teaching evolution just after Tennessee had enacted a law prohibiting the teaching of evolution (1925). The court found Scopes guilty of breaking the law, but later the verdict was reversed on a technicality. However, the press gleefully made this a *cause célèbre*, portraying the prosecution lawyer, William Jennings Bryan, as anti-intellectual and bigoted. The stereotype has persisted to this day. An interesting sequel: in the mid-nineties a Canadian community challenged, on the basis of human rights, a school board ruling that *excluded* inclusion of creation in classroom teaching.

[8]Carl F.H. Henry's prolific writing reached its peak in 1983 with the completion of the six-volume treatise, *God, Revelation, and Authority*, called 'the most important work of evangelical theology in our times.' (Waco: Word Books, 1976–1983).

[9]Arthur H. Matthews, *Standing Up, Standing Together*, the Emergence of the National Association of Evangelicals (Carol Stream: National Association of Evangelicals, 1992).

London to get the advice of Britain's Evangelical Alliance went Harold J. Ockenga, NAE's first President and pastor of Boston's historic Park Street Church (Congregational), with T. Christie Innes, Scottish minister of Knox Presbyterian Church in Toronto, Canada.

Since early in the century, the British Evangelical Alliance had been calling itself 'The World's Evangelical Alliance (British Branch)' keeping alive the global concept of 1846. The British agreed it was time to establish the worldwide network desired by national fellowships.

That was in 1946, centennial of the original vision. Later that year, the energetic Elwin Wright, NAE's first Executive Director, also visited national fellowships in Europe, finding the same interest. Wright and his colleague, Clyde W. Taylor, proposed an exploratory meeting, which was held in Clarens, Switzerland. Other international discussions in both the UK and the US led to the August 1951 International Convention of Evangelicals, in Holland.[10] It was there that delegates voted to establish the World Evangelical Fellowship.[11]

Delegates received good wishes from international figures, including Princess Wilhelmina of the Netherlands and President Chiang Kai-shek of Nationalist China. The Conference approved a statement of faith, based on the statement drawn up by the 1846 Evangelical Conference.[12] Two staunch evangelicals, A. Jack Dain (a member of the Brethren who became an Anglican Bishop) and John Stott (an Anglican who has ministered as a Bible expositor at such interdenominational events as InterVarsity's Urbana Missions

[10]For the full history of WEF, see *The Dream that Would Not Die* by David M. Howard, (Exeter: WEF/Paternoster, 1986). *The Elusive Dream* by the same author is a précis. (Grand Rapids/Exeter: Baker/Paternoster, 1989).

[11]Two years later, in 1953, the World's Evangelical Alliance (British Organization), reverted to the original name used in 1846, the Evangelical Alliance, in order to avoid possible confusion. Although the WEA was British-based, it maintained international connections because of Britain's globe-encircling Commonwealth ties. WEF has always recognized the leading part that the British EA played in keeping alive the vision of the global unity of believers in Christ. However, the British EA saw itself as only one of several EAs worldwide. When in 1852, the Swiss requested a constitutional change, the British EA replied that it had no authority to make such a change, 'inasmuch as the British organization is not *the* Evangelical Alliance and has no competency whatever to alter any of its resolutions or documents.' (Proceedings of the Sixth Annual Conference, Dublin, 1852. Italics supplied by the author.)

[12]For WEF's Statement of Faith, see Appendix C. WEF's Statement of Faith expresses the basic tenets historically held by evangelicals. In spite of having to withstand a wide spectrum of theological climates in different nations through the years, it has weathered every storm. In fact, it has become a 'bell-wether' statement. AD2000 and the International Institute for Christian Studies are among more recently formed organizations using the WEF statement.

Conference),[13] put forward a biblical outline of the three-fold purpose of WEF:

a. The furtherance of the gospel (Phil. 1:12)
b. The defence and confirmation of the gospel (Phil. 1:7)
c. Fellowship in the gospel (Phil. 1:5)

A VISIBLE UNITY

Although until 1951 evangelicals had no international office, the individual national fellowships had a sense of being linked around the world. Typical was a letter from East Africa following the annual Week of Prayer. It concluded with the wish: 'May God bless his work through the Alliance, carried out round the globe!'[14]

Ever since its inaugural meeting in 1951, WEF has had a sense of fulfilling the ultimate vision of 1846: a global fellowship. At the Sixth General Assembly (1974), WEF President Imchaba Bendang ('Ben') Wati referred to WEF's roots growing out of the 1846 Conference.[15] 'WEF', he told delegates, 'provides the only visible unity and solidarity among evangelicals.'[16]

But translating WEF's purpose statement into specific goals took the next 35 years. In their preliminary visits around the world, Wright, Taylor, and others were very careful to listen and observe, not to impose their plans on others, but gently to encourage fellowship and co-operation.

After WEF's formation, an Englishman, General Sir Arthur Smith (WEF's first President) and a Canadian mission-minded pastor, Oswald J. Smith, toured the USA to spread word of the new global

---

[13]Dr. Stott also became Chaplain to Queen Elizabeth II of England.

[14]J.W. Ewing, *op cit*, p.37.

[15]WEF President's Report, Sixth General Assembly, Chateau d'Oex, Switzerland, July 1974. A publication marking the 20th anniversary of the Evangelical Fellowship of India (founded in 1951) states: 'The birth of the National Association of Evangelicals in the United States led to something more: a revival of the vision of 1846 of an international fellowship of evangelicals. . . . The link with 1846 was preserved, for it was at the centenary of the Evangelical Alliance in 1946 that conversations began between the Americans and the [British] Alliance about the possibility of a new world fellowship.' Robert J. McMahon, *To God Be the Glory*, (New Delhi: EFI, 1970), p. 3. In his definitive study of Evangelicalism, Mark Ellingsen reinforces the concept that WEF was not a new movement but rather an organizational fulfilment of 1846: 'No history of the Evangelical Movement can ignore the founding of an international organization of Evangelicals in 1846, the Evangelical Alliance (the predecessor body of the present-day World Evangelical Fellowship).' Mark Ellingsen, *The Evangelical Movement* (Minneapolis: Augsburg Publishing House, 1988), p. 116.

[16]David M. Howard, *op cit*, p. 107.

body. They addressed large crowds in 37 cities. Later that year, Wright and an American pastor, Paul Rees, toured 24 nations on behalf of WEF. They ended their tour impressed with the vibrancy of national fellowships such as they found in India. Their recommendation: Western groups, although often better financed than Third World groups, needed to take a servant role to churches in the rest of the world.[17]

This low-profile approach has continued through the years and helps to explain the fact that most people do not know what WEF is. For WEF leadership, the order of priority has been to promote (a) Christ as Head of the Church, (b) the National Fellowships as the main agent in developing the churches to accomplish their task, and (3) WEF as an international servant to strengthen and equip the National Fellowships.

Involved in this process are countless schools, agencies, and missions (church and para-church) – each with its distinctive ministry of evangelism, church-planting, and discipling. Understandably, supporters are much better acquainted with their ministries than they are with the end results seen in evangelical co-operation through WEF.

WEF has adhered to the 1846 Conference principle of not interfering in the affairs of its members.[18]

WEF's distinctives may be partly defined by what it is not, as well as by what it is:

1. WEF is not a council that exerts authority over its members, but a fellowship that receives its mandate from its members.
2. WEF is not an *ad hoc*, transitory agency; it exists because the churches exist.
3. WEF 'fellowship' is not a comfortable end in itself; it is an active partnership with a task – churches helping each other disciple the nations.

The first 'General Committee' responsible for the work of WEF included members from Asia, Europe, and South America. At first, executive leadership was provided jointly ('Co-Secretaries'), then by a 'General Secretary', eventually titled 'International Director'.[19]

[17]Matthews, *op cit*, pp. 109,110.
[18]This was in keeping with the resolutions of 1846, which emphasized that the Evangelical Alliance was not establishing a new church, did not intend to rupture current churches, and did not interfere in the affairs of its members. J.W. Ewing, *Goodly Fellowship* (London: Marshall, Morgan, & Scott. 1946), p. 19.
[19]The sequence of International Secretaries/Directors since 1951: Roy Cattell and Elwin Wright; A.J. Dain and Elwin Wright; Fred Ferris; Gilbert Kirby; Dennis Clark; Gordon Landreth (Acting); Clyde Taylor; Waldron Scott; Wade Coggins; David Howard; Agustin 'Jun' Vencer.

Each brought talents and experience that contributed to the development of the global body.

Here was a low-profile organization, thinly spread around the world, composed of a wide spectrum of evangelicals, without adequate funding, and staffed (for the most part) with part-time leadership. Its continued existence has been somewhat of a miracle. Certainly its survival has evidenced the Holy Spirit's blessing.

WEF'S LOWEST MOMENT

Of course, there have been the low points as well as the high points.

'For me, WEF's lowest point came in 1985,' recalls David Howard, who became International Director in 1982. 'WEF had not developed a solid support base. We knew our dependence was on God, and that it was the Holy Spirit who prompted people to give. But responsible stewards are not going to support a work that they know very little about or do not understand. Foundations will not give to a ministry that has not precisely defined its goals and its proposals for reaching those goals.'

Howard sent urgent reports to the Executive Council, impressing on them the seriousness of the financial situation. But the picture only worsened. All reserves were exhausted. Howard cut his own salary by half but still had to let three staff members go. WEF was not only bankrupt but also in debt. Finally, with no resources to keep his office open, Howard felt unable to continue. Perhaps WEF needed a different kind of International Director, he thought. By the end of 1985, Howard had sent his resignation to the Executive.

That emergency brought together WEF's top leadership plus three experienced WEF colleagues to meet with Howard in Elburn, near Chicago, USA, in January 1986.

'We are not here primarily to handle administrative matters,' WEF Chairman, Tokunboh Adeyemo, told the group. 'Our first priority is not even to consider the resignation. First we must seek the face of God and his will for the future. I am asking David Howard to put his resignation on hold while we do that.'

Howard agreed, and the group spent the next day-and-a-half in heart-searching, prayer and Bible study. Then followed an intense evaluation of WEF. What was God trying to tell them? Why was there never sufficient support to keep the office operating, let alone develop ministries to serve the national fellowships? Had WEF completed its purpose? Was it time to close down?

One discouraged Executive member thought so. There were other, newer agencies that seemed to have the financial support of God's people. Why not turn WEFs office and ministries over to one of them?

'Younger leaders are more interested in these newer, more attractive organizations than they are in WEF,' he continued. 'Look at Brian Stiller in Canada, Clive Calver in the UK, and Ramez Atallah in Egypt. They are all leaving WEF.'

AIRPORT TELEPHONE CALL

Just then Howard was summoned from the room to take a telephone call. He was glad to escape from the discussion's pessimistic pall.

'David Howard?' the voice on the telephone was asking. It was Brian Stiller, Executive Director of the Evangelical Fellowship of Canada. 'I phoned your office and they gave me this number to reach you. I just felt that the Holy Spirit wanted me to talk with you.

'Dave, I heard a rumour that you have resigned. Tell me it isn't true!'

'It is true, Brian,' replied Howard. 'I feel that WEF needs someone else to lead it. I obviously don't have the right gifts.'

'You can't do that!' exclaimed the 43-year-old Canadian, who had been Director of Youth for Christ in Canada before leading EFC. 'You can't resign. We all think you are God's man to lead us. I've been talking with Clive Calver, Ramez Atallah, and Ajith Fernando. They are my friends, and I know they feel the same as I do. WEF needs you, and we need WEF. Dave, please do not resign. We're backing you!'

After ten minutes of pressing his point, Stiller hung up. Somewhat stunned, Howard walked back into the room to face the sombre group.

'You aren't going to believe what has just happened!' Howard told them. When they heard what Stiller had said, the gloom suddenly lifted. The timing was remarkable. So was the fact that Stiller, unaware of the discussion that had just taken place, named three of the people (including himself) who had just been reported as disillusioned with WEF. Actually, they positively supported it.

'We had prayed for God clearly to show us his will', recalls John Langlois, WEF Treasurer. 'It could not have been clearer! The attitude of the meeting turned completely around – 180 degrees! We all thanked God for his unmistakable guidance.'

MOVE TO SINGAPORE

Howard withdrew his resignation. Jun Vencer, present as a consultant, led a planning session to develop WEF. A major step was to move the International Director's office out of the USA to Singapore. This emphasized the global nature of WEF, and aroused greater interest on the part of non-American fellowships.

'It was the right move', comments Howard. 'Until then, the image of WEF tended to be American, although we really were an international fellowship. The office had been located in the USA, and the International Directors had so far come from there. Moving to Singapore erased that image and brought us all into closer contact with the rest of the world. National Fellowships realized they were on the same footing; we all shared responsibility for WEF.

'Being in Singapore certainly renewed my vision for the church worldwide. Supporters saw us in a new light, too. The Maclellan Foundation provided a grant to enable us to move to Singapore and to rent office space. People such as Benjamin Chew ("father" of evangelical work in Singapore), and other capable leaders serving on the Singapore Council have been a great strength to WEF.'

Another important step was to develop the North American office more as a support base, along with increasing contributions from other areas of the world (see Chapter 6). To assist this process, Howard and the International Council approved a Statement of Mission that helped supporters to understand WEF's objectives.

During his ten years as International Director, Howard developed the administration of WEF and its Commissions. From the central location of Singapore, he was able to travel extensively, encouraging the development of national fellowships in many lands. A major contribution was to write WEF's first history (1951–1986).

GRASS ROOTS ORGANIZATION

'The thing that excites me about WEF is the fact that it is not something imposed from the top down,' Howard sums up. 'WEF has its roots in the local churches through their national fellowships. They appoint delegates to the General Assembly, which in turn appoints the International Council, to which the International Director is accountable.

'I have been a mission director, and an agency director. I thank the Lord for evangelical ministries. Each makes its own contribution to world evangelization and discipling. WEF helps consolidate and extend the results of their ministries. It provides the worldwide network of fellow-believers the churches need. It helps them get on with the task of discipling their nations and reaching out to others. They strengthen each other in the global task.'

David Howard's greatest moment? Perhaps, after all, it was in Manila in 1992, when he had the joy of handing over the torch to

WEF's first non-Caucasian International Director, Agustin 'Jun' Vencer.

'We have made history today, and the Lord is pleased!' announced WEF Chairman Tokunboh Adeyemo, who gave the inaugural message. Adeyemo had himself helped shape WEF's history.

CHAPTER 4

'It Takes Two Hands'

People in one-time enemy countries work together to meet the vast needs of their regions.

Tokunboh Adeyemo sat under a mango tree on top of the rocky hill. He was grateful for the tree's shelter from the African sun. It was not the mango season, but even if there had been fruit, he would not have eaten it. The young man was fasting and praying – and mulling over the collapse of his familiar world ever since he decided to follow Christ.

'How can you do this to your family!' his father had shouted. 'You have disgraced us all by becoming a Christian. We Adeyemos are Muslims. We belong to the royal line and are destined to lead our people. Stop this talk about Jesus, or I shall disown you!'

As a child, Tokunboh had learned to recite the Koran in Arabic. He was a teenager before attending an elementary school. But he soon coped with studies in English – the official language of Nigeria. His father, a farmer-exporter of coconuts and cola nuts, had drilled into his eldest son that he should work hard and hold his head high. Adversity was only something to overcome. Success was the most important goal.

'Remember who you are', reminded his uncle, with whom his father had sent Tokunboh to live. It was customary for uncles and aunts to raise their nephews and nieces. Yoruba Muslims are more tolerant and syncretistic than northern Nigerian Muslims, and Tokunboh's uncle had married a non-Muslim. His uncle and aunt provided Tokunboh with a loving family environment.

In five years, 'Toks', as his close friends called him, went through both elementary and teacher's school. He became headmaster (principal) and got involved in local politics. With the goal of becoming President of Nigeria in ten years, he was flying high – until the military toppled the government and imprisoned many politicians, including his uncle, a Member of Parliament.

UNDER ARREST

Because of his political activism, Toks himself was placed under house arrest. One of his teaching staff, John, dropped in to visit him regularly. That was kind of John, but the thing Toks thought most about were John's prayers. On each visit John would pray for his friend's release and also his salvation – and he prayed in the name of Jesus.

When Toks was freed, he agreed to attend an evangelistic service. The speaker was quoting Jesus' words: 'I have come that they may have life, and have it to the full' (John. 10:10). Toks knew he needed just that. Afterwards he talked with the evangelist and asked God to give him eternal life.

'I hardly understood what I was doing, but I sincerely prayed the sinner's prayer', Adeyemo recalls. 'I started reading the Bible, from Genesis to Revelation. I searched the word of God. The change in me was tremendous.'

The church he started attending mixed charismatic Christianity with traditional spiritism. As Adeyemo shared what he was discovering in the Bible, pastor and members began to understand the purity of the gospel. They stopped praying to the river spirits and sprinkling holy water on sick people.

'That church was changed,' Adeyemo says. 'It became a Bible-believing evangelical church, just from reading the word of God. Although I did not know the meaning of "syncretism" then, I learned that the solution is through studying the Bible.'

But now, sitting on the hilltop under the mango tree, Adeyemo knew that his family members were discussing what to do with him. He would probably be disowned, no longer eligible for the chieftaincy title. As he prayed, he sensed a voice quoting the words of Psalm 27:10: 'Though my father and mother forsake me, the Lord will receive me.' Peace filled his heart.

His family did throw him out. The young teacher rented an apartment, and after his teaching duties studied the Bible by correspondence. He showed such insight that his course mentor at Back to the Bible Broadcast (BBB), USA, wrote, 'Why don't you consider going to Bible college?'

The upshot was that BBB awarded him a scholarship to attend Igbaja Theological Seminary in Nigeria. There he met visiting professor Byang Kato, General Secretary of the Association of Evangelicals in Africa (AEA).[1] Impressed by the life of the young

[1] Igbaja Theological Seminary was founded by the Society for International Ministries (SIM – originally Sudan Interior Mission) and carried on by the SIM-related denomination, Evangelical Church of West Africa. Byang Kato, a member of ECWA, became General Secretary of the Association of Evangelicals of Africa in 1973, and Secretary of the WEF Executive Council in 1974.

Nigerian theologian, Adeyemo said to himself, 'I would like to work with that man.'

BATTLE FOR AFRICA'S HEART

Adeyemo took to heart Kato's forecast, 'Over the next ten years, the battle for Africa will be fought on the theological battleground.' The aspiring young politician suddenly had a greater goal than being President: the war of truth against error.

In typical fashion, Adeyemo threw himself into his studies, graduating in two-thirds of the normal time in spite of starting late in the school year. The same thing happened when he went on to Talbot Seminary in California, USA. He then earned a Doctor of Theology degree from Dallas Seminary, Texas. Meanwhile, he kept in touch with Kato, whose writings on religion in Africa helped him in his own research. Eventually he did post-doctoral studies at Aberdeen University, Scotland.

But while still in the US, Adeyemo received the shocking news that the leader who had inspired him back in Africa, Byang Kato, had drowned while on holiday with his family.

'O Lord!' Adeyemo cried, sinking to his knees in his dormitory room. He realized the vacuum left by Kato's death. 'Lord, help us prepare many more Katos.'

Before Adeyemo had completed his studies in the USA, AEA called him to take Kato's place as AEA General Secretary. This meant representing evangelicals throughout Africa. But he carried with him two concerns that dated back to his formative years in Nigeria.

His own family was one concern. He prayed for their salvation and witnessed to them. His father passed away without making a profession, but Adeyemo had the joy of leading his mother to the Lord, and seeing his brothers and sisters trust in the Saviour.

His other major burden was for Muslims. Because of his own Islamic background, Adeyemo understands Muslim intolerance of his Saviour; they think he is blaspheming when he talks about the Son of God. He understands their fatalism and fanatic devotion to Islam as they feel assailed by a changing world. But from personal experience, he knows they can be won to Christ. He challenges Christians to reach out to Muslims – who represent well over a third of Africa's population.[2] Under AEA, Adeyemo has

---

[2]Other than South Africa and Egypt, African nations have no reliable statistics on population or religion. Patrick Johnstone's *Operation World* figures for Black Africa do not include North Africa, which is 99.9 percent Muslim.

initiated a task force to plan strategy for sharing the gospel with followers of Islam.

'CAN AFRICA BE SAVED?'

Adeyemo had no illusions that the task before him, as AEA General Secretary, would be easy.

For starters, he realized the vastness of Africa – one fifth of the world's land mass. One out of every ten of the world's population lives in Africa. Its peoples are fragmented, with over two thousand languages, plus another thousand ethnic dialects, dividing its 600 million people. Traditional ethnic strife fractures relationships within the artificial political boundaries of its more than 50 nations. These tensions have broken up regional co-operatives in currency, trade, defence, and education. Communication services – postal, telephone, and travel facilities – between countries are often inadequate. Corruption is endemic at all levels in public as well as private life.

Add physical conditions to the continent's problems: drought, floods, desertification, locust plagues, tropical fevers, AIDS, and poverty. Then there is the religious element: Islamic fatalism and animistic[3] superstition, which not only resist the gospel but also militate against improving communal living.

'Can Africa be saved?' Adeyemo asked in the AEA Newsletter, *Afroscope* (June 1993). 'We answer emphatically in the affirmative because the power to save Africa from material and spiritual collapse does not reside in men but in God. Genesis 18:14 asks, "Is anything too hard for the Lord?" He who created the heavens and the earth can surely turn around the captivity of Africa!'

As an example of what God can do, Adeyemo referred to the remarkable turnaround in India's Nagaland after a spiritual revival there. He quoted Imchaba 'Ben' Wati, former Director of the Evangelical Fellowship of India, who came from the area: 'Now Christianity makes an impact at all levels of society in Nagaland. Awakened from deadness, churches are alive in the Spirit and sensitive to the social, economic, and political issues of their society.'

To challenge Christians in Africa, Adeyemo quoted from 2 Chronicles 7:14: 'If my people, who are called by my name, will

[3]Animism (from Latin for 'breath of life, spirit') is used to describe traditional religions, distinct from Islam and Christianity. Animists (often referred to as pagans) believe that ancestral and other spirits inhabit people and objects, cause phenomena (such as a storm, an eclipse) as well as illness and accidents. Spirits are believed to control people and events, and must be placated and worshipped.

humble themselves and pray and seek my face, and turn from their wicked ways, then will I hear from heaven and will forgive their sin and will heal their land.'

STANDING TOGETHER

The Association of Evangelicals in Africa (AEA) was formed in 1966, at a consultation of evangelical leaders from across Africa. They knew that the gospel could make a difference in their continent, but the churches first needed to overcome their isolation and factionalism. They had to meet on the common ground of God's word, and together they had to face the daunting task of ministering to a continent in turmoil.

They were also faced with the growing influence of liberal theology. Although grass root Christians were mostly evangelical at the time, liberal theology was gaining ground in the institutions of higher learning. Churches felt pressured into alliances that did not stand for the biblical faith. Individual groups of believers were in danger of being picked off by the 'savage wolves' the apostle Paul warned about (Acts 20:29).

'Before we leave here, we must establish an association that will reflect and strengthen our unity in Christ', Aaron B. Gamede of Swaziland urged the consultation. He put forward a motion that led to the formation of AEA.

'It takes both hands to lift a heavy load!' said David Olatayo, who was elected as the first AEA President. 'Evangelicals have a heavy load to lift; we cannot do it if we remain isolated from each other.'

OUT OF THE SIDELINES

'Since then, God has done amazing things for his church,' comments Adeyemo. 'Even when I took office nearly 20 years ago, evangelicals had the image of being only negative – against this and against that. But I realized we had to establish our identity by what we are for, not what we are against.

'Over the years, God has taken evangelicals out of the sidelines into the centre of the arena, standing in the gap for the nations, living as salt and light.'

Adeyemo points out that governments and agencies used to ask advice from the All Africa Council of Churches and Roman Catholic bishops, but not from evangelicals. Now they seek the opinion and assistance of AEA as well. During the Rwandan genocide, AEA hosted a non-sectarian consultation of agencies, including AACC and RC groups, to plan how best to handle the tragedy. AEA recognized that in the face of human suffering, evangelicals needed to take the initiative. The other groups thanked them.

When Adeyemo became General Secretary, there were only eight national fellowships in existence. None had a full-time executive officer or office. Now there are 34, half of them with full-time leaders. AEA would like to see four new national evangelical fellowships (NEFs) formed per year. At that rate, every African nation would have an NEF by the year 2000.

'Many things seem to be falling apart in Africa, whereas evangelicals are coming together', reports Adeyemo. 'The church of Jesus Christ is gaining strength. Now we want to see it make an impact on the continent, to help overcome the destructive forces.'

To further this end AEA has departments for Communications; Discipleship and Leadership Training; Ethics, Peace, and Justice; Evangelism and Missions; Relief, Development, and Social Transformation; Prayer and Renewal; Theology and Christian Education; Women and Youth.

AEA not only has its own headquarters buildings, but also sponsors two graduate schools of theology, one for French-speaking Africa and the other for English-speaking Africa. (See Chapter 10, Theological Commission.) The Accrediting Council for Theological Education in Africa (ACTEA) helps Bible schools and seminaries to develop quality theological education.

DEVASTATING CRISES

At the Pan-Africa Christian Leadership Assembly II, held in 1994, more than 800 delegates from 42 countries discussed the topic, 'Developing Godly Leadership for Africa'. Among the findings, PACLA II pointed out that 'the impact of the Christian faith has not gone deep among many Africans'. It emphasized the need for 'a thoroughgoing application of the Bible in daily decision-making and lifestyle.'

It is true that Christianity in Africa has been growing phenomenally, so that it has become the majority religion south of the Sahara.[4] However, much Christianity is nominal or uninstructed, and is not 'the salt and light' that Africa desperately needs.

[4]Statistics need to be qualified. British statistician David Barrett's Christian growth rates cover the widest possible use of the term 'Christian,' including syncretistic groups that use the cross in animistic ritual. Also, as Barrett explains, the oft-repeated growth rate of 16,000 new Christians per day is mostly biological increase (the population increase, or birth rate, in communities that are considered 'Christianized'). A very similar percentage increase could be claimed by Muslims in some countries.

'God is calling all of us to life-giving action at a time when our continent is surrounded by devastating crises spiritually, socially, politically, and economically', the Assembly report concluded.

That same year, just after South Africa's first black President was installed, Potchefstroomse University awarded Adeyemo an honorary Th.D. in recognition of his 'important contribution . . . towards the development of the AEA, an organization which aims at uniting Christians faithful to the word of God through the continent of Africa.'

Although Adeyemo already had an earned doctorate, this presentation held special significance for him as an African and as an evangelical. Potchefstroomse was founded in 1869 by white Boer settlers, members of the race that later established apartheid. By the award, the university was signalling recognition of black evangelical leadership. As Adeyemo said, 'We accept it for all evangelicals throughout Africa.'

In the midst of Africa's political crises, Adeyemo has at times felt the Holy Spirit prompting him to speak directly to national leaders. When former President Kaunda of Zambia published a book endorsing the use of violence for political ends, Adeyemo visited him to express the concern of evangelicals.

'Jesus is called the Prince of Peace, and we who follow him must live in peace', the AEA leader told the President, who called himself a Christian. 'There is more power in love than in a bullet.'

When Kenya was about to change to a multi-party system, Adeyemo went to encourage that nation's President. At that time, the land was suffering drought. Adeyemo stressed that if President Moi would walk humbly with the Lord and do what is right and just, he could trust God to provide political stability and also rain.

'At the time, the national tension did subside – and the rains came!' Adeyemo recalls.

THE ASIAN GIANT

The Association of Evangelicals of Africa is but one of seven WEF Regional Associations that provide geographic groupings for National Evangelical Fellowships. The Evangelical Fellowship of Asia (EFA), formed in 1983, is another example of the networking and mutual assistance that goes on within these regional groupings.

The area covered by EFA is colossal, spanning nine time zones. The demographics are staggering – more than half of the world's population. Its rapidly developing economy increasingly competes with Western nations for world markets.

All major religious movements have started in Asia: Judaism,

Hinduism, Buddhism, Christianity, and Islam (in that order). These have influenced the course of world history.

Knowledge of the one true God accompanied descendants of Abraham who wandered eastward across the continent to the Yellow Sea. We do not have records of who they were, but Jewish traders seemed to turn up everywhere. Inevitably, they would have with them the Law and the Prophets and the Psalms of Zion.

Christianity itself is no newcomer to Asia. In fact, the Apostle Thomas, it is said, preached the gospel in India (1st century) before St. Patrick made it known in Ireland (423) or Columba took it to England and Scotland (560). Alban took the message of Christ into the heart of China (635) before Boniface reached Germany (716) or Anskar preached in Denmark (827).[5]

History thus gives the lie to the charge that Christianity was first introduced to Asia by 'the Western imperialist'. The incursion of Western powers was only the most recent wave of invading armies (most from within Asia) that have swept over the nations during the past six thousand years. Each had its own form of imperialism. As a result, racial, religious, political, and economic fault lines run deep. Figuratively, they can be as violent as an earthquake, as explosive as an erupting volcano.

APOLOGY AND FORGIVENESS

But the gospel is even more powerful – the power of God for . . . salvation (Romans 1:16). It can overcome the greatest hurts. Tadashi (Joshua) Tsutada of Japan experienced that, when he stood before delegates to the Evangelical Fellowship of Asia (EFA) conference in 1987. At that time, it seemed unthinkable that a Japanese would apologize to fellow Asians for atrocities his nation committed during World War II. But Tsutada did just that.[6]

The Japan Evangelical Association (reconstituted in 1986) sent Tsutada to the EFA conference, held in Singapore. Arriving by air, he flew over the beach where Japanese invaders had gunned down

[5]Henry L. Rowold, 'Lord of the Reach', in *Missio Apostolica*, Journal of the Lutheran Society of Missiology, (St. Louis, Missouri, USA, Nov. 1994).
[6]It was seven years later, on June 6, 1995, that the Japanese government for the first time expressed 'deep remorse' for attacking its Asian neighbours. On August 14, 1995 (the fiftieth anniversary of Japan's surrender), the Prime Minister made a further apology to the whole world, for the 'tremendous damage and suffering to the people of many countries' caused by Japan's 'mistaken national policy' of 'colonialism and aggression'. The Japanese Evangelical Association added its own apology for the failure of many Christian churches to protest at the time.

thousands of Singaporean defenders. Later, as he passed the shrine built to their memory, Tsutada wondered how he would be received. His listeners would be polite, but could they really forgive his nation? How could any nation in South-East Asia forget the atrocities, in which tens of millions of Asians died?

During the conference, Tsutada read an official letter of greeting from the Japan Evangelical Association to the churches in Asia.[7] It offered sincere apologies for the war crimes committed by Japan, asking for forgiveness, and expressing hope that they could be united as brothers and sisters in Christ, for the furtherance of his kingdom.

'We do not offer any excuse', Tsutada continued; 'but Japanese Christians were very few in number then. The church was small and could do nothing to stop the war. However, I want you to know there were pastors who died in prison because they refused to obey the Emperor's war edicts. My own father languished in prison throughout the war, because he disagreed that the war was divinely inspired. After the war was over, he started a church denomination that is still growing. Now to you and other nations we want to express our deep sorrow for our nation's actions. Many of you and your relatives suffered. . . .'

The Japanese church leader could not continue speaking. He wiped tears from his eyes.[8] But before Tsutada could sit down, a Singaporean pastor stood up beside him and said, 'You are my brother in Christ. I forgive you!'

The Singaporean went on to tell how he had once hated the Japanese invaders. They had shot his brother, who was hurrying home a few minutes late for curfew, after buying medicine for his sick wife. 'But when I found Jesus as my Lord and Saviour, I also found grace to forgive,' the pastor told the Japanese guest.

THE SOLDIER WITH A BIBLE

The atmosphere was electric as Benjamin Chew, the patriarch of Christians in Singapore, got up to speak.

'I was a young medical doctor during the Japanese invasion', he

---

[7] See Appendix F for a copy of the letter, which was signed by Tsutada on behalf of the Japan Evangelical Alliance.

[8] The memory of the war was especially poignant to Tsutada, who married the daughter of the captain of Japan's largest submarine, the I-26. Captain Yokota became a Christian after the war and took his Christian bride's family name, Hasegawa, to dissociate himself from his wartime past.

told the hushed gathering. 'I saw the atrocities. I hated your people. I wished I could forget my medical oath to save lives and instead kill every wounded Japanese soldier lying in the hospital!

'Then one day I noticed a black, leather-bound book beside the bed of a dying soldier.'

'Are you reading that Bible?' the Singaporean doctor asked.

'Yes', responded the Japanese lad weakly.

'Are you a Christian?' Chew pressed him.

'Yes, I am a Christian', the mortally wounded soldier answered huskily but with conviction.

Chew told the conference how his hatred and anger melted away. The love of Christ was stronger than the hostility of war. Doctor and patient ministered spiritually to each other until the lad died of his wounds.

There were few dry eyes in the conference hall. A public show of emotion is not very oriental, but people forgot their inscrutable culture and hugged each other as tears flowed.

After the war, Tsutada studied at Bible college and then served as a missionary in India for 17 years. Back in Japan, he became principal of Immanuel Bible Training College, senior pastor of the College church, Chairman of the EFA, and a member of the WEF International Council.

When the Evangelical Fellowship of Asia elected him, a Japanese, as Chairman of the Executive in 1989, Joshua Tsutada saw the grace of God at work. 'The unity of the Spirit through the bond of peace' had overcome the antagonisms left by war.

Japan's Evangelical Association, though small, has been effective as an evangelical voice in its own land. For instance, JEA helped to persuade the Japanese government to compensate Korean girls who had been forced into prostitution as 'comfort women' for Japanese troops who invaded Korea.

Although Japan is a wealthy land by world economic standards, many of its evangelical churches number only a dozen or so members, and the average Sunday attendance would be fewer than 50 per church. Most Christians are in a low wage bracket. Yet JEA has raised major funds to assist evangelical projects in poorer nations.

GREAT CONTRASTS; MUTUAL ACCEPTANCE

The role of Japanese Christians in the Evangelical Fellowship of Asia is but one example of National Fellowships assisting each other. For instance, Korean churches are sending missionaries to neighbouring lands, as well as worldwide. (See Chapter 5 for examples from other countries.) EFA has itself provided great strengths to WEF through its Commissions, including Theology and Missions.

Countries within the Asia Region represent great contrasts, from China's massive size to Bhutan's tiny kingdom. Pakistanis pray for water; Bangladeshis wish for less. In South Korea, Christians enjoy religious liberty; in Vietnam they still face restrictions. India dates its first attempt to form a National Fellowship back to 1849, whereas Cambodia's is in the formative stage. But old or young, large or small, they all find mutual acceptance within WEF, and are helping to build each other up in the faith.

This was apparent at the Asia Church Consultation sponsored by EFA in 1994 in Indonesia.

'The consultation was unique', reported Francis Sunderaraj of the Evangelical Fellowship of India, who was General Co-ordinator of the Consultation. 'This was the first time that key evangelical leaders of Asia gathered together to focus comprehensively on the biblical understanding of the nature, life, and ministry of the Church in the Asian context. The theme was from Jesus' declaration: "I will build my church." '

The 320 delegates from 19 Asian and six non-Asian countries – including once restricted nations such as Mongolia, Laos, Vietnam, and Nepal – affirmed 'that the mission of the Church is to make disciples of the Lord Jesus Christ from among all nations of the world, including the Asian peoples'.

Islam presents its own challenge to Christianity. Sunderaraj points out that in several Islamic nations, Christians are restricted to preaching and teaching the gospel only in church buildings and Christian institutions. However, there are a few congregations made up entirely of converts from Islam. A few nations increasingly restrict visas for Christian missionaries. One concern of the EFA is the lack of witness by Asian Christians to their Muslim neighbours.

WEF REGIONS SPAN THE GLOBE

WEF's regional groupings, similar to AEA and EFA, encompass the world:

AFRICA: Association of Evangelicals in Africa
ASIA: Evangelical Fellowship of Asia
CARIBBEAN: Evangelical Association of the Caribbean
EUROPE: European Evangelical Alliance

LATIN AMERICA: Latin American Evangelical Confederation
SOUTH PACIFIC: Evangelical Fellowship of the South Pacific

The WEF Office in North America functions in a role supportive of
WEF worldwide. It works in co-operation with the National Asso-
ciation of Evangelicals (USA) and the Evangelical Fellowship of
Canada.

WEF's Regional Fellowships encompass more than 100 National
Evangelical Fellowships that represent 150 million evangelicals
worldwide. WEF Commissions (featured in chapters 6–12) work
with these Regional Fellowships and their National Fellowships to
help them develop specific ministries: Missions, Religious Liberty,
Theology, Women, Youth.

In addition, Departments represent special needs, such as Church
and Society, Communications,[9] and Prayer and Renewal Ministries.
Commissions and departments make available the expertise of
specialists, produce materials, help plan strategies, and conduct
seminars that assist WEF member bodies worldwide. Regional and
national bodies may set up their own commissions, which interact
with the global commissions.

REGIONAL CONCERNS

Each Regional Fellowship has its own special concerns.

AFRICA and ASIA have already been referred to in this chapter.

EUROPE: The European Evangelical Alliance (EEA) was not
formed until 1952, but among its members are some of the oldest
national fellowships: Britain (1846), Switzerland (1846), Sweden
(1853), Germany (1857), Norway (1858), and Spain (1887). Stuart
McAllister, EEA General Secretary, points out that today the
Alliance faces new challenges in the post-communist era, with
secularism on the one hand and on the other hand the Orthodox
and Roman Catholic churches trying to regain their former powerful control. Meanwhile, long-festering ethnic hostilities break out
in open violence.

Particularly in the former Eastern *bloc*, biblical Christianity must
present its message of hope for disillusioned men and women who
ask, 'What is capitalism? What is democracy? Exploitation? Poverty? Immorality? Violence? Drugs? Cultural destruction?'

LATIN AMERICA: The Latin American Evangelical Confedera-

---

[9]Communications matters are handled by a WEF associate, International Christian
Media Commission.

tion (CONELA) is strengthening churches dealing with a climate of poverty, religious superstition (including voodoo cults), and influential drug barons. J. Norberto Saracco of Argentina and Key Yuasa of Brazil, represent the Spanish and Portuguese language nations on WEF's International Council. They point out that the rapidly growing number of evangelicals needs Bible teaching. Increasingly, churches realize their responsibility to evangelize their nations and reach out to other countries. CONELA President Hector J. Pardo of Colombia and General Secretary Ruben N. Proietti C. are encouraging training programmes.

CARIBBEAN: The Evangelical Association of the Caribbean faces great logistical problems affecting travel and communication, with its membership stretching 2,000 miles along a necklace of islands. Nevertheless, General Secretary Gerry A. Seale points out that EAC is gaining strength through their Commissions: Communications (radio, in particular), Evangelism and Missions, Theology, and Women's Concerns.

NORTH AMERICA: The two associations in North America, the National Association of Evangelicals (NAE) in the USA and the Evangelical Fellowship of Canada (EFC) are both seeking to defend biblical values assailed by humanistic trends in the courts. EFC's Executive Director Brian Stiller gains public hearing with his weekly televised panel discussions, while EFC's Commissions earn a hearing in the courts over issues such as euthanasia, sexual-orientation rights, and religious instruction in schools. NAE's Executive Director Don Argue continues the strong leadership shown by former Executive Director Billy Melvin.

'The highlight of my time leading NAE was an invitation by the Russian government to share spiritual insights after the collapse of Soviet Communism,' says Melvin, who was among a group of 19 evangelical leaders invited to Moscow in 1991. 'Former Communist officials were asking us to help them introduce biblical values that were being excluded from our American schools and society.'[10]

BEARING ONE ANOTHER'S BURDENS

In cultures where people carry heavy head-loads, a bystander will voluntarily spring to help lift a load on to a person's head – or to

---

[10]The vice-chairman of the former Soviet Secret Police (KGB), who met with the group, called this 'a plot twist that could not have been conceived by the wildest fiction writer.' The story is told in Philip Yancey's book, *Praying with the KGB* (Portland: Multnomah Press, 1992).

set it down on the ground. Metaphorically, WEF Regional and National Evangelical Fellowships are doing just that for each other. As churches help each other, they fulfil Jesus' command: 'Bear one another's burdens.'

'It takes two hands to lift a heavy load!'

CHAPTER 5

Reversing Babel

*Christians in a cultural mosaic find they can disciple their own
nations and help other nations too.*

Paul Negrut was feeling suicidal. He knew he had just failed the
written entrance examination for a Psychology course. He had
spent his father's last *leu* to travel from the impoverished family
farm to the Romanian capital, Bucharest. How could he face his
father?

Negrut returned to his tiny room in tears. Delia, his girlfriend,
had often told him about God, but Negrut had been brought up to
believe there was no God and that Jesus was a myth.

'You will never find God until you come to the end of yourself
and confess you are a lost sinner', Delia said. Negrut could never
admit to failure, let alone to being a sinner. But now Delia's words
confronted him. He started praying, and after several tearful hours,
he found forgiveness and salvation through faith in Christ as
Saviour.

Returning to the university the next day to take the oral portion
of the examination, Negrut was amazed that his answers came so
easily. The professor was impressed. He accepted Paul as one of 90
students from among 5,000 applicants.

At university, the Communist Party pressured Negrut to become
a member. He refused, knowing it would compromise his new-found
faith. He endured the taunts of the lecturers, but they could not
ignore his high academic standing on the course. After graduation,
Negrut worked as a certified clinical psychologist, but he was a
marked man.

By 1982, Negrut had decided the best way to serve his nation was
as a pastor. But the state would not register him, and it was illegal
for an unregistered person to preach. Negrut preached anyway and
ended up in a military concentration camp. When Romania's
dictator Ceausescu visited Canada, evangelicals there raised
Negrut's case as a human rights issue, and within 24 hours the young

pastor was released. But harassment continued until freedom came to Romania.

OUT OF THE CATACOMBS

When it did, evangelicals were ready for it. The Communist regime fell in December 1989 – the end of 45 years of severe repression. The next month, January 1990, evangelicals met to discuss forming a fellowship. In March they officially registered the Evangelical Alliance of Romania. In May they held a nationwide evangelistic campaign, with Luis Palau as the speaker. In October they held their first national assembly and elected their first full-time chairman – Paul Negrut.

'All at once, our churches had to move out of a catacomb mentality into a public-square mentality', Negrut says. 'It was not easy, after 45 years of isolation and persecution. But maybe we were more ready than evangelicals in some other countries.'

Negrut explains that repression of evangelicals did not start with the Communist regime. The Romanian Orthodox Church, untouched by the Reformation that took place in other parts of Europe, had always been hostile. In the early 20s, an Orthodox priest, Iosif Trifa, came to saving faith in Jesus Christ while translating the Bible into contemporary Romanian. But when he preached that salvation was to be found in Christ alone, and not in church membership, the Orthodox Church defrocked him.

Protestants, especially evangelicals, have been oppressed by Orthodoxy as much as by Communism. One Orthodox leader has called Protestantism 'the biggest heresy in Europe.'[1]

'That history has made believers feel united', says Negrut. 'Denominational labels did not keep believers apart. For instance, Joseph Tson, a Baptist pastor, prepared teaching materials that evangelicals of all denominations used. We studied together and prayed together. When believers are persecuted, they turn to the Word for comfort and instruction. People see Christ in their lives and turn to him.'

When liberty came, it was natural for evangelicals to form their own national fellowship.

'I have never seen anything like it in any other evangelical alliance', reported David Howard, when he attended the very first national assembly of the Evangelical Alliance of Romania. 'It was absolutely amazing. There were four thousand people in Bucharest's

[1]Patrick Johnstone, *Operation World*. (Carlisle, UK: OM Publishing; Grand Rapids: Zondervan, 1993).

great Palace Hall, where less than a year before, Ceausescu had declared that atheistic Communism would never be swept aside in Romania.'

Romanian evangelicals felt the embrace of the rest of the evangelical world. One of the speakers at that inaugural assembly was Sam Kamaleson of India. Another was Peter Kuzmic, of the Protestant Evangelical Council of Churches of Croatia. Paul E. Toms represented the National Association of Evangelicals, USA.

Howard accompanied Evangelical Alliance of Romania (EAR) leaders to an audience with the nation's new head. Vasile Talos, interim chairman of the EAR, reminded the President that the Alliance represented three million evangelicals in Romania. Howard added that WEF, of which the EAR was a member, represented one hundred and fifty million evangelicals worldwide. Joseph Tson, founder of the Romanian Missionary Society, presented the President with an inscribed Bible. Christianity in Romania was by no means a museum exhibit. Now evangelicals alone account for 5 % of the population.

THE GLOBAL FAMILY

The Evangelical Alliance of Romania, one of the newest among WEF's 110 national fellowships, illustrates the networking and reciprocity of the worldwide body. The concept of the Alliance started from a need felt at the grass roots. Its leadership is homegrown, and it speaks to the challenges of Romanian life – seeking to be 'salt and light' in the community, among people in all walks of life.

It produces a gospel television programme in government time five days a week, and sponsors a secondary school and a Bible college. The State recognizes the latter's teaching degree. The Alliance also plans to develop a Christian university.

While addressing their own nation's needs, Romanian evangelicals are not isolated from the worldwide body of Christ. Their first action was to join the regional body, the European Evangelical Alliance (EEA), which is part of the global body of WEF. Before the new Romanian Alliance was able to develop its own support base, a donation through WEF's office in the USA enabled it to secure office space (see Chapter 6). After 45 years of isolation, it meant a great deal to relate to fellow believers in the rest of the world.

'WEF is very important to us in Romania', says Paul Negrut, who is a member of WEF's International Council. 'In WEF we can relate to the body of Christ worldwide in meaningful ways.

'But apart from the sense of spiritual belonging, we benefit from the work of the Commissions. The Religious Liberty Commission spoke up for us evangelicals, even before we formed our Alliance. In 1994 the Theological Commission held a consultation here on Theological Education in Post-Communist Europe. It has also advised us on curriculum and faculty and library development, and helped us with scholarships for leadership development. We know we can call on any of the Commissions to share the experience and skills of other alliances.'

At the same time, the courage of Romanian Christians under persecution is a strength to believers suffering in other lands. And its missionary vision – for Europe, Russia, and North Africa – is an inspiration to all.

'My hope is that the West will not only assist but will also benefit as the East European church tells what it has learned through persecution and suffering', says Peter Kuzmic of Croatia. 'Perhaps we can also share our values of community, to help Christians in the West who over-emphasize independence and individualism.'

That is one of the greatest benefits of national fellowships – they minister to each other. They have different needs and different gifts to contribute – a principle of the Body of Christ, which the apostle Paul pointed out to the Corinthians (1 Cor. 12:12–26).

Worldwide, there is a tremendous variation in the size of national fellowships. For instance, the Evangelical Fellowship of India has a membership of more than 24 denominations, plus 20 independent congregations, 62 agencies, 13 institutions, and 3000 individuals – in a nation of about one billion people. In contrast, the Evangelical Fellowship of Fiji is made up only of individual members in a country with fewer than one million people.

There are other obvious contrasts between national contexts. Religious liberty is one. The National Association of Evangelicals (USA) represents a nation that was founded on the principle of religious liberty. Over 86% of the population calls itself Christian, and 30% claims to be evangelical. By contrast, The Evangelical Fellowship of Pakistan seeks to survive in an Islamic state, in which, unofficially, evangelicals are looked upon as a threat to national stability. They face marginalization and sometimes death. They register barely 0.29% of the population, and all Christians combined total less than 2%.

THE ECONOMY, DRUGS, AND CRIME

National economies provide another sharp contrast. The Dutch Evangelical Alliance operates in a nation with a strong economy.

The National Association of Evangelicals of Bolivia, on the other hand, struggles in a nation that has experienced hyper-inflation (it once hit 26,000%), and has an income per person only one thirtieth of Holland's.

The world drug trade not only points up contrasts between producer nations and consumer nations (unfortunately, the latter make the former profitable), but also provides a common challenge for evangelical fellowships.

In Europe, evangelicals minister to young people trapped in the drug culture as consumers. In South America, evangelicals are battling against forces that control drug production and the lives of the farmers who grow the drug-related crops. In some Latin American countries, the illegal drug trade involves more money than the national budget. Poor farmers can make ten times more from drug crops than food crops. National fellowships in Latin America, assisted by missions and aid agencies, help farmers plant alternative crops so they can provide for their families.

Evangelist Caio Fabio D'Araujo Filho recently found himself in the middle of a live-ammunition drug war in the slums of Rio de Janeiro. Brazil's President had placed the six-million population under an emergency military regime, to clean out the violent armed gangs controlling the slums. The drug Mafia retaliated, and a veritable hot war was ready to explode.

As the tense population watched in amazement, Fabio, whose evangelistic agency, VINDE,[2] teams work in the worst slums, persuaded a major drug lord to surrender his cache of weapons. That set the stage for a negotiated peace. Impressed, Rio officials asked for Fabio's help city-wide.

'The rapid spread of the gospel in the slums opened a window for us to help solve violence', states Fabio, who is also President of the Brazilian Evangelical Association (BEA) and a member of WEF's Religious Liberty Commission.

The BEA, founded only in 1991, represents 35 million evangelicals and 220 denominations. Ministries of VINDE include broadcasts over 14 Christian radio stations, and 'The Factory of Hope', a city block of services for the poor, providing skill-training and jobs.

Evangelicals in Asia, Africa, Europe, Latin America, North America, and the South Pacific face distinctive needs in their nations. But they have a common mandate to apply the gospel in their society. They find strength by working together through their national fellowships, regional associations, and the global body of WEF.

[2]VINDE: An acronym for 'Vision for Evangelizing a Nation.'

NEW LIFE IN AN ANCIENT LAND

The Evangelical Fellowship of India (EFI) provides one of the oldest examples of a national fellowship. EFI was formed in the same year as WEF was officially launched. More than a century earlier, a committee of the 1846-launched Evangelical Alliance had been formed in India,[3] but in January 1951, EFI as a national body held its first annual meeting – seven months before the inaugural meeting of WEF (August 1951).

EFI's formation was closely linked with preparations for the founding of WEF. As the 1846 vision of a global alliance developed, two of the main promoters of the concept, J. Elwin Wright and Clyde W. Taylor (see Chapter 3), had circled the globe to share the idea with other evangelicals. In 1950 they held two meetings in Calcutta and met with a favourable response. In January 1951, leaders in India met at Yeotmal and officially founded EFI. At the inaugural meeting of WEF later that year, EFI became a charter member.

EFI elected A. Jack Dain as Chairman. At the time, he was Overseas Secretary of the Evangelical Alliance (Britain), and later played an important part in WEF, Lausanne, and the Billy Graham Evangelistic Association. Since 1951, India has provided two presidents for WEF: Ben Wati and Theodore Williams.

An Indian bishop, Alexander Mar Theophilus, led the opening 'procession of nations' at the 1966 World Congress on Evangelism (Berlin) sponsored by the Billy Graham Evangelistic Association. In 1970, EFI followed this up with the first All-India Congress on Evangelism – four years before the International Congress on World Evangelism (ICOWE) that met in Lausanne.

THEOLOGICAL 'CHEMISTRY'

Today EFI's General Secretary is Francis Sunderaraj, a graduate in Chemistry as well as Theology. He became a Methodist missionary pastor in Malaysia, where his English-speaking congregation also included Chinese and Tamil people. Returning to his home city of Madras, he was assistant pastor to a powerful Bible preacher, Samuel Kamaleson. Joining the staff of EFI's Christian Education Department (CEEFI) in 1976, he was appointed General Secretary of EFI in 1984, and has since taken further graduate studies.

[3]John W.Ewing, Goodly Fellowship. (London: Marshall, Morgan, and Scott, 1946), p.22.

'My life verse is 1 Thessalonians 5:24', Sunderaraj says: 'The one who calls you is faithful and he will do it.'

That verse gives him courage in the face of the enormous needs of his nation – an already crowded land that is projected to bypass China in population in the coming century.

Public morality is concerning even secular leaders. *The Times of India* recently quoted a former Chief Justice of the Supreme Court of India: 'The judiciary in India has deteriorated in its standard because such judges are appointed as are willing to be influenced by lavish parties and whisky bottles.' Another former Chief Justice (Patna) has stated: 'Corruption is now a way of life, and there is corruption in the judiciary also.'[4]

Degeneracy in morals, reflected in India's booming movie industry (Bombay is dubbed 'Bollywood') and the increasing crime rate concern Sunderaraj, as does the violent hostility between Hindus and Muslims. But he is most concerned about the growing ineffectiveness of many churches in dealing with these spiritual and social evils.

MANY GODS VERSUS ONE SAVIOUR

Sunderaraj recently warned theological educators that the witness of India's church will be destroyed if syncretism is not confronted. He noted that during a synod prayer meeting of the Church of South India (the church in which he was brought up), one prayer was in the names of the Hindu god Shiva, the Gautama Buddha, and Islam's Allah, along with the name of Jesus Christ. He also noted that by the end of this century, India will have the largest Islamic population in the world – and there is very little Christian witness directed to reach it.

To help local churches teach biblical truth and also witness to neighbours of all faiths, EFI's Theological Commission holds consultations on such issues as syncretism. Other EFI Commissions and Departments minister in the areas of Christian Education, Missions, Revival and Evangelism, and Women's Ministries, to build up the churches. Agencies such as the Theological Research and Communication Institute (TRACI), produce videos and publish a 'Christian Mind Series' that applies the Christian faith to Indian society. Christianity in India, dating back to the first century, is being revitalized by today's generation of believers.

'I am thankful that EFI has the vision to strengthen the churches

[4]Valson Thampu, 'Christian Response to Corruption,' *The Christian Mind Series* (New Delhi, TRACI, April 1995).

and also the people to give leadership', says the energetic EFI General Secretary, who is also General Secretary of the Evangelical Fellowship of Asia. 'This is where WEF is so meaningful to us all. It puts us in touch with evangelicals who are facing similar problems in other parts of the world. We can share materials and strategy with each other.'

'The strength of WEF is that it is based in the church. Through WEF, churches around the world network together, to help equip the national fellowships, which in turn strengthen the local churches.'

The story of India is just one among the more than one hundred stories of national evangelical fellowships (NEFs) all over the globe. Although space does not permit those stories to be told here, WEF's *Evangelical World* magazine regularly reports on the work of NEFs. (See Appendix B for a list of countries in which WEF has member bodies.)

THE ENABLERS

WEF sees itself as a coalition, a consortium, a fellowship of grass roots churches seeking to build up themselves and each other in the faith, so that the nations will be discipled. WEF's part is to be an enabler of the national fellowships, to accomplish this goal.

'Our immediate task is to strengthen the national fellowships, so they can plan and implement nationwide strategies of co-operative evangelism', explains Jun Vencer. 'Our goal is for every NEF to have a full-time general secretary by the year 2000.

'The long-range goal is to enable the organization of effective national fellowships in the remaining countries that do not have a co-operative framework for united evangelical action. We would like to see a WEF-affiliated fellowship organized in each of the world's 237 nations by the year 2004.'

Those twin goals are a colossal challenge not only organization-ally but also in developing leadership. Since WEF is not a council of churches that can set policies for member churches, Vencer realizes that he has a major task in communication. At the grass roots, many pastors do not understand biblical principles of leader-ship: how to develop a plan to evangelize their communities, how to motivate and organize believers to accomplish the task, how to disciple those who respond.

At the national level, NEFs face the task of showing member churches and agencies how they can make a spiritual impact on the nation by working together. Many NEFs have the skills to do that; others need to know how to develop a national strategy, how to equip the churches to meet their goals of evangelizing and discipling, and how to communicate evangelical concerns to the nation.

'NOW I SEE WHAT CAN BE DONE'

To help meet the need, WEF sponsors the Leadership Development Institute, conducting seminars for regional and national fellowships. A Christian foundation has funded some costs on a matching donor basis. Experienced executives from other NEFs give their time to assist in leading the workshops. Vencer and LDI Co-ordinator Rafael Navarro developed a Training Manual[5] that includes an organizational chart for strategic planning. It shows participants the sequence of putting into effect the vision: A Discipled World for Jesus Christ.

'The key to the whole strategy is a strong NEF', the Manual states, showing how WEF donors, ministry partners (missions and agencies), and Commissions enable NEFs to mobilize churches to reach their communities, nations, and even other countries. Included in materials is a Bible study on the effective use of spiritual gifts, written by Vencer.

'The participants in these seminars develop a greater awareness of the church and appreciation of working together', reports Navarro, whose experience includes leadership and management in the church as well as in the corporate world. 'They end up with a larger vision of discipling their nation and how to go about it.'

Response has been enthusiastic as overburdened leaders have seen what can be done. They have learned not only from the visiting lecturers but also from one another. At one seminar in South-East Asia, participants came from Bangladesh, Indonesia, Kampuchea, Laos, Mongolia, Nepal, Pakistan, Sri Lanka, and Thailand.

'WEF is giving a valuable treasure to the national church by holding these seminars', said a Kampuchean leader.

'This first seminar motivated me to equip leaders from the 120 tribes I am working with', enthused an Indonesian evangelist. 'Now I want to attend seminars II and III.'

After a seminar in South America, a discouraged leader revealed that he had come with a motion to dissolve his regional association. 'But after this session on strategic planning, I have a new vision of what can be done', he testified.

'Traditionally we have perceived Latin America as reliant on outside help', another explained. 'This seminar changes our way of

---

[5] Augustin Jun Vencer , *The World for Jesus Christ*, a Primer for Leaders of National Evangelical Fellowships, (Manila: WEF, 1994).

thinking. We never thought we could do the work of God in this way.'

The Papua New Guinea Christian National Evangelical Council sponsored a seminar, during which two national newspapers and a TV station carried interviews with Jun Vencer. The Prime Minister (recently converted), the Chief Justice of the Supreme Court, two Cabinet Ministers, and two Associate Police Commissioners personally welcomed Vencer's team.

'The most exciting thing for me is building relations with my brothers – linking visions together', stated a pastor from the Pacific Island of Samoa.

'The Leadership Development seminar was the best thing that the Association of Evangelicals of Africa ever did for us', reported a Zambian pastor. The WEF LDI seminar was held in Kenya under AEA sponsorship. Co-teaching, along with Navarro and Vencer, was a Singaporean businessman, Keith Chua, who paid his own way to East Africa.[6]

'For me personally, that seminar experience sealed my love for the African people', reported Chua. 'I can see how churches in the non-Western world will play an increasing role in world evangelization. Developing leadership is an important step in that direction.'

Those responses find an echo around the world. Manfred Kohl of Germany put it this way while studying theology at Gordon-Conwell College, USA: 'The Christian church of the entire post-Communist world has no greater need than qualified national leadership at every level. We do not want Western Christianity to be dumped on us. We would love to have the tools, and then we will work it out for ourselves.'[7]

Providing tools for churches in each nation to help themselves and help others – that is the goal of WEF. To do that requires resources, as the son of a tomato-grower on a tiny island in the English Channel discovered (Chapter 6).

---

[6]Under WEF's Global Leadership Network (GLN), selected business and professional men and women contribute 15 days a year to WEF, at their own expense. GLN plans to recruit 300 of these resource people, to help develop National Evangelical Fellowships and their churches/agencies. Concerning all who help WEF, Vencer quotes 1 Chronicles 12:22: 'Day after day men came to help David, until he had a great and mighty army.'

[7]Quoted in *Contact*, Spring 1994, Gordon-Conwell Theological Seminary, Boston, USA.

CHAPTER 6

'The Lord's Conveyance'

*The bank of heaven keeps WEF afloat in rough
waters.*

'Your ticket to Africa will cost £455', the travel agent told the young lawyer, John Langlois.

John's problem was that he did not have £455. He had just started his own law practice in his native island of Guernsey, and money was scarce. Besides, anything left after living expenses went into printing and posting WEF publications.

Clyde Taylor, WEF's International Director at the time (1972), had asked John to accompany him on a tour of Africa, to share the vision of evangelicals working together. John had no money, but he could pray about it. The next morning an estate agent telephoned to ask him to handle the papers for a client purchasing a large property. The man's lawyer had been called to court for a case, and the buyer was in a hurry.

'I agreed', recalls John. 'The amount a lawyer receives for a property conveyance is determined by the value of the property. Imagine my surprise when my payment came to £454.60! It was pretty clear indication God wanted me to buy the ticket to Africa. All I had to add was 40 pence.

'And as if God had a sense of humour, the client's name was Mr. Lord. Thereafter we called it "The Lord's Conveyance".'.

Answers to prayer have been prominent in the story of John E. Langlois, member of the Guernsey Parliament, lawyer, lay preacher, and International Treasurer of the World Evangelical Fellowship. Since the late 60s, Langlois and WEF have been an inseparable part of each other. Through times of joy and times of difficulty, when WEF seemed about to die, Langlois has hung on to the call he heard while studying at London Bible College in England: to serve the Lord in WEF.

TOMATO GROWER'S SON

John's father grew tomatoes – at one time the major export of Guernsey, one of the mild Channel Islands off the coast of France. When his ancestors arrived from England in AD 1100, they were dubbed 'L'Anglois' (Norman-French for 'The English,' pronounced 'Longlay' by the islanders).

John always had an analytical mind. Even at the age of fourteen he wrote to the youth director of his denomination, 'This denomination is rotten from top to bottom!' He learned a lesson in Christian grace when the director wrote back that although he did not agree with the young upstart's judgment, he did wish him well in serving the Lord.

'Serving the Lord' meant being a missionary teacher, John decided after sensing a call to missions in 1963. He had heard of such a need through his father, who was the representative for the Worldwide Evangelization Crusade in the Channel Islands. A man of action at 21 years of age, John left his government job as a legal draftsman and enrolled at London Bible College (LBC). He also gave up the studies in Law he was taking on the side.

Missionaries and other friends advised him to continue his Law studies; they could become valuable in Christian service. So without announcing it, John quietly studied Law externally while studying Theology at college. Meanwhile his critical analysis of the church at large continued.

'I could see evangelicals drifting, as the mainline denominations had done through the years', John Langlois recalls. 'Singing choruses and listening to sermons would not protect the next generation. We were constantly evangelizing the world, but each generation seemed to lose the vision of its forefathers. If we wanted to preserve the fruit of missionary labour, we needed to make disciples as well as converts. Matthew records Jesus' command, "Make disciples." Why weren't we doing that more?'

In his last year at LBC (1969), Langlois shared his concern with the Principal, Gilbert Kirby, who had formerly been WEF's General Secretary (International Director). He asked Kirby to let him know of any suitable opportunity for Christian service. At the same time, a young New Zealander, Bruce Nicholls, was also at LBC, working on a degree in Theology. He asked Kirby if he knew of any graduate suitable to help him in the Theological ministry of WEF.

'Bruce and I had only half an hour together before he flew back to India, where he was teaching', recalls Langlois; 'but from then on, I knew God had called me to serve with WEF.'

'Why should God give me a part to play in this worldwide fellowship?' John Langlois asks when he looks back on his ministry with WEF. 'Like Gideon, who felt he was unworthy because he was the least of his father's household, I am from one of the smallest island states in the world. I am not even from a major denomination. My father was only a tomato grower. I realize that God uses those who, like Gideon, do not come in their own strength but "with the sword of the Lord". Their trust is in God.'

TENTMAKING

This Guernsey lawyer-theologian has known the inside story of God's provision for WEF over a longer period than anyone else still living. In 1969, he began serving in WEF's office, located in Lausanne, Switzerland, but lack of funds closed the office in 1971. It was a low moment in WEF's history. Dennis Clark, International Director, and the office secretary resigned. Langlois found himself the sole full-time staff member of a world organization – and without a budget.

Remembering the apostle Paul's example of tentmaking for support, he went back to Guernsey, completed his law degree, and set up his own law practice. Lawyer friends warned him that his prospects for making money were not very good. Employed by law firms, his friends enjoyed the security of salaries, whereas after meeting expenses, a self-employed lawyer might clear only a sixth of a salaried lawyer's income in the first year.

'Instead, I ended the first year with twice the amount of my friends' salary, and the next year five times as much', Langlois remembers. 'I can only account for that income as God's provision. I was able to give the larger portion of my earnings to the Lord, and live off the rest.'

By the third year, Langlois decided to merge his expanding practice in a partnership with a lawyer who had larger staff resources. The two not only agreed they would split the income evenly, but also that Langlois would take all the time he needed for WEF ministry.

However, Clyde Taylor's invitation to accompany him to Africa came before these developments, just after Langlois started his law practice. Neither man had funds for the ticket.[1] That is when 'the Lord's conveyance' came to the rescue.

Taylor, an outgoing six-foot-four American, and Langlois, a quiet

---

[1]Clyde Taylor himself received no salary from WEF, serving on a part-time basis while continuing as General Director of the National Association of Evangelicals (USA).

Channel Islander, complemented each other as they travelled through Africa. By the time they reached Zambia in the south, Langlois had heard Taylor's message so often that he was able to repeat it *verbatim* when Taylor lost his voice to laryngitis. Langlois not only spoke in Taylor's place, but also added his own testimony of personal calling – a powerful endorsement of the vision.

'Some had questioned whether it was appropriate for an American and an Englishman to travel on behalf of WEF in the post-colonial era in Africa', Langlois recalls. 'But the trip taught me that God's plans are not limited by nationality or geography. He is colour blind. He used the Africa trip to affirm my calling to serve with WEF.'

NO GIVING UP

Following the closure of the WEF office in Lausanne, finances continued to be scarce in the worldwide organization. Even Taylor, the irrepressible American optimist, became discouraged when there were no funds to finance the International Director's office, and yet there were such tremendous opportunities to strengthen the church around the world. At one particularly low period, he told Langlois that he was going to resign if there were no improvement in finances. It simply did not make sense for him to continue if he could not meet expenses.

'If you pack it in, I still won't', the Guernsey tomato grower's son told Taylor. 'I believe God has a purpose for WEF, and WEF has a future.'

First from his grandmother's barn and then from his home, Langlois distributed a quarter of a million copies of WEF publications in a ten-year period. He and Bruce Nicholls (who was teaching Theology in India), even developed an exigency plan to continue the strategic work of the Theological Commission, should WEF have to close down.

'We felt that central to our evangelical existence is our stand for the truth and our understanding of the Bible through the indwelling of the Holy Spirit enlightening our minds', Langlois still emphasizes. 'We have seen too many denominations go downhill, with people not believing anything because they have forsaken the Scriptures.'

Langlois' work as Treasurer of the Theological Commission gave him insight into WEF as a whole, and in 1980 he became International Treasurer for WEF. At times he has felt like Old Mother Hubbard, going to the financial cupboard and finding it bare. But at such times he has remembered 'The Lord's Conveyance'.

STANDING ON PRINCIPLE

It was in 1980 that friends persuaded Langlois to enter politics. He was elected to the Guernsey Parliament (known as the States), where he has headed several government ministries. His role as a senior statesman has opened up other orbits of witness, not only in public debate but also as he and his wife, Pat, have entertained political figures on state visits.

Member of Parliament Langlois is known for standing on principle, unswayed by convenience or compromise. A book exposing the use of Guernsey as a shelter for tax evasion in Britain cites Langlois as one of the lawyers who exposed the fraud.[2]

While applying his Christian principles to politics and jurisprudence, Langlois has made sure he has first applied them in his Christian ministry.

As WEF Treasurer, he ensures that the organization maintains financial accountability through internal and external audits. Each WEF office receipts donations made to it and ensures that the funds are used as designated. National offices are careful to fulfil the financial legal requirements of their governments.

FUNDING A WORLDWIDE BODY

In spite of continued financial strictures, WEF did not close down. However, lack of funding continued to slow it down. This was not a new problem for evangelicals. Back at the time of the 1846 conference, many overseas delegates spent their life savings to travel there (although the Conference was able to fully cover its own expenses). After the exhilarating inaugural assembly, by 1849 the Evangelical Alliance faced a serious financial crisis. National alliances that helped to keep the international vision alive had their own struggles for financial support. Offices had to function without adequate staff, and in extra lean years, conferences and even council meetings were postponed.

Christians, struggling to fund their local churches and denominational offices, found it difficult enough to contribute to their own national fellowship. It was even harder for them to see the need to fund a worldwide fellowship. When WEF was formed in 1951, membership fees were expected to meet the expenses of the central office. However, the annual fee was kept low in recognition of the poverty of some member countries. Members from more affluent countries were expected to give above the annual fee, to make up

[2]Gillard, *In the Name of Charity*. (London: Chatto and Windus, 1987).

the shortfall. Regrettably, it took nearly forty years for this to happen.

Part of the reason was the worldwide fiscal situation. Europe was struggling to rise from the rubble of World War II, and apart from North America, most countries were facing economic hardship. Support for the United Nations reflected the economic disparity: the USA had to bear 50% of the UN's budget in its early years, to ensure it survived. Even now, the US funds a quarter of the UN's budget.[3]

That disparity in financing a secular world organization helps to give perspective to the source of WEF finances in the 50s. Evangelicals in most countries simply did not have the funds to give. At first, over 98% of WEF's income came from the USA,[4] and even that did not cover expenses, let alone fund the development of ministries. In the US, the National Association of Evangelicals was facing its own financial needs: in some lean months, the founder and first Executive Secretary, J. Elwin Wright, did not even claim his salary.

Even if WEF could keep an office open and distribute its many significant publications, its International Director was constantly frustrated at not being able to travel and meet the membership. In the late 60s, the Billy Graham Evangelistic Association gave a grant to WEF, enabling Dennis Clark, then International Director, to circle the globe encouraging churches to reach out in mission.

When those funds ran out, there was no adequate constituency to continue support. Waldron Scott outlined three reasons for the difficulty in developing public support among Christians:

1. Pervasive apathy toward evangelical unity and co-operation in general;
2. Misunderstanding regarding the role of WEF in particular;
3. For many ordinary Christians, the strategic role of WEF is too vague and indirect to comprehend.[5]

'When I became Treasurer', recalls Langlois, 'I felt that WEF's financial shortage was not primarily a question of money. There was a tremendous amount of goodwill towards WEF, but we had to convey our statement of mission, our goals, our objectives, our long-range plans, and our aspirations in a credible programme, before people would get behind WEF financially.'

---

[3] Annual Reports of the Secretary-General of the United Nations, 1949 and 1995.
[4] WEF Executive Council Minutes, Nov. 20–22, 1976.
[5] Waldron Scott, 'General Secretary's Report,' September 25, 1979. Waldron Scott was General Secretary (now termed International Director) 1974–1980.

'GLOBAL DEACONS' AND A BLIZZARD

Scott did try to communicate the WEF vision. One method was through the concept of Global Deacons – men and women who would commit themselves to supporting WEF in prayer and by finance. They would be involved in ministry tours and special projects. One supporter who became interested was Betty Wehr in Minnesota. On one occasion, Scott took Theodore Williams, visiting from India, to express to Wehr WEF's appreciation.

A winter blizzard had knocked out electric power lines and almost buried the town. The two men abandoned their car on the main road and waded through deep snow to reach the house. Amazed that anyone would battle through the winter storm to visit her, Betty Wehr invited the two in.

Because there was no electric power to heat the house, Scott gallantly offered to light a fire in the spacious hearth. But he forgot to open the chimney damper. The visit ended unceremoniously as everyone fled outside to escape the choking smoke.

Betty Wehr's vision for WEF did not go up in smoke, however. She continued supporting it until her death. One sizable donation she sent in 1990 enabled evangelicals in Romania to establish their office.

Scott's Global Deacon idea was great, but unfortunately the number who enrolled was not. The WEF Council passed motions with great vision, but there were no funds to implement them.

A LOW POINT

In 1980 WEF proposed a merger with the Lausanne Committee on World Evangelism (LCWE), which at the time seemed able to attract funding. However LCWE did not agree, and WEF struggled on. The operating deficit continued to grow, necessitating a 50% cut in office staff in 1983. The crisis caused WEF leaders to redefine their purpose and goals, and to state them more clearly so that supporters would share in the vision of WEF. The Executive also streamlined the administrative structure.

A communications professor, James Engel of Wheaton College Graduate School, USA, noted WEF's struggles. In one of his Development classes he used WEF as a case study on viability. Comparing WEF's mission statement with its donor base, two-thirds of the class found WEF not viable. It should shut down, according to development theories. The other students thought there were some ministries WEF could continue.

Engel had a different idea. He urged David Howard, recently

appointed International Director of WEF, to draft a proposal to establish a Finance Development Department for WEF, and to submit it to the Maclellan Foundation, which supports evangelical projects.

'I presented my proposal to the Maclellan Foundation board', Howard recollects; 'but I was not too hopeful. In fact, I was putting on my coat to leave the building when Hugh Maclellan, Sr., called me back to tell me the board had decided to make the grant, and had added $20,000 for WEF to retain Engel as consultant for a year.'

1986 was the turning point in the support of WEF, states Howard. WEF's goals were better defined, and people began to see it as strategic to strengthening evangelicals worldwide to further the outreach of the church and defence of the gospel.

To emphasize its international character, WEF decided to move the International Director's office to Singapore. To head up the new Financial Development Department in USA, Howard had already appointed Galen Hiestand, who had a background of both pastoring and development. Hiestand became WEF North America Director (1986-1994), building up WEF's constituency in the USA and, in Howard's words, 'forging the North American Council into an effective, committed, hard-working body'.

'WHAT IS WEF REALLY DOING?'

Hiestand knew that Christian funding agencies sincerely want to advance God's work, but they have to ask tough questions to be sure their investment is being used in the most effective way.

'We're sure you are doing a lot of good things,' the Maclellan Foundation told Hiestand in 1988, 'but we do not know *what* it is you are doing.'

In other words, it was not enough to have a lot of useful projects. The foundation had to know how those projects furthered the overall strategy: *enabling the national associations to motivate and equip their churches to evangelize and disciple the nations.*

Hiestand and his colleague, Dwight Gibson, went to work preparing funding 'proposals' (detailed descriptions of projects), along with David Howard (up to 1992) and Jun Vencer (after 1992). They helped each Commission Director to assign quantifiable goals to their budgetary figures. Other foundations funded studies, training, and strategic planning sessions. If a foundation turned down a proposal as inadequate in detail, the North America staff went back to the drawing boards and worked on it until it was satisfactory.

The hard work satisfied the foundation. In 1992, one of its

Directors told Howard, 'Ten years ago we thought that WEF was about dead. We were wrong; you were right. If WEF is not already the most important international evangelical organization in the world, it will be by the end of this century.'

The experience with the Maclellan Foundation was typical of relationships with a number of supporters who have provided vital funding and continue to do so. One very analytical contributor announced he was coming to a WEF North America Council meeting, to check on procedures first hand. 'Is WEF handling grants as required by the donor and by the U.S. government?' he wanted to know.

At the end of his visit, he stated: 'I am completely satisfied!'

It was understandable that the foundations would have confidence in the leadership of David Howard, the well-known figure whom God had used to resuscitate WEF in the difficult 80s. But how would they view the change in leadership in 1992? As the foundations got to know Jun Vencer and sensed his vision, their confidence continued. 'We are extremely pleased with the leadership Jun Vencer brings to WEF', Hugh O. Maclellan, Jr., wrote.

THE BANK OF HEAVEN

Grants from several different foundations enabled the Commissions to develop and equip national associations, but funds to keep the North America office open came mostly from the sacrificial giving of individuals and churches.

'In the 80s, three sacrificial women, unknown to each other, practically kept the WEF North America office afloat, as far as general fund expenses were concerned', recalls Hiestand. 'They reminded me of the women who supported Jesus. Then God raised up other men and women, and opened up the bank of heaven. We started out one year with an operating deficit of $40,000, but by May we had $100,000 in the bank.'

Floyd Keck, an Iowa farmer, was another sacrificial supporter. When J. Elwin Wright, whose vision led to the forming of WEF in 1951, called for lay people to go with him around the world to encourage evangelicals to work together, only Keck volunteered. From then on he gave away most of his money and lived in a humble shack – 'more like a chicken coop', recalls Hiestand.

As Keck passed the age of 90, his daughters tried to persuade him to buy better glasses

'I don't need to see better', replied Keck. 'There are so many people in this world who do not have spiritual sight. I'd rather spend the money on them.'

The Wheaton office staff joined in the sacrificial living. There were months when they drew only part of their salaries. At times vital staff in Wheaton had to be let go, because of lack of money for salaries. One staff member and her husband took out a second mortgage on their house, in order to provide a low-interest loan to meet office expenses.

In Singapore, Administrative Officer Chuang Toy Him has persevered in spite of shortage of personnel and finance. 'The only thing that has kept me here is my commitment to the Lord and the vision of WEF', she says.

Staff everywhere have willingly made sacrifices, but they have been frustrated as they realize how much more WEF could do for evangelical associations if funding were available. They knew that in one year, the World Council of Churches raised $50 million just in the USA, for their worldwide operation. In the same year, WEF North America was able to channel only $1 million to evangelical projects.

KEEPING STRETCHED

'A critical problem is the lack of any financial reserve that would enable us to plan more strategically', states Dwight Gibson, North American Director. 'We are thankful that God has brought to us funds just at the right time, but they have had to go out as soon as they have come in. That has kept us stretched–which isn't bad, but it does create problems in planning.

'What WEF needs is the support of hundreds of churches, who will realize they can link arms with thousands of churches in other lands needing strategic development in missions, theology, leadership training, and ministries to youth and women. Or they may need direct help with religious liberty problems or in ministering to relief needs. By funding WEF, churches here can make that happen. Some pastors or lay people may also be able to give time to assist directly in these projects.'

Gibson points out that at first people may think of WEF as just another mission agency looking for support.

'But their eyes light up when they realize that it is not another mission', he explains. 'It is not a committee or council in the West trying to serve the churches "over there". It really is evangelical churches worldwide helping each other to be effective, to win their nations for Christ. Supporters begin to see its significance to all the mission and church work they have been involved in.'

Some people may misinterpret the word 'Fellowship' in WEF's name as a kind of cosy togetherness – an end in itself. 'But no one wants to give to unity – our unity has already been established in the Spirit', comments Vencer. 'Supporters need to see what we are doing with that unity – how it enables us to fulfil the mandate God has given to evangelize and disciple the nations.'

THE GIANT GUEST

Chairing the North America Council is a man who personally understands financial struggles as well as faith in God's provision. David Detert, with a doctorate in electrical engineering, owns a small communications marketing company. His business regularly takes him to Europe, where he uses the opportunity to interest people in their national associations and WEF as a whole. He understands the European church and culture, chairing the board of his local church, which has a strong Old German tradition.

During times of economic downturn in the world, Detert's business accounts have been in the red. Those times have cast him and his wife, Joyce, upon God. So he understands the financial struggles of WEF, and applies to its needs the same principles of faith and organizational integrity.

Detert's first contact with WEF goes back to the early 70s, when a guest speaker at his church stayed with the Deterts. That started a long friendship which contributed to the Deterts' spiritual growth. The guest was a giant of a man. His name: Clyde Taylor, International Director of WEF.

'Wouldn't it be great to have a part in the work that Dr. Taylor is doing!' Dave said to Joyce at the time. Today, as North America chairman, he adds, 'Imagine – what a privilege God has given us!'

Without exception, North American Council members feel the same way about their own participation. They include a seminary president, two corporate directors, an insurance broker, the owner of a bakery chain, the executive directors of two missions associations, a missionary author, a pastor, and executives of the US and Canadian evangelical associations. They have placed their organizational skills in the hands of their Lord, and they depend on him for his financial provision for WEF.

'WHAT YOU NEED, I WILL GIVE'

While that has been the experience of evangelicals in North America, in other nations also, God has been raising up men and women who have the grace of giving.

'My calling is to provide logistics for God's people to advance the

Kingdom', a Jamaican chicken rancher told Jun Vencer. Each week he ships half a million chicks to buyers, and passes on most of the profits to fund Christian work.

A grant from Germany paid for the WEF head office space in Singapore. The Wuerttemberg Synod, Stuttgart, has supported the Theological Commission significantly. Koreans help fund Theological scholarships.

Substantial funding for the 9th General Assembly, held in Manila, Philippines in 1992, came from Britain, Germany, Japan, Korea, Singapore, and the USA, with other nations assisting. As the economy of poorer nations improves and as they catch the vision, they too are increasing their giving to WEF. And their national fellowships are seeking to be self-reliant as much as possible. Vencer was impressed when a delegate from the Evangelical Alliance of Angola – a country still suffering the effects of a devastating civil war – handed him a cheque for US$425 – the Alliance's annual membership fee. That amount would equal a teacher's annual wage in Angola.

'We in Africa were very encouraged at the way a recent March for Jesus in Nairobi was funded', WEF's Chairman, Tokunboh Adeyemo, reported to the International Council during a budget session. 'The pastors said they would raise the money among the churches, in spite of the poverty of the people. They worked on the budget and whittled it down. For several weeks, we met for special prayer. I was amazed at the way the money came in – not a single penny from outside the country.'

Tadashi (Joshua) Tsutada, Chairman of the Evangelical Fellowship of Asia, shared with the Council what he felt was the secret of raising finances for the Lord's work:

'People in other countries look at Japan and say, "You are rich and can easily raise funds, but our country is poor." True, Japan is rich now, but it was not always so. After World War II, our economy was in ruins. But the Japanese churches, although few in number and membership, started sacrificial giving right then. If they had not established a pattern then, they would not be giving now, when they are better off.

'There are two essential keys for giving to God's work:

'First is the need for faith – to trust God to supply.

'Second is the biblical principle of giving to meet someone else's need.

'We tend to think of our own needs, but those may just be "wants". Instead, we should be thinking of the needs of other churches in other lands that do not have what we have. Our principle should be: What you need, I will give. By faith.'

INTERNATIONALIZING THE SUPPORT BASE

Jun Vencer finds that he can easily talk about finance with leaders in poorer countries, because they know the background of poverty from which he came. And he knows from experience that even the poorest Christian can contribute something.

'When I accepted the position of International Director of WEF, I woke up the next morning without a guaranteed salary,' he recollects. 'I thought back to my roots – how God provided for me in many difficult circumstances. I asked him to show me that support could come from the Third World, not only from the West. Now more than a third of my support comes from my own nation, the Philippines.'

Vencer challenged a group of Asian businessmen with statistics showing that the majority of the world's unevangelized people live in Asia.

'At the same time, the most rapid economic growth area is the Pacific and South-East Asia,' he reminded them. 'God must have a plan for Asian Christians to be more involved in meeting financial needs.'

That is what happened in planning the Asian Missions Congress sponsored by the Evangelical Fellowship of Asia in 1990 in Korea.

'We had the conviction that Asian Christians should underwrite most of the budget, but the initial estimate was far beyond our capabilities,' says Tsutada. 'The treasurer pared it in half by cost-cutting measures. I then presented it to our EFA assembly, representing 17 Asian nations. I asked them to discuss what they could do, and then make a faith pledge.'

A hum of discussion ran among the delegate groups, followed by an embarrassing silence. Finally a hand went up.

'Let me tell you,' Tsutada recalls; 'that first hand was not from the richer nations, like Japan or Korea or Singapore. They probably did not want to dominate the process. The first hand was from one of the struggling nations – India. The second hand was from the Philippines.'

After several delegates pledged in faith, the Korean delegation spoke up: 'We do not have the money to do this, but in faith we have decided that we should pay for the accommodation, the food, and the transport within Korea, of the entire 5000 delegates to the Congress.'

'Japan and Singapore then made their pledges,' says Tsutada. 'By the end of the Congress, all expenses had been covered, and 94% came from Asia. That was a great encouragement to us all.'

As Vencer travels to other parts of the world, he is conscious that until recently many developing countries have looked upon America and other Western countries as 'money bags' available to the rest of the world – and that perception can affect Christians, preventing them from putting their resources, however meagre, at God's disposal.

To stress this point, Vencer once told evangelical leaders in Bulgaria that he was not there because of American money but because of Filipino money. When he returned to the Philippines, he told about Bulgaria's struggle to establish an evangelical office. Two Chinese businessmen wrote cheques that covered the Bulgarian office budget for its first year.

Later, a church in the USA helped to support the office under WEF's Adopt-a-Nation plan, which encourages short-term support of developing national fellowships. After three years, the assisted fellowship is supposed to begin paying back the amount, in order to assist another new fellowship.

On one visit to WEF's International Office in Singapore, someone suggested holding a dinner for donors.

'But we have no money to pay for the dinner', Vencer pointed out.

'We will take care of that', replied a WEF Singapore board member.

After the dinner, a guest remarked that it was the first dinner sponsored by a Christian organization at which he had not been handed a donation pledge card. And when Vencer went to pay his room bill at the hotel, he found it was already paid. The hotel owner, a member of the board, had covered it.

THE WEST STILL SHARES RESPONSIBILITY

Internationalizing WEF's support base is a welcome development. But it is no reason for Christians in the West to let up in their own giving. The fact is that, regardless of remarkable growth rates elsewhere, the 'G7 Nations' (six in the West plus Japan) dominate the world economy.[6] This places the major share of responsibility on evangelicals in these nations to help finance the outreach of the

---

[6]The 'G7 Nations' (Britain, Canada, France, Germany, Italy, Japan, USA) are members of GATT: the General Agreement on Tariffs and Trade. G7 members account for nearly half of the world's economy. In 1995, the USA led with 21.2%, followed by Japan (8.4), Germany (5), and the others ranging between 3.6 and 1.9. (Sources: World Bank, IMF, *The Economist*.) Although Japan is included among the G7 as a nation, it must be remembered that evangelicals account for only 0.32 of the population, with most of them among the lower income bracket. Thus their giving has been remarkable.

gospel in countries of economic need. Men and women without current hope and eternal life cannot await the development of national economies.

The apostle Paul put together the equation of giving when he reminded the Corinthian believers of their giving out of poverty and in affliction. He pointed out the reciprocity of one church meeting another's needs and vice versa, and the stimulation and encouragement that the giving of one church can be to another. (2 Cor. 8:2, 14; 9:2.)

Langlois also knows that support for WEF and its programmes requires a worldwide partnership – 'fellowship in the gospel'. It demands commitment, sacrifice, and sometimes a miraculous provision – like *'the Lord's conveyance.'*

CHAPTER 7

A Task as Big as the Globe

A Brazilian witnessing in Albania is just part of today's exciting missions scene.

'Socialism has triumphed!' declared Comrade Envir Hoxha, President of Albania. 'The nation has at last achieved atheism. Religion is banished. There is no God.'

That was in 1967. For the next 24 years, Dictator Hoxha continued to silence opposition and stifle religion by imprisoning or killing one fifth of Albania's three million population. At one time the nation, tucked between Greece and the former Yugoslavia, was 40% Muslim and 18% Christian (Orthodox and Roman Catholic). Albania became Europe's poorest and most repressive nation, rejecting the cautious reforms that several other Communist states allowed.

Prospects for Christian witness were dismal. Bibles were banned; worship had to be in secret; Christians faced discrimination and persecution. A pastor who was found praying or singing a hymn in public, or handing a religious book to one of his church members, could face a prison term.[1]

As to visitors' witnessing, any Albanian seen speaking at length to a foreigner could be sentenced to prison for three years. Unable to obtain visas to enter the country, mission members prayed and awaited the day when they could enter.

Hoxha's regime fell and Albania did open up in 1991. Missions, especially short-term projects, poured into the country – some thirty of them. But they discovered a young Brazilian missionary was already quietly living there, witnessing in the Albanian language.

---

[1]Persecution of evangelicals in Albania was not a new phenomenon. One hundred years before, the Albanian evangelist Gjerasim Qiriazi had attempts made on his life for preaching the gospel. Papers given at the 'One Hundredth Anniversary Celebration of the Death of Gjerasim Qiriazi, 1894–1994' (Tirane: Albanian Evangelical Alliance, 1994) trace the lengthy contact Albania has had with Christianity – ever since the apostle Paul's time.

SPIRITUAL TRANSFORMATION

The story of that Brazilian missionary, Najua Diba, goes back across the Atlantic to the sprawling industrial city of Sao Paulo in South America. Born of Lebanese immigrants, Najua grew up to become a teacher, but one who lived for the pleasures of the world. At first, it seemed to be an exciting life for her and her friends, but this lifestyle eventually became frightening to Najua.

Finally Najua gave in to a friend who pestered her to attend a church where young people were finding deliverance from sin.

'Jesus Christ became my Saviour that night', says Najua. 'He cleansed me and changed me. It was amazing – I never again craved drugs or drink!'

Najua's partying friends were stunned by the dramatic change in her. She boldly witnessed about her Saviour wherever she went. Longing to spend her life as a missionary among people who had never heard the gospel, she believed that God could do for others what he had done for her. Her pastor told her about the Antioch Mission School in Sao Paulo. There she met a missionary teacher, Barbara Burns, who helped her grow spiritually.

Burns' journey from USA to Sao Paulo had taken a few un-anticipated twists. Unable to practise as a missionary nurse in Brazil because of government regulations, she accepted an invitation to teach at a Bible school in the interior.

'I jumped at the chance, because I really wanted to teach missions', recalls Burns. 'But the Brazilian principal would not let me. To him, the concept of missions was truly a "foreign idea". He thought that only foreigners, not Brazilians, were meant to be missionaries.'

But Burns was able to weave in a lot about Christ's Great Commission as she taught Bible survey and church history. Students became concerned for unreached peoples. When a graduate went to Africa as a missionary, ending up in jail during a revolution, students and staff joined in regular prayer for him. From those prayer meetings arose a greater burden for the unevangelized in Brazil and the rest of the world, and the founding of Brazil's first mission agency, the Antioch Mission.

'It was a small beginning for what is now a much larger movement', says Burns, who became a training consultant to the WEF Missions Commission. 'Candidates needed to be equipped, so we started a missionary training school, and at last I was able to teach missions.'

Today there are more than twenty such schools in Brazil, but it was to that first little school that Najua Diba came. She studied statistics on countries all over the world and decided that Albania was probably one of the hardest to reach with the gospel.

TOUGH ASSIGNMENT

'The Lord is calling me to be a missionary to Albania!' she announced to Burns one day, her brown eyes sparkling at the thought. Burns had become Najua's close friend, more than just her teacher.

'Albania?' Burns repeated incredulously. 'You've never been out of Brazil, and you want to go to the toughest mission field in Europe? Forget it! Missionaries can't even get into Albania.'

Burns told herself that Najua was just an immature Christian, idealistic, with lots of enthusiasm but not the stuff needed for a land like Albania.

The Brazilian girl listened politely and continued her witness at home. Still, in her prayer times her burden for Albania grew, and she read everything she could find about the country. When an opportunity opened in the late 80s for her to study English in Britain, she took it. Albania was a lot closer now!

Someone told her about an Albanian community in the south of what was then Yugoslavia, so off she went – closer still to Albania.

While studying the language, *Tosk Albanian*, Najua joined forces with an expatriate Albanian couple, John and Von Quanrud working with the Frontiers Mission. Soon she had made friends with Albanian college students, and with a small group of Albanian believers. The young Albanian who pastored that group had been led to Christ in 1975 by a Slovenian evangelist named Peter Kuzmic, who would one day be called 'the Billy Graham of Eastern Europe' (see Kuzmic's story in chapter 10).

Najua went on field trips with her new friends across the border into Albania. On these forays, they left their own Bibles behind in inconspicuous places, praying that the Lord would lead prepared people to find them. However, they were very discreet in making any personal contacts, aware that secret police were watching. They kept in mind that three years in prison could await anyone seen conversing at length with a foreigner; possessing a Bible could bring fines and imprisonment.

THE HOTEL MAID

At the end of one 'tourist' visit to Tirana, the capital, Najua picked up her bags to leave her hotel room. As she swung open the door, a maid entered to clean the room. Najua stopped in the doorway as an inner voice urged her to witness to the maid.

This is just a crazy impulse, she told herself. It could get the maid into trouble — dismissal, and maybe three years in prison. Anyway, 'hit and run' witnessing was not the team's policy. In Albania's atheistic climate, it was important to establish friendship before witnessing. Besides, Najua's companions were already on the bus and the driver was impatiently blowing his horn. There was just no time.

But the impression grew so strong that Najua dropped her bags, closed the door, and faced the startled maid.

'Do you know God?' Najua blurted out, wishing she had time to build up a little rapport.

'I have heard of God', replied the maid in a low voice, glancing nervously around the room. 'This morning I prayed that if he exists, he would show himself to me!'

While the bus driver continued to honk, Najua hurriedly explained the way of salvation to the maid, and left her a Bible. Then Najua ran downstairs and jumped on the departing bus, wondering how such a brief encounter could have any lasting results. But she kept praying for the girl, whose name was Lumi.

Seven months later, the Brazilian missionary slipped across the border again and went to look for Lumi. The girl's face was radiant as she told Najua about her joy in Christ.

'Now I want to take you to meet my family', Lumi said. 'They have all come to know God too! But we need someone to teach us the Bible. Can't you stay?'

As Najua was debating what to do during those months, Hoxha's hated regime collapsed (1991), and so did restrictions on foreigners. So the Brazilian missionary moved into Albania. She stayed with Lumi's delighted family until she could find a room to rent.

'That's how a Brazilian came to be the first resident foreign missionary in Albania', explains Barbara Burns. 'When I went to visit Najua in Albania, I found this young woman, who I thought would never make it, witnessing to everyone she met. She was deeply involved in a rapidly growing church.

'We went to the beach one day for a break. To Najua, that was another prime opportunity for witnessing. She started talking with a woman, and in no time men and women, all in swimsuits, were crowding around to hear this Brazilian girl tell how to find eternal life. They listened intently for at least forty minutes. There is such a spiritual hunger in Albania today!' Burns concluded.

Najua is one of a small army of Brazilian missionaries Barbara Burns knows, for no longer do Brazilian churches think of missions as an imported concept. They are sending workers into some of the most difficult spots, including North Africa, Israel, and China.

'FROM MISSION FIELD TO MISSION FORCE'

It was in Sao Paulo that the first all-Latin-America missions conference took place in 1987. Called COMIBAM,[2] the conference at-
tracted men and women from all over the continent, as well as from
Portugal, Spain, and other countries.[3]

'COMIBAM marks the transition of Latin America from a
mission field to a mission force!' declared Argentinian Luis Bush,
who had grown up in Brazil. Bush had seen that transition coming.
While pastoring in San Salvador, he had been challenged by the Bible
messages of WEF's Wade Coggins at a WEF Missions Commission
seminar.

At the time, most Latin Americans thought of themselves only as
recipients of missions. A missions conference would not succeed,
pastors predicted. But with a sharpened vision himself, Bush proved
them wrong. He organized the first missions conference for Central
America – and a thousand people packed out the sessions held in
his church.

Brazil's Edison Queiroz, Barbara Burns' pastor at the time, told
the crowd how his expanding flock had built a 'left-over' church
building. 'They did not think they could keep up their missionary
giving and also build a larger church. But we made a commitment
to meet our mission responsibilities first. So our new church was
built from left-over money.'

Queiroz then asked delegates to stand if they were committing
their lives to God for missions. Nearly everyone stood. When he
asked how many had previously done so, most of the rest of the
audience stood up.

Bush and his colleagues marvelled at the response. However, they
knew it represented a tremendous challenge.

'In Latin America, we are behind some other parts of the world
in understanding missions', Bush explained. 'Eager volunteers want
to get up and go to other lands, but they will come back disillusioned
if they are not properly trained. And then their churches will be
turned off missions.

---

[2]COMIBAM: Congreso Misionero Ibero-Americano, or Ibero-American Missions
Conference. ('Iberian' is used as a generic term for the Portuguese and Spanish
languages, which emanated from the Iberian Peninsula in Europe.) Following the
successful conference, COMIBAM has continued as a Latin American missionary
movement.

[3]COMIBAM was assisted by Partners International, the Latin American Evangelical
Confederation (CONELA), the Lausanne Committee for World Evangelism, WEF,
and other agencies. Most of the 3000 delegates or their supporting churches paid for
travel and accommodation.

'Our research uncovered 180 Latin American organizations that call themselves "missions" but most do not know how to prepare missionaries, how to support them, or how to administer their work. That is where we need help from experienced groups.'[4]

ACHILLES HEEL OF MISSIONS

William (Bill) D. Taylor,[5] Director of the Missions Commission of WEF, hears other Christian leaders voice these needs as he travels the globe, assisting national fellowships and mission associations in the churches' outreach.

'Adequate preparation is the most critical need', says Taylor. 'Take the case of a Brazilian missionary we'll call Salinas, who went to West Africa all by himself. He was full of zeal, but he had no training, no orientation to Islamics, and no one to shepherd him.'

The local Muslim priest debated with the Brazilian missionary, and finally set a challenge. They should both spend time fasting and praying, and then decide which way – Islam or Christianity – was the way to God. Depending on the outcome, one of them would convert to the other's way.

The young Brazilian had little knowledge of the Islamic meaning of the familiar terms he heard – words such as God (Allah), sin, salvation. They sounded biblical but had very different meaning. Lonely, uninstructed in the Bible, and influenced by a strong Muslim priest, Salinas publicly converted to Islam. Today he is a prime opponent of the gospel in that area – a tragic setback for Christian witness there, and for the missionary vision of the church that sent him from Brazil.

'Churches and missions in the Two-Thirds World are learning that responding to a call is perhaps the easiest part of missions', comments Taylor. 'Preparing, orientating, coaching, administering, and caring for the missionary are equally important. The cases of Najua and Salinas show a crucial contrast: one was prepared, discipled, supported by prayer and care; the other was not. As churches catch the vision of missions, they need help in developing basic mission infrastructures to support the vision.'

Dr. Young Jun Son, Director of the Korean Missionary Training Institute, agrees. 'You have heard of thousands of Korean men and women volunteering for missions?' asks Son, who has been a missionary in Japan and in USA. 'Praise God for that response! But

---

[4]W. Harold Fuller, *Tie Down the Sun* (Scarborough: SIM, 1990).

[5]Bill Taylor was born of missionary parents in Costa Rica, Central America, and brought up in Guatemala, where he later served as a missionary.

have you seen the casualties returning, because although they had zeal, they had little understanding of what was involved?

'That results not only in spiritual defeat for the young missionary who has failed. It also causes confusion in the ranks of other missionaries and the emerging churches, and it demotivates the supporting churches. They have sent unprepared men and women out, with great expectations, but some of those have come back broken in spirit. The churches do not understand what has happened, and they do not want to risk another defeat. So they give up on missions.'

As more Korean missionaries returned home in confusion or defeat, Son decided to do his part to overcome the problem. He set up the Missionary Training Institute under the Presbyterian Church of Korea General Assembly – a short-term, intensive missions programme for seminary graduates. It includes English language immersion, essential for international travel and ministry. To staff the Institute, Son calls on established missions to supply visiting seminar lecturers.

'Dr. Son has met a great need in Korea,' says James Hudson Taylor III of the Overseas Missionary Fellowship. 'Many Koreans are serving effectively in other cultures because of the preparation MTI gave them.'

INTERNATIONAL TEAM

The Missions Commission has been thoroughly international from the start. A Korean Theologian, Chun Chae Ok, was its first Director, from 1974–1979,[6] with Wade Coggins as Chair. Chun was followed by Theodore Williams, founder of the Indian Evangelical Mission (1979-1986), and William D. Taylor (1986 to present). The Commission's Purpose and Vision statements read:

PURPOSE: *To equip the Church and, in particular, the regional and national missions alliances to carry out the Great Commission.*
VISION: *To serve as an international partnering-networking team that shares ideas, information, and resources to empower the global missions movement to effectively train and send missionaries. We do this by affirming and facilitating the vision of regional and national missions leaders.*

---

[6]Dr. Chun was the first female doctoral graduate of Fuller Theological Seminary. After serving as a missionary in Pakistan, she became Principal of Ewha Woman's University in Korea.

'WEF does not send out its own missionaries', Taylor points out. 'Nor do we take the place of missionary societies. We exist to help the churches that missions establish, to continue the missionary vision. Our role is to enable the national associations to mobilize their own member churches to do that effectively. Call us enablers, catalysts, mobilizers, motivators – we exist in order to help the churches themselves fulfil the Great Commission from their own national bases.'

Through seminars, conferences, newsletters, and training manuals, the Commission starts right at grass roots level, with material to help the local church stimulate prayer and missionary vision. It provides tools through the various levels of training, planning strategy, and mission-church partnering. It also publishes 'how to' books to strengthen the global missionary movement.

'For instance, we have an International Training Programme that provides scholarships for developing missionary trainers', Taylor explains. 'We have a team of experienced volunteers who visit missionary training centres as consultants, mentors, and teachers. Our *Training for Cross-Cultural Ministries* bulletin goes to more than five hundred training centres worldwide and over one thousand individuals.'

One of the most strategic training seminars was held in Pasadena, California, USA, in 1994, for WEF's International Missionary Training Associates. It brought together 96 key leaders from 32 nations, who worked on plans for developing training programmes in their own contexts.

'The seminar opened my eyes to the need to link up with others who are doing missionary training', reported Met Castillo, President of the Asian Missions Commission. 'WEF provides linkages at the international level, but we also need to do this regionally and nationally.'

Rodolfo Giron, President of COMIBAM, hit home with a message about David and Goliath. 'David refused to put on Saul's armour. Instead, he chose stones for his sling. Methods, tools, and strategies that were of great value in the historical missions movement may not fit the needs of emerging Two-Thirds World missions.'

Taylor and his staff saw that principle applied in the South Pacific Missionary Training Consultation held in New Zealand in 1995. It involved 60 key leaders from eight islands in WEF's South Pacific Region.

'My wife, Yvonne, and I will never forget the background to this', Taylor says. 'Our Consultation was preceded by the annual South Pacific Prayer Assembly, attended by some 250 believers from the islands. The spiritual leader of the Solomon Islands, Michael

Maileau, invited Australian and New Zealand delegates to come forward and pray with delegates from the smaller islands, committing themselves to missionary outreach together.

'It was a partial prelude of the majestic worship scenes in heaven. But it was much more: the reality of such diverse believers united in the spirit of partnership, each bringing strengths to the missionary movement.'

ALARMING CASUALTY RATES

Mission-minded churches in all continents hope that the emphasis on better preparation will overcome an alarming trend they have been noticing: the number of missionaries who came home early or who did not return for another term of service.

For instance, in the 80s, Hong Kong missions leaders noted a 'casualty rate' of 55%. (This is gradually lowering.) In Brazil in 1993, a speaker at the National Missions Congress stated that of the 5,400 missionaries sent out in the last five years, a large percentage returned to Brazil after less than two years of service. Of these, most would not return as missionaries. To help reduce this attrition rate, the Association of Brazilian Missions Teachers (APMB) was formed in 1992.

North American and European missions are also concerned about their attrition rates. The reasons given for high casualty rates are lack of effective training, inadequate on-field pastoring, and unsustained financial support.

Responding to these concerns, WEF has launched the International Missionary Research Project (IMRP). Taylor is excited about its newest focus, called ReMAP: Reducing Missionary Attrition Project.

'It is unique because it includes missions worldwide', Taylor explains. 'This enables researchers to identify the causes of undesirable missionary attrition in different situations, under different types of missions – Western and non-Western. The goal is to help missionaries sustain effective ministry over a long-term period.'

'We feel that this study will be very important to the whole missionary movement', states ReMAP Co-ordinator Giron, a Guatemalan who has been a pastor and missionary. 'Although we are excited about the numbers of missionaries we hear about, we are also shocked to learn about the numbers of casualties – those who last only a year, or who don't continue after one term. That represents a great loss to the outreach of the church of Jesus Christ. We want to help overcome that loss and the harm it does.'

The ReMAP survey formed the core of the Missions Commission

plenary seminar in 1996. For some time to come, missions and churches worldwide will be analysing the results and their application to different contexts. Mike Stachura, President of Advancing Churches in Missions Commitment (ACMC) says: 'I wholeheartedly endorse WEF's ReMAP plan to both analyse missionary attrition and to create a forum for addressing how we can prayerfully turn around this problem.'

MAJOR ISSUES

The Missions Commission is concerned about more than missionary recruitment, training, and care. A rapidly changing world is challenging the most basic assumptions of evangelical missions. WEF's Theological Commission (see Chapter 10) has worked closely with the Missions Commission to provide biblical answers to the critics of Christian mission.

One common charge is that it is arrogant or culturally insensitive to take the gospel to people of other faiths. To answer that criticism, the Theological Commission has published biblical studies on *The Uniqueness of Christ in a Pluralistic World*. Another study discusses *The Gospel and Culture*. WEF's international membership lends great strength and credibility to these and other studies involving theologians from all parts of the world.

WEF's Missions Commission publications and seminars reflect the conviction that it is the responsibility of the church to give everyone – whether non-Christian or 'Christianized' – opportunity to hear and understand the gospel of Jesus Christ. After all, that viewpoint is one of the distinctives of being an evangelical (see chapter 14).

As to cultural arrogance, WEF does not condone cultural insensitivity on the part of Christian missionaries from any nation. (Today's missionaries are not only from the West, but from all continents.) They need to respect the cultural heritage of their host country, ministering with a servant attitude. At the same time, the gospel will always confront harmful practices such as female circumcision and widow-burning. 'The gospel must judge every culture', stated the African theologian, Byang Kato (see chapter 4).

The globalization of vibrant Christianity, accompanied by an increasing missionary vision for unreached peoples, is the most encouraging fact of our times. Half of the total number of Christians live in the developing world.[7]

[7]Bryant L. Myers, *The Changing Shape of World Mission* (Monrovia, Ca: MARC, 1993).

Increasingly, missions from West and East, North and South, work in partnership, each contributing its strength. WEF's 1992 consultation, 'Towards Interdependent Partnerships', in Manila, Philippines, brought together 95 missions leaders from 35 nations to explore the topic.[8]

The biggest factor is the size of the task itself, increasing exponentially because of population growth. People who argue that the day of missions is over forget that we do not live in a static world. They also ignore the globalized Christian mission vision and force.

'Don't think the day of missions is over', says Panya Baba, Nigerian mission leader and former WEF Missions Commission member. 'Experienced Western missions should not think they can leave the task up to the rest of the world. The task is greater than any one of us can face alone. The church of Jesus Christ must work together to evangelize those who are still unreached, as well as the millions who are coming into the world all the time.'

It is true that some governments restrict Christian missionaries. But Loh Hoe Peng, a Singaporean architect who co-ordinates the WEF Task Force on Tentmaking,[9] does not think of any country as completely 'closed'. Loh's parents came from China, and he himself moved from another restricted country to Singapore.

'Most countries will give visas for experienced men and women in professions or industries', says Loh. 'Even if open witnessing is discouraged, the Holy Spirit can use the presence of a Christian to make a powerful statement for the gospel.'

Loh and his colleagues invited suggestions from around the world, and Jonathan Lewis, Missions Commission Publications Co-ordinator, compiled them into *Working Your Way to the Nations: A Guide to Effective Tentmaking*, published by WEF.

A GLOBAL NETWORK

'I am thankful for the vision of Christian leaders who initiated the World Evangelical Fellowship', says WEF International Director Jun Vencer. 'It provides a non-denominational body able to help the church worldwide. It does not come with its own agenda but helps churches, missions, and associations to fulfil their agendas. It also provides scope for agencies with evangelistic and missionary

---

[8]William D. Taylor, Ed., *Kingdom Partnerships for Synergy in Missions* (Pasadena, Ca: William Carey Library, 1994).

[9]'Tentmaking' is used to describe Christians who take up employment in restricted countries, instead of entering as members of a mission. Their witness is on a personal, not public, basis. The term refers to Acts 18:3.

distinctives that can strengthen the national associations in their outreach. God has raised up several very effective groups that work along with WEF – such as DAWN, Lausanne, and AD2000.'

DAWN is the acronym for Discipling a Whole Nation, initiated by Jim Montgomery in the Philippines in 1975. It uses a nationwide, comprehensive, rather than piecemeal, approach to evangelism. DAWN now represents a special-interest-evangelism arm of WEF, under the Missions Commission.

LAUSANNE is the ongoing evangelism consortium that grew out of the International Consultation on World Evangelism (ICOWE) sponsored by the Billy Graham Evangelistic Association in Lausanne, Switzerland, in 1974. That seminal gathering motivated evangelicals in a number of nations to form evangelism committees. The Lausanne Committee for World Evangelism (LCWE) has provided a broad umbrella for these committees, and has sponsored important discussions on major issues, including Evangelism and Social Responsibility, The Gospel and Culture, Christian Witness to Jews, Muslims, Nominal Christians, People of Traditional African Religions, and Secularized People. These have been published in a series titled *Lausanne Occasional Papers*.

AD2000 AND BEYOND was initiated at the first Global Consultation for World Evangelization (GCOWE), held in Singapore in 1989. Under the leadership of Thomas Wang (Chinese) and Luis Bush (Argentine), AD2000 has the goal of 'a church for every people and the gospel for every person by the year 2000'. AD2000 co-ordinates the activities of key 'tracks' and networks that contribute toward this goal, including mobilization of new missionaries, urban evangelism, church planting, prayer, and specialized media.

In May 1995, 4000 participants from about 180 countries gathered in Seoul, Korea, for GCOWE II, to plan strategy up to the end of this century. WEF's Jun Vencer praised the organizational skills of the Korean hosts in caring for their visitors and making the massive conference run smoothly. Two-thirds of the participants were from Africa, Asia, and Latin America, and three-quarters of the funding came from those areas. A number of WEF people and related agencies have participated in the realization of this end-of-the-century vision. Before departing from the Conference, delegates declared: 'We resolve, by God's grace, no longer to ignore the challenges, nor miss the opportunities set before us. This is the time for which we were born.'[10]

MISSIONARY MEDIA: *World By 2000* is a consortium initiated by four radio agencies (FEBC, HCJB, SIM, TWR) in 1985 to produce a half-hour daily programme in every language spoken by

[10]From the GCOWE '95 Declaration.

at least one million people, and to achieve this goal by the end of the century. *The Jesus Film* is Campus Crusade's strategic audio-visual ministry to reach the same major linguistic groups (some three hundred remaining) with the video film, *Jesus*. The language versions of the film are having an unprecedented viewing audience worldwide, even in several restricted countries.

In 1988 researcher David Barrett and editor James Reapsome (of *Evangelical Missions Quarterly, Pulse*) identified 387 end-of-the-century evangelism projects sponsored by denominations and organizations. Patrick Johnstone's *Operation World* (Fifth Edition, 1993)[11] lists these special efforts as well as the broad spectrum of missionary programmes throughout the world. Johnstone's well-organized, detailed statistics and summary reports have done much to increase effective prayer and vision for missionary outreach.

Most people are familiar with the development of European missions, including the pioneering Moravians who sailed to the Pacific Islands, William Carey who translated the Scriptures (whole or portions) into 35 of the languages of India, Hudson Taylor who ventured into the heart of China, and David Livingstone who fought the slave trade in East Africa. Sending agencies in Europe and North America (with a total of perhaps 90,000 missionaries) are still active, but increasingly their supporters are asking, 'What are Christians in other lands doing to spread the gospel?' The development of indigenous missions in India helps answer that question.

INDIA CASE STUDY

As the Evangelical Fellowship of India (EFI) developed in the 1950s, Ben Wati, then Secretary-Treasurer, challenged EFI to have a missionary vision. In 1954, its first missions project was to support an independent Indian missionary in Kenya. In 1957 the project was called 'Indian Evangelical Overseas Mission'. In 1965 EFI launched the Indian Evangelical Mission, under the leadership of a Methodist Bible teacher, Theodore Williams.

He urged churches all over India to evangelize nationwide. The population, second in numbers only to China, was expanding at the rate of 13 million a year. Communication was a major obstacle among the 1650 languages and dialects, requiring cross-cultural missions. Missionaries met with hostility in their own land when they ventured into the strongholds of other religions, including Hinduism and Islam.

[11]Patrick Johnstone, *Operation World* (Carlisle, UK: OM Publishing, 1993).

The current General Director, Theodore Srinivasagam, had committed his life to the work of missions while doing research in Britain for a Ph.D. in Marine Biology. Returning to India, he and his wife, Diana, a medical doctor, became IEM's first 'overseas' missionaries, as they were seconded to work in Thailand with the Overseas Missionary Fellowship. Later they returned to IEM administration, and in 1993, Srinivasagam became General Director.

Today, IEM fields some 450 missionaries. However, it is one of 80 Indian missions included in the India Missions Association. These field a total of 9600 cross-cultural missionaries, most serving in India and supported mainly from within the country.[12]

India is not a wealthy country, and Christians certainly are not in the big money bracket. But EFI has always sought to develop the principle of giving in its churches. Finance from overseas can be attractive and has its place, but EFI is conscious that it can also cripple church giving and create foreign dependency if not handled wisely.

While he was General Secretary of EFI, Wati was offered $1 million by an overseas industrialist to use in his ministry. It was a generous and sincere offer, but Wati relates how he felt that the gift could harm his work in the end. The industrialist then offered the money to the Evangelical Fellowship of India (of which Dr. Wati was then General Secretary), but EFI turned it down, saying, 'Big money would kill EFI.' The same amount was offered to another indigenous mission (see chapter 13 re. Friends Missionary Prayer Band), which also declined.

'It was a major test,' commented John Richard, 'but Wati and his colleagues chose the way of faith rather than materialism.'

INTO THE NEXT MILLENNIUM

'India is just one example of how the church of Jesus Christ is rising to the challenge of missions', states WEF's Bill Taylor. 'In every land, the church must live and thrive in a changing context. It must proclaim the changeless gospel and the unique Christ of the Scriptures.

'We cannot be triumphal as we face the spiritual need of the world. Religions which deny that Jesus Christ is the Saviour are themselves engaged in active "missionary" outreach – even in Western nations that have traditionally been called Christian.

'However, we do praise God for the Christian missionary vision that has transformed churches in many nations into potential

[12]*Indian Missions*, India Missions Association, Delhi, April—Sept. 1995 issue.

mission-sending bases. We praise him for the spirit of inter-dependent partnership that must guide and control the global outreach of the church as it moves into the next millennium.

'WEF's Missions Commission is one more example of the global church in partnership.'

CHAPTER 8

'Bind Us Together, Lord'

Love transforms hostility as churches help overcome tragedy.

'Please forgive me!' cried the white-haired Episcopalian bishop, Adonia Sebununguri. He was taking part in the Rwanda Church Leaders' Meeting in 1994, to seek 'healing and reconciliation' following the tragic genocidal war between Hutus and Tutsis.

Forty-five delegates from seven denominations and several para-church groups met in Nairobi, Kenya, for four days of prayer, Bible study, reconciliation, and planning. All had lost relatives or friends among the one million Rwandans who had been massacred. They knew many among the two million others who had fled to neighbouring countries. They were ashamed to admit that not only had Hutus and Tutsis mercilessly killed each other, but also that among the killers were Christians.

In many cases, the killers had slaughtered men, women, and children in the churches where they had desperately sought refuge. Tribal resentments of three centuries, marked by atrocities on both sides, had boiled over in one of history's bloodiest ethnic wars.

At the Nairobi conference, Moise Napon, a West African, had just preached powerfully on 2 Corinthians 5: 'God . . . reconciled us to himself through Christ and gave us the ministry of reconciliation.'

No one moved after the message. The silence was broken only by sobs. Then the senior bishop of Kigali, Rwanda, slowly rose to his feet and announced in a tremulous voice, 'My brothers and sisters, I have a confession to make.' Bishop Adonia, a Hutu, told how bitterness had filled his heart. Adding to his pain, some Tutsis accused him of siding with Hutu authorities. 'I turned my back on the cross, the way of forgiveness', continued the Bishop, stooped with age and sorrow. 'I have confessed my sin to God, who, according to his word, has forgiven me. Now I also confess my failure as a Christian leader and ask your forgiveness.'

'Bishop', responded a tall young Tutsi, rising to his feet; 'I was one of your accusers, and I want to ask your forgiveness for my sin.'

The two men, a Hutu and a Tutsi, publicly embraced in reconciliation. Tears flowed down the faces of many delegates.

Chairing the session was Rene Daidanso, Associate General Secretary of the Association of Evangelicals in Africa (AEA), which sponsored the meeting. Daidanso had seen God bring reconciliation to church leaders in his native Chad in the 70s, after the murderous persecution of Christians by the nation's President in the name of 'cultural authenticity'.[1]

'GOD MELTED OUR HEARTS'

Tokunboh Adeyemo, General Secretary of the AEA, had invited Reg Reimer, Director of WEF's Church and Society Department, and Michael Cassidy of African Enterprise to put together the Rwanda meeting and other reconciliation efforts. Cassidy, a South African, had seen miraculous reconciliation take place in his own nation. Reimer, a Canadian who once served as a missionary in Vietnam, had seen the gospel bring reconciliation to warring factions in Asia.

The 45 Rwandan leaders first took part in the Pan-Africa Christian Leadership Assembly being held in Nairobi, attended by several hundred Christian leaders from all over Africa. Then they gathered for the Rwanda consultation – the first time that refugee leaders from Kenya, Rwanda, Tanzania, and Zaire had been able to meet together.

'The Rwandan conflict was especially difficult', explained Reimer. 'Sadly, the churches often mirrored the ethnic hatreds, instead of speaking boldly against them. Some leaders were accused of allowing themselves to be used by the former government; others were blamed for fleeing their parishes instead of staying with their flock. Only the Holy Spirit, using his word, could remove the hostility, fear, and distrust. After four days God began to melt hearts and gave the group new hope to move forward out of their darkest hour.'

Visiting Rwanda, Reimer entered the bullet-scarred shell of a

[1] A few months after the Rwanda Reconciliation meeting, Daidanso demonstrated the same principle of God's grace in a personal family tragedy back in Chad. His son and another young man had accidentally drowned while crossing a river. Although the two were Christians, their families came from opposing tribes – traditional enemies – who insisted on separate burials, along with sacrifices to placate the river spirits. Flying to Chad, Daidanso and his wife, Marteen, instead conducted a joint Christian funeral. 'Our sons became close friends because of their love for Jesus', Marteen declared. 'We buried them together as a witness to the power of Christ to make peace among enemies.' Pagan villagers were amazed. 'We will follow this God of Daidanso's family!' some declared. 'Even in tragedy, they have given us Good News.'

church. Trampled underfoot was part of a wall motto, 'GOD IS'. Dangling from the charred wall behind the pulpit was the rest of the banner, bearing only the word 'LOVE'. Amidst the rubble of another church, Reimer and a few other expatriates joined with a group of Tutsi and Hutu believers singing, 'Bind us together, Lord, bind us together!'

'BURDENS WERE LIFTED'

Reimer recollected another reconciliation gathering, one that took place on the opposite side of the continent, in Liberia. For five years that nation had been racked by a hideous civil war, during which a quarter of the population had fled the country. World Relief asked Liberian Christians what would be their priority project for aid funds: food, clothing, shelter?

'There are other agencies ready to help with food and clothing', they replied. 'But we have a greater need – reconciliation! There are churches on both sides of the war. We can't describe the awful things going on. Yet we Christians have been given the ministry of reconciliation in Christ. We need help to do that.'

As a result, World Relief sponsored a conference in which 694 key leaders, representing 26 tribal groups and 23 church denominations, met to discuss national reconciliation. A visiting black American pastor brought a series of Bible studies. On the third day, during a time of sharing, two women from opposing tribes went to the speakers' platform and asked forgiveness of each other. As they embraced, the whole assembly was moved, confessing and forgiving with tears.

A Krahn told how he had been waiting to ambush Gio villagers. Suddenly he thought of a Gio boyhood friend. The Krahn dropped his gun in the forest and ran off. Now he was at the reconciliation meeting.

'I am that very Gio friend!' cried a man in the conference. 'We played together when we were boys.' It was a dramatic moment as the Gio and the Krahn embraced.

A Muslim, one of several non-Christians present, remarked, 'I have heard many new things. I am convinced we need to talk about tribal reconciliation.'

'Burdens were lifted that day', reported Liberian Brian Johnson, General Secretary of the Association of Evangelicals. 'We saw Christians and churches being unified. This could be a catalyst for reconciliation in the rest of Liberia.'

Indeed, it may have been that. Six weeks later the Liberian warring factions signed a peace accord. Many Liberians felt that the

Bible-based reconciliation seminar helped to pave the way, as delegates went back to persuade their communities to seek peace.

'GOD MADE THE PLANE TURN BACK'

In South Africa, unreported by the world's press, evangelicals played a pivotal role in the transition from *apartheid* to democracy. The first post-apartheid election was threatened by the refusal of the Inkatha Freedom Party to participate. Without Inkatha's co-operation, the election results would only herald further violence.

The Evangelical Fellowship of South Africa, along with African Enterprise, called for special prayer. On one occasion, 30,000 people gathered in the Jesus Peace Rally to pray for peace. Meanwhile, Washington Okumo, a Kenyan diplomat who is also an evangelical Christian, sought to meet with the indomitable Inkatha leader, Chief Mangosuthu Buthelezi. The Chief, about to leave for his homeland, agreed to meet Okumo at the airport, but the Chief's flight departed before the diplomat arrived. Christians wondered why God had not answered their prayers for the proposed meeting, but they prayed on.

After take-off, the pilot announced that the aircraft had a mechanical problem, requiring a return to the airport. Upon landing, the Chief was amazed to find Okumo awaiting him.

'God made our plane turn back!' the Inkatha leader said afterwards. 'Mr. Okumo and I had a long talk, and I came to realize that Inkatha needed to be part of the election.'

The result was a transition to full national democracy, more peaceful than most people would have dared hope.

BALTIC BOMBARDMENT

Peter Kuzmic, Croatian evangelist and theologian, saw an instance of reconciliation during the ethnic warfare between Bosnians, Croatians, Hungarians, and Serbs in the former Yugoslav area.

'As I was preaching from Ephesians 2 on Christ the Reconciler, air raid sirens went off,' recalls Kuzmic. 'Many of the 200 people present started screaming – they had been traumatized by the 150,000 shells that had bombarded our city. I appealed to them to stay and pray, rather than flee into possibly greater danger outside.'

After a lengthy prayer time, the preacher opened his eyes to see a Hungarian family embracing a Serbian family, and people of other ethnic groups tearfully asking forgiveness of one another for the hostility between their nations. Kuzmic led in public prayer:

'Oh Lord, outside they kill each other. They hate each other; here people love each other. Outside there is revenge; here there is reconciliation. God, you do not kill the enemy, but the enmity!'

Evangelicals have turned out to be the only effective bridge-builders between the ethnic religious groups, Kuzmic states.

In other countries, there have been numerous other examples of reconciliation based on confession and forgiveness. The outstanding instance was Japan's, on the 50th anniversary of World War II, mentioned in chapter 4.[2]

A CUP OF COLD WATER

Reconciliation is but one emphasis of WEF's Church and Society Department. Helping churches reflect the Saviour's concern for the poor and destitute is another.

The Church and Society Department was originally called Relief and Development, but in some countries that label was difficult for Christians to understand. Also, it could lead people to think in terms only of foreign aid for their nations. WEF changed the name not only to reflect its own church-based structure, but also to emphasize the role that churches can have in their own nations – bringing the influence of the gospel to bear on society.

The Department is also concerned for the welfare of believers living in countries where Christians are more than marginalized – their very existence is threatened by repressive regimes and intolerant religions.

Reg Reimer has lived among Christians who suffer great persecution. Recently he returned to Vietnam, where he had once lived as a missionary of the Christian and Missionary Alliance. At an Easter service in the Hanoi Evangelical Church, he met men and women he had known a decade earlier. Their faces showed the strain of years of ostracism and suffering, but their eyes glistened as they told of God's grace.

'We have the truth', one of them told Reimer; 'so we must tell others. They cannot stop us believing!'

In neighbouring Laos, a Christian leader who spent 13 years in correction camps and prison told Reimer: 'We have learned to trust in God.'

---

[2]When the Japanese Diet finally did apologize, on the 50th anniversary of Japanese surrender, the Japanese Evangelical Association issued its own confession that during the war many liberal churches had left the historic Christian faith and lost their power to protest against nationalistic policies: 'We are indignant with the government's actions. . . . We repent and confess our faith concerning the sins we as churches of Japan committed at the time of World War II and in the process which led to the war.'

BELEAGUERED BELIEVERS

WEF's Religious Liberty Commission helps defend the human rights of Christians in such countries, seeking to bring pressure on governments in appropriate ways (see chapter 9). Meanwhile, the Church and Society Department has a very special ministry that can make a significant difference for persecuted believers.

'In restrictive nations, Christians feel isolated and helpless to make any impact on their society', Reimer explains. 'Just existing consumes all their energies. When drought or flooding or other human disasters strike, outside agencies hasten to provide aid, but that does not improve the acceptability of local Christians in the eyes of the community or government.

'Through our Church and Society Department we help national associations and their churches realize they can play a major part in meeting needs during natural disasters – and even preventing them. They can mobilize their people and can network with aid agencies. Among resistant people, help in the hour of need makes a more lasting impression than all the preaching in the world – and it also prepares people to listen to the gospel. It raises the credibility of believers.'

In many different circumstances, evangelicals have proved that. In Sudan, one drought-stricken community expressed surprise at the magnanimity of Christians. 'Muslims tell us that their aid must be given only to Muslims, but you Christians provide food for anyone who needs it – Christian and non-Christian alike!' village elders exclaimed.

At the beginning of the Cuban Communist revolution, evangelicals were labelled as 'counter-revolutionaries', facing imprisonment, unemployment, and social ostracism. Through their integrity and industriousness, however, they proved that they were dependable citizens. After 25 years, Fidel Castro publicly challenged Communist youth to emulate the work ethic of Christians. They had won their way in society and earned a hearing for their witness.

In India, the Evangelical Fellowship established a Committee on Relief (EFICOR) in 1967. It is often first on the scene of community disasters. One prominent Christian woman personally runs a school for the children of 'rubbish-heap scavengers'.

Evangelicals have been foremost in concern for deprived and suffering people, including the street children of London and Calcutta, the landless peasants of the Andes, the leprosy patients of Africa, and waves of refugees worldwide. In the 18th century, William Wilberforce's crusade against slavery epitomized evangelical social action for an unpopular cause, a cause based on biblical values of justice. William Carey in India and David Livingstone in

Africa battled against public opinion and government intrigue to crusade for oppressed peoples. Two supporters of the 1846 Evangelical Conference went on to establish agencies that have touched the world for good: George Williams founded the Young Men's Christian Association, and Jean Henri Dunant founded the Red Cross. Over the past century most missions have been involved in health, education, and agricultural projects among some of the poorest communities in the world, as they have also given them the hope of eternal life.

Today alongside these missions there are numerous evangelical relief and development agencies, with combined budgets of millions of dollars. Their work in relieving emergency and chronic disasters reflects Christian compassion and generosity. However, WEF cautions against unwise use that can produce harmful side-effects. For instance, hundreds of aid agencies swarmed into Eastern Europe after Communism fell. They were well-intentioned but often misguided.

'Ten percent of the help we received was positive,' states Pastor Nikolai Nedelchev of Bulgaria. 'Ninety percent was negative. There are great needs here, but it is better when donors ask how they can help.'

Nedelchev points out that aid unwisely given can destroy the spiritual ministry of pastors and corrupt the recipients. WEF and its national fellowships advise aid agencies to listen to the advice of local leaders and to work through them. 'When agencies do that, they are most effective,' says Paul Negrut of Romania.

HEARTS AND HANDS

In the light of such a record, it is surprising that evangelicals have often been stereotyped as caring more for 'spiritual scalps' than for the welfare of 'the whole man'. When Vencer told an official of the World Council of Churches about WEF's Church and Society Department, the WCC man expressed surprise. 'He did not seem to expect evangelicals to be concerned about people who are hurting', recalled Vencer.

Some liberals have depicted evangelicals as uninterested in social conditions, whereas theologically liberal groups have postured as the champions of human rights.

Liberal allegations reflect a misunderstanding of the mainstream evangelical position. It is true that in the 1920s most evangelicals backed away from anything that might be construed as 'the social gospel'. That was a reaction to increasing liberal emphasis on an earthly, temporal 'salvation' through social change, without the eternal spiritual dimension of the new birth. Fundamentalists, in particular, over-reacted, causing some evangelicals to become defensive and apologetic for combining evangelism with social action.

For the most part, responsible evangelicals have not neglected humanitarian needs, but their social acts have been subsumed under their overwhelming concern for the eternal destiny of men and women. To them, that reflects their concern for the whole person – a wholistic, biblical gospel. As Commissioner Earle Maxwell, Chief of Staff of the Salvation Army, puts it, 'We face two tragedies: Those who have no bread, and those who attempt to live by bread alone.'

Debate about how much emphasis the church should give to social action and how much to evangelism is based on an unbiblical division. A false dichotomy is created by those who say that evangelism and social action are like the two wings of a dove or the two blades of a pair of scissors. That is like comparing mouth and hands with the blood system. They are not comparable.

A more appropriate illustration is the blood coursing throughout the human body, enabling the mouth and the hands to function effectively. In the same way, the spiritual heartbeat that drives the blood of compassion through the arteries of Christ's disciples today, moves their lips to share the way of salvation and their hands to meet physical needs.[3] WEF put it all together in the slogan, 'Spiritual unity in action'.[4]

'I believe in the primacy of evangelism within the overall mission of the church in the world', says Peter Kuzmic. 'But the tragic bloodshed in Bosnia taught me that the Good News of our Lord cannot be preached in antiseptic conditions. Those who need it most have not only ears and souls but also eyes and minds, bodies and stomachs. Their receptivity to the Word is greatly conditioned by their painful context and the ability of both the message and the messenger to touch them at the point of their greatest need.'

PRACTICAL CHRISTIANITY

Kuzmic practised what he preached. He and other evangelicals in Croatia launched Agape Ministries – a relief agency that provides war-ravaged civilians with a hot meal a day (117,000 were fed

[3]The evangelical view of the relationship between evangelism and social action is explained in a paper presented at the 1981 General Assembly of the Association of Evangelicals of Africa, under the title, 'The Church and its Mission and Ministry', by W. Harold Fuller.
[4]The slogan was introduced in 1962 by WEF leader Gilbert Kirby. J.B.A. Kessler, Jr., *A Study of the Evangelical Alliance in Great Britain* (Netherlands: Oosterbaan and le Cointre N.V. 1968), p. 94.

regularly in one recent year), clothing, and even furniture. Agape has opened an orphanage and replaces the shell-shattered windows in the homes of the poor.

Meanwhile, the agency also seeks to meet spiritual needs through radio broadcasts and with Bible and other Christian literature distribution. For many, this has been their first Christian literature since the Communist era.

The concept of Croatia's Agape is being repeated all over the world as evangelicals minister to hurting people. WEF's Theological Commission has put this in a biblical context. As a corollary to concern for the poor, WEF and Lausanne co-sponsored the International Consultation on A Simple Lifestyle, in 1988.[5] In 1996 they published *Sharing the Good News with the Poor*.

In that study, WEF's Bong Rin Ro cited a slum in New Delhi with more than 7,000 poor families, totalling over 50,000 people. In the midst of these Hindus and Muslims was a tiny Christian church of five or six families.

Those Christians feel much like believers all over the world, helpless in the face of overwhelming needs. But through its national fellowships, WEF seeks to enable local churches to play their part in protecting the environment and in overcoming poverty as they share the good news of eternal life.

SALT AND LIGHT

'When Jesus said that the poor will always be with you, he was stating the obvious fact', says Jun Vencer. 'But that was not a fatalistic condemnation of masses of people to live in poverty. Jesus did something about their needs. The biblical norm is that "there shall be no poor among you". Because poverty is an aberration from God's ideal society, then it becomes an evangelical agenda.

'Evangelicals are to close the gap between the ugly face of reality and the desired ideal of eradicating poverty. Far from complacency, this is a call to action. It is not an option between social concern and ultimate concern. They are the two things we do. Jesus' life models both. To be Christlike is not just to be a gospeller but to be concerned with justice and poverty issues also.'

Vencer speaks from personal experience of poverty, and of mobilizing the Filipino churches to do something about it.

'We must convince churches that they *can* make a difference,' Vencer adds. 'To do so, they need to change community values –

[5] See 'A Simple Life Style – How?' by D. John Richard of India: Appendix G. Also in 1993, WEF and Lausanne published *Evangelical Christianity and the Environment*.

and only the gospel can do that with lasting impact. In this way we can be a significant force for good in the world.

'Evangelicals can also influence their own governments to pressure oppressive governments to ensure religious freedom and to strengthen non-government structures that are committed to the alleviation of poverty and the eradication of injustice.'

WEF's Church and Society Department (CSD) puts the mission and ministry of the church together in action. As with all WEF ministries, CSD does not try to do the work directly or unilaterally. Its whole focus is on enabling the national fellowships (the church) to minister to the needs of their nations (society) in the name of Christ.

Enabling the national fellowships also involves increasing their awareness of opportunities within their nations, helping to network with other nations which have workable models or which can provide material assistance, and developing leadership to manage programmes.

To accomplish the latter, WEF's Leadership Development Programme (described in Chapter 5) interconnects with the Church and Society Department, to enable the national associations to minister to their nations more effectively.

A CASE STUDY IN NETWORKING

The Rwandan emergency provided a case study in how WEF networks to enable churches to meet national needs – whether in crises or in normal times: faced with an overwhelming emergency, and with church leadership in shock, the Association of Evangelicals in Africa set up a conference to help church leaders plan a comprehensive strategy for reconciliation, healing, and rebuilding. AEA, a member of WEF, called on WEF's Church and Society Department to be a catalyst in the process.

The CSD had already been networking with Christian aid agencies. For instance, Hong Kong Christians were among those who sent financial aid. The Religious Liberty Commission monitored Rwanda's human rights abuses. Key leaders attended a Leadership Development Seminar conducted in Kenya by a WEF team.

The healing process will take much time. Hatred, fear, and revenge still pit Hutu and Tutsi against each other. Christians on both sides are having to work through grief, acceptance, confession, forgiveness, and reconciliation. But Rwandan church leaders know that Christ can enable their people to face the future with hope – the hope of the gospel applied to their desperate national calamity and personal pain. Meanwhile, it is strengthening to them to know that evangelicals worldwide, through WEF, are concerned for them and ready to help. 'Please thank God's people in other lands for remembering us,' Bishop Adonia told Reg Reimer. 'God has spoken to me personally.'

WEF's Church and Society Department is helping churches apply God's grace to some of the most difficult situations in the world.

'Bind us together, Lord! Bind us together!'

CHAPTER 9

Faith Without Fear or Favour

Oppressive powers take notice when believers stand together

'HALT!' commanded the masked terrorists at the barrier they had thrown across the winding mountain road high in the Peruvian Andes.

The battered bus in which Romulo Saune was travelling skidded to a stop on the gravel road. He and family members were returning from visiting the grave of his grandfather, who had been tortured and killed by Shining Path guerrillas five years earlier. It was the first time Saune had ventured back.

Brandishing sub-machine guns at the travellers, the terrorists made everyone climb down from the bus and stand by the roadside. Romulo's young nephews shivered in the frosty wind blowing from snow-covered peaks.

'The downtrodden masses will triumph!' chanted the guerrillas as they checked the vehicle and passengers for weapons.

Romulo recognized the tactics of the Maoist Shining Path. Started by university intellectuals and students, the brutal movement sought to overthrow the government by inciting rural people, mostly illiterate, to revolt. They gunned down anyone who resisted intimidation, including teachers who refused to parrot their Maoist lessons. They especially targeted Christian leaders. During 25 years of conflict, 25,000 Peruvians were killed.

Romulo's thoughts must have flashed back to his grandfather Quicana. He praised God for the courage of the 83 year old, who had witnessed to his torturers and had left word that his family should wear white, not black, at his funeral. 'I am going to glory!' Quicana had shouted. 'This is victory, not defeat.'

Now the guerrillas were relaxing, apparently satisfied that the vehicle was not carrying weapons. Romulo breathed deeply. But suddenly out of the sky came the whirr of a helicopter.

'Militia!' shouted the terrorists. Panicking, they opened fire on the passengers and fled. As the dust and smoke cleared, Romulo and

14 other passengers sprawled in death. Their blood soaked into the dry earth as condors wheeled high above.[1]

RELIGIOUS LIBERTY CITATION

Just three months earlier, Romulo (aged 39) had received the bi-annual WEF Religious Liberty Award presented during the 9th General Assembly of WEF. It cited the Quechua leader for 'consistent and courageous efforts to proclaim and maintain a witness of Jesus Christ amidst harsh repression and terrorism.'

'We were impressed with Romulo's life and ministry,' recalled John Langlois, Chairman of the Religious Liberty Commission. 'We felt not only that Romulo deserved this recognition, but also that the award would send the right signals to people in other repressive situations. It would encourage suffering believers, to know that the rest of the evangelical world was standing with them. It could also make oppressive forces more hesitant to deny human rights.'

Romulo himself had expressed the hope that the award would lead to greater safety among his people. His own town of Ayacucho ('Corner of the Dead') had become a focus of Shining Path attack and government counter-attack – both violent and indiscriminate in brutality. Tragically, Christians suffered from both sides. One July, terrorists opened fire in a church, killing six worshippers. A few days later, government troops raided another church and ordered the congregation to sing loudly while soldiers hauled six believers outside to their deaths.

The drug trade added to Peru's nightmare. Poverty-stricken peasants were pressed to cultivate coca (from which cocaine is produced), and were caught in the battle between drug lords and narcotics squads.

In the midst of the terror, Romulo and his wife Donna assisted in translating the Quechua Bible into the Ayacucho dialect and taping Quechua sermons for radio broadcasts. He helped lead a Quechua mission, TAWA, founded by his uncle, Fernando Quicana. TAWA means 'four,' a reference to the four corners of the ancient Inca Empire, which Quechua Christians want to reach with the gospel. TAWA maintains links with Amerindians in South and North America.

'Any one of us could have been killed as Romulo was,' commented Quicana, who survived the terrorist road attack. 'This

---

[1] Although Saune had previously faced violence because of his faith, his death and that of his companions resulted from random violence by terrorists.

kind of violence is an ever-present reality. But we must continue to minister in conflict areas. We trust the sovereignty of God.'

Monitoring the violence in Peru is the National Evangelical Council of Peru (CONEP), a member of WEF. WEF's Religious Liberty Commission helps CONEP and other national fellowships by responding to their needs and alerting world opinion concerning abuses of human rights, especially those affecting religious liberty. In many situations, WEF maintains a low profile, preferring to work co-operatively behind the scenes in order to enhance the effectiveness of other groups.

NETWORKING OVERCOMES ISOLATION

'WEF hopes to co-ordinate an international response network that can help evangelicals facing religious liberty challenges,' says the Commission's Research Associate, Mike Morris of Britain's Evangelical Alliance. 'National fellowships can feel very isolated. They know the local situation better than anyone, but sometimes their hands are tied locally. There are times when outside information and representation can achieve a lot. When they ask us for help, WEF's Religious Liberty Commission wants to be ready.'

Increasingly, evangelicals living in oppressive situations are asking for that kind of help. In some countries, oppression is religio-political, as in the case of Islamic or Buddhist regimes. In Eastern Europe and Latin America, inter-religious tensions affect Christians. The Religious Liberty Commission (RLC) is often involved in advocacy for the people affected.

Shortly after the collapse of the Soviet Union, evangelicals in the area found themselves under new forms of attack. The Russian Orthodox Church pressed for legislation restricting other religious groups. (Russia's President twice vetoed a restrictive bill.) In Bulgaria, newspapers publicly attacked evangelicals. The Polish government is more tolerant, but Roman Catholic bishops have attempted to re-establish their control as the State church. A draft law in Albania would have discriminated against Protestants by recognizing only Muslim, Catholic, and Orthodox faiths.

The European Evangelical Alliance, regional WEF body, asked the RLC for advice on how national fellowships should respond. They knew that RLC leaders had experience in other continents, and they also knew that action taken by one member could have adverse effects on other members. Concerted action helped modify the Albanian law.

'It is very encouraging to see this kind of networking,' comments Religious Liberty Commission Director Brian O'Connell of the

USA. 'National fellowships with problems sought advice from their regional fellowship, which in turn kept in touch with the worldwide body through the Religious Liberty Commission. That kind of co-ordination leads to better strategic planning and strength.'

DEVELOPING LEADERSHIP

In protesting against infractions of human rights, WEF seeks to keep positive and not be labelled by governments as a reactionary troublemaker. WEF's primary role is not to criticize a government but to help Christian citizens use tools, such as constitutional rights, to encourage freedom. One major need is for evangelicals to communicate more effectively within their nation as to their plight and their rights as citizens, advises the RLC.

'Leadership development is a strategic aspect of our work', says O'Connell. 'Very often Christian leaders do not understand the best channels and approaches to the government, or even such basics as documenting infractions of human rights. Yet it is important that protests come from within the nation, rather than appearing as outside meddling. Our regional consultations are proving helpful in developing effective first-line defence of liberty from within a country. When necessary and desirable, we can help apply pressure from the outside.'

WEF also emphasizes that it is not concerned about the rights of Christians only, but of everyone, regardless of their religious affiliation. 'Unless there is religious liberty for all, there will be religious liberty for none – except the religion of their oppressors', O'Connell explains.

'WEF is not a powerful organization', adds Jun Vencer. 'Evangelicals are usually a minority. But evangelicals do not have to be powerful to be effective. By God's grace, they function under repression. Yet, all minorities need to protest, because any society that ignores minorities becomes repressive.

'However, religious freedom is the foundation of all other freedoms in society. It stems from mankind being made in the image of God. It gives men and women their intrinsic value as free moral agents to believe or not to believe in a deity. It distinguishes them as being created a little lower than the angels – not a little above the animals.'

To WEF, religious liberty is an essential concern not just for evangelicals freely to proclaim the gospel and publicly worship the Lord. It is religious freedom for all to express their beliefs in public.

CLASSIC CASE STUDY: IRAN

Iran is a classic case study of a totalitarian government denying religious liberty. Since the Islamic revolution in 1979, religious liberty has been increasingly restricted. Iran established an Office of Religious Minorities in the Ministry of Islamic Guidance that has monitored and controlled all religious activities – even requiring permits to conduct church weddings, and identity cards for church worshippers. Christian leaders have been interrogated and harassed; increasingly, Christian employees have been dismissed from their jobs.

In 1989 the government prohibited the printing of Bible portions, unless references to Jesus as 'Son of God' and 'Lord' be substituted with 'prophet'. Later that year, the government padlocked the office of the Iranian Bible Society, removing its files and ordering staff not to return to work. The Office of Religious Minorities announced that the Iranian Bible Society had been dissolved and would not be allowed to operate again.

Although Christians constitute only 0.4% of the population, Muslim authorities are concerned about the increasing number of Muslims who are turning to Christ. At the time of the revolution in 1979, no more than 300 Muslims were known to have become Christians. Fifteen years later the number was 6000, with urban churches overflowing. By 1992 an estimated 10,000 Muslims had turned to the Christian faith.[2]

In 1993 the government pressured church leaders to curtail the large number of Christians congregating on Fridays – the official day of rest and worship, and also Islam's holy day of the week. They commanded churches to sign a statement promising not to evangelize Muslims, and to provide identity cards for church worshippers. This would expose converts from Islam to persecution and even death – the penalty for 'apostasy' (abandoning Islam for another faith).

'You can arrest us, put us in prison, or execute us, but we will not close our churches', several Christian leaders responded. They reminded authorities that government regulations permit Christians to preach and teach inside their churches.

In 1993 the United Nations Special Envoy to Iran, Reynaldo Galindo-Pohl, published a report on human rights abuses in Iran. It included religious rights infractions over several years. The Iranian government reacted by pressuring non-Muslim religious leaders to

---

[2]*International Institute for the Study of Islam and Christianity Bulletin*, (Feb.–March 1994).

sign a statement declaring they enjoyed religious freedom. Several religious leaders signed, for, after all, the constitution does provide for religious liberty – and the leaders did not want to lose any they already had.

But for minorities, such as Jews, Parsis, Baha'is, and Christians, 'religious liberty' is only a technicality, meaning permission to practise one's faith privately, within a registered building. It forbids public witness, evangelism, and conversion from Islam. The theocratic state has enforced an Islamic dress code on all women, Islamic education for all students, and the Koranic court system. Christians have been pressured out of government jobs and harassed by arbitrary arrest, interrogation, and beatings. Publicly witnessing that Christ is the Saviour (blasphemy to a Muslim), can incur the death penalty for 'insulting Islam'.

DEATH SENTENCE

Bishop Haik Hovespian-Mehr, chair of the Council of Pastors of the Iranian Protestant Churches, was instrumental in requesting the UN investigation. He also publicized the nine-year imprisonment of Rev. Mehdi Dibaj, who at the age of 15 had turned from Islam to Jesus Christ. Dibaj became a pastor of the Assemblies of God and a Bible translator.

An Islamic court imprisoned him for insulting Islam, the prophet Muhammed, and the Ayatollah Khomeini; for spying for the West; and for apostasy. In his defence, Dibaj testified: 'Jesus paid the penalty of our sins. . . . He has asked me to deny myself and be his fully surrendered follower, and not fear people even if they kill my body.'

Three times during his imprisonment, the pastor was sentenced to death. The Supreme Court overturned each order, but the powerful Islamic courts refused to release him. He underwent several mock executions, and for two years was in solitary confinement.

'Two years blindfolded in solitary confinement did not hurt me', Dibaj later attested. 'They were the most beautiful years of my life, because the Lord was with me.'

International pressure on Iran to honour its commitments under the Declaration of Human Rights finally brought about release for the 60-year-old pastor in January 1994. Christians hoped that this signalled a let-up in persecution. But three days later Bishop Haik himself was abducted; his family identified his body ten days later. He had been stabbed to death.

Rev. Tateos Michaelian took Bishop Haik's place as chair of the Protestant Council of Pastors. He had told his congregation that

Christians, instead of fearing martyrdom, should be prepared for it. Ten days later he too was murdered.

Six months after Pastor Dibaj's release from prison, he was stabbed to death.[3]

Iran's government refused to take any responsibility for the killings. If the Christian leaders had been executed as a result of a court order, government culpability would have been obvious. Instead, the government could blame the assassinations on unknown criminals. The fact is, any Muslim can claim God's favour for killing a person accused of 'insulting Islam'.

COMPLEX CASES

Article 18 of the *Universal Declaration of Human Rights* adopted by the United Nations is specific:

> Everyone has the right to freedom of thought, conscience, and religion; this right includes freedom to change his religion or belief, and freedom, either alone or in community with others and in public or private, to manifest his religion or belief in teaching, practice, worship, and observance.

In the Iranian situation, WEF's Religious Liberty Commission could demonstrate clear-cut infractions on the part of the government. The Commission worked closely with human rights groups such as Amnesty International and other agencies that track religious persecution – including Jubilee Campaign, the Institute of Religion and Democracy, Middle East Concern, and Christian Solidarity International. They made representations to the United Nations and the Iranian government, and circulated news releases to the media worldwide.

Most of all, WEF helped to mobilize prayer worldwide. 'I thank all the churches for their prayers, fasting, tears, and groaning', Pastor Dibaj had written from prison before his release and subsequent murder. After the three leaders had been murdered, WEF organized an international day of prayer for Iran (November 20, 1994). It involved the widest global participation of any single WEF event, and the greatest press coverage.

On behalf of WEF, Sir Fred Catherwood, a former vice-president of the European Parliament, awarded the Religious Liberty Award posthumously to Bishop Haik.

'God has taught me many lessons during this tragic time', testified

---

[3]Sources include News Network International, Middle East Concern, and Voice of the Martyrs.

the murdered bishop's widow, Takoosh Hovespian-Mehr, who received the plaque. 'At first I could not forgive the murderers. Then one day God enabled me to forgive. I thank WEF for honouring my husband. May this bring glory to God's name.'

The Iranian persecution points up the complex situations the Religious Liberty Commission faces. On the one hand the government professes freedom of religion, but on the other hand the theocracy accuses Christians of undermining the state (a political crime) when evangelicals witness that Jesus is the Saviour. Even the charge of 'causing political unrest' is easily levelled, since there are usually a number of opposition political parties eager to overthrow the government of any nation.

In Iraq, the Baathist party, currently in power, is actually secular-socialist in ideology but uses Islam to control the population. The minority Sunni Muslims oppress the majority Shi'ite Muslims, who have sectarian ties with the dominant Shi'ites in hostile Iran. In 1995, Saddam Hussein's 'barbaric cruelty' received the strongest condemnation ever made by the United Nations Human Rights Commission concerning a nation's human rights record.[4]

TARGETING CHRISTIANS

In a theocracy, Islamic courts can pass the death sentence on Muslims who convert to Christianity. At the same time, the government blames random violence for the murder of Christians, and tells pastors that it cannot take responsibility for their safety.

That makes Christians 'fair game' for zealots who believe that killing an 'infidel' will ensure the assassin direct access to heaven at the time of his own death. Worshippers meet behind closed doors, checking all who enter. Church car parks are closed for fear of car bombs.

Even harder to prove is the covert discrimination that Christian students and employees constantly face in Iran and some other lands. In Pakistan, a leading figure in the Evangelical Fellowship of Pakistan received anonymous threats that his son, who was quietly witnessing to fellow students, would be sent home 'in little pieces in a box'. The young man fled to Russia to continue his studies in medicine.

Persecution of Christians in Pakistan came to international attention after a Christian boy, although illiterate, was charged with 'insulting Islam' by writing graffiti on a mosque. (One report is that the boy, Masih, and a young Muslim playmate had a dispute over pet pigeons, and in anger the Muslim boy alleged that Masih had defaced the mosque.) An uncle and a friend were charged along with Masih. While on bail, the friend was shot by an assailant. The other two were eventually sentenced to death.

After an appeal backed by a co-ordinated public campaign of international condemnation, the High Court quashed the sentence because of 'irregularities'. Christian friends whisked Masih and his uncle out of the country to protect them from vengeful Muslim fundamentalists.

Prime Minister Benazir Bhutto, although a Muslim, had not been in agreement with the death sentence. However, her political position was precarious. Moderate leaders like her may want to introduce reforms, but unless they have the backing of the powerful religious leaders (who oppose reform), they cannot stay in office.

The powerful economic influence of Islamic leaders can even cause an open society to restrict overt criticism of abuses by other nations. For instance, Christian agencies in Singapore, a stable and politically neutral nation, have to be discreet about exposing Islamic abuses elsewhere. The city-state is economically dependent on neighbouring oil-producing nations that use its refineries and shipping facilities.

Oil supply and regional stability have muted criticism of Saudi Arabia by Western democracies, who support the Gulf nation even though it has been cited as the world's most repressive regime vis-à-vis religious liberty.

Several totalitarian governments (particularly Islamic) now hide behind their own 'Bangkok Declaration' on Human Rights. This argues that cultural, religious, and regional factors should override the provisions of the Universal Declaration of Human Rights accepted in 1948.

Sudan uses the protracted North-South civil war to defend its slaughter of largely Christianized Southerners. Truckloads of Southern refugees have been dumped in the desert without food and water. Many non-Muslims, especially Christians, are harassed, raped, and tortured. Middle East Concern and a German press agency cited the forcible removal of Christian communities and five crucifixions in one month. The widows and children of the victims were sold into slavery, reports state.

UNDERSTANDING SENSITIVITIES

Cases like that are well documented. However, pinpointing *bona fide* denial of religious liberty in other cases is increasingly complex worldwide. For instance, in the former Soviet Union and Eastern

Europe, there is some backlash against Christian evangelism. But Christian observers can, in all honesty, understand the reason for some visa restrictions.

Before the collapse of the Soviet Union, David Howard, then WEF International Director, wrote to President Mikhail Gorbachev:

> On behalf of 100 million evangelical Christians around the world, we urge you to support the legislation which will guarantee human rights to all believers in the USSR and eliminate unjust discrimination which has restricted full expression of Christian faith.

The liberty that did come was beyond the greatest hopes of Soviet believers. They immediately made good use of the new freedoms. But after the Berlin Wall collapsed, a flood of religious projects poured into the area. Much of it was responsible, but certain Christian agencies were culturally insensitive and blatantly unwise. Along with them entered sects and cults of every persuasion. Muslim fundamentalists made inroads.

Adding to the confusion, Western culture accompanying foreign assistance often brought with it crass materialism and flagrant immorality. Governments that initially welcomed any kind of help soon had to impose constraints.

In Nigeria, Islam has traditionally sought to marginalize Christianity, and there have been periodic outbreaks of violence between Muslims and Christians. Yet a recent restriction on missionary visas was originally aimed at Muslim fundamentalist missionaries, after Islamic extremists had fomented riots in the North.

Similarly, India and China are apprehensive of any group – religious or secular – that might unsettle or exploit their massive, restive populations. Religious liberty infractions have to be very clearly described in order to put pressure on the perpetrators; yet detailed description could single out individuals for greater persecution. In such cases, WEF tries to be guided by local advice before taking action.

John Langlois sized up the situation in China after a personal visit: 'Unfortunately Chinese Christians have had to bear the brunt of being seen as allies of national enemies who humiliated China for 150 years. Oppression of the church since 1949 has been both anti-Western and anti-religious, so that Christians have endured double persecution – unlike Buddhists, who had no foreign involvement to contend with.

'In the last few years, there has been enormous growth in the Christian church and relative freedom for Christians – as long as they keep a low profile. While there does not now seem to be any centrally-orchestrated programme of harsh repression, local officials often persecute Christians.' As China-watchers have learned through the years, pressures on Christians can be turned on and off at the will of the government.[5]

In several countries of South-East Asia, Christians experienced some liberty after the fall of Communist dictatorships. However, secular and religious leaders have little love for Christians. In Northern Laos, in spite of a new constitution supposedly guaranteeing religious liberty, 'hundreds of Christian families have been forced to sign statements saying they will not spread their faith, will not assemble for worship, and will not even pray for healing when sick! Forty churches have been closed.'[6]

But in Vietnam, members of a minority ethic group, the Hmong, are turning to Christ in the midst of severe persecution stirred up by Buddhist leaders.

CONCERTED ACTION EFFECTIVE

Early in the history of the Evangelical Alliance, when slavery was a major issue, British evangelicals were the first Protestant body to encourage the formation of 'national leagues of liberty'. They remembered the 17th century legacy of John Bunyan, who was imprisoned for his faith and helped secure religious freedom in English law. The German Alliance, which had the heritage of Martin Luther's struggle for liberty, encouraged the establishment of East Africa's first settlement for liberated slaves.[7]

Later, individual national fellowships became active in monitoring religious liberty affecting citizens of their countries, as well as questions of justice.

Wade Coggins remembers how the National Association of Evangelicals (NAE), USA, obtained action on behalf of evangelicals in Colombia, South America. It was when Catholic persecution of evangelicals was still intense. At the time, Coggins served with the Christian and Missionary Alliance in Colombia. In an Andean village, a mob incited by the local priest attacked him and a Colombian colleague with long knives. Escaping, Coggins later learned that the assassins had planned to kill them at a bridge, but God had led them to take another route home.

---

[5] See Tony Lambert, *The Resurrection of the Chinese Church* (Wheaton: Harold Shaw Publishers, 1994).
[6] Report by Reg Reimer, Director, WEF Church and Society Department, after a personal visit to South-East Asia, April 1995.
[7] J.W. Ewing, *Goodly Fellowship* (Edinburgh: Marshall, Morgan and Scott, 1946), p. 95.

'On another occasion, a pastor was killed in the presence of his wife', Coggins recalls. 'The killers then forced her to cook food for them. This violence could not be blamed on the drug trade – it was before that developed. The cause was open hostility to evangelicals. In those days, government officials did the bidding of the local priests. They made no arrests for atrocities against evangelicals.'

WEF did not yet have a Religious Liberty Commission, but Clyde Taylor of NAE presented a formal protest to US President Harry Truman, who in turn lodged a diplomatic complaint with the Colombian government.

MANDATE FROM THE GRASS ROOTS

Since its constitution in 1951, WEF has sought to address these issues. However, the Christian public has often been unaware of the background issues that affect Christian freedoms; moreover, evangelicals needed guidance in presenting a co-ordinated response. In 1990 the National Association of Evangelicals (USA) funded a survey of all National Evangelical Fellowships, to see if a co-ordinating commission was needed.

'We were amazed at the response – 75% of the questionnaires sent out', said O'Connell. 'Significantly, 99% of those replied in the affirmative. This was a mandate from the grass roots membership.'

WEF assigned O'Connell, Langlois, and 'Mike' Morris to draft a proposal. In 1992, the 9th General Assembly of WEF, held in Manila, approved the establishment of the Religious Liberty Commission, with Morris as its first Director.

'We recognized that a global body could bring pressure to bear on oppressive regimes much more effectively than believers struggling under those regimes,' said Langlois.

'Religious conflicts and persecution in Africa, Asia, Latin America, and the Middle East are actually on the rise,' reports Canadian Paul Marshall, Academic Advisor to the Commission. 'Unfortunately some Christian circles too easily accept unreliable information, but on the other hand, they don't properly use the information they do get.

'Some religions receive official backing from certain governments; Christianity usually does not. Evangelicals usually take the brunt of hostility, because other religions oppose conversion. The right to change religions is enshrined in the UN Bill of Human Rights, but some nations, or extremist groups in government, do not permit that right, and liberal attitudes in the West regard attempts to convert as arrogant. So it is difficult to get action on evangelical cases. Governments and agencies tend to ignore us. We have to be very sure of our facts and need to understand the most effective approach.'

National fellowships welcomed the new Commission. Said Daniel K.C. Ho, former General Secretary of Malaysia's National Evangelical Christian Fellowship and an executive member of the Commission, 'Religious liberty is tied up with what it means to be human.'

REPROACH OF THE CROSS

WEF realizes that the cross of Christ will always bring reproach. The Commission is not seeking to avoid that. The apostles suffered beatings, imprisonment, and even death for their faith. Commission members remember Paul's words to Timothy: 'Everyone who wants to live a godly life in Christ Jesus will be persecuted' (2 Tim. 3:12). Peter urged godly patience under persecution.

However, WEF also notes that Peter refused to be silenced by a religious fiat, and Paul used his citizenship to defend religious liberty and to witness at the highest levels of the Roman Empire.

With this in mind, the Commission states its Purpose:

To strengthen a local church's ability fully to express its faith by fostering a freer social and political environment in the nation and throughout the world, and to equip WEF regional and national alliances in dealing with government.

The RLC Vision Statement further defines its role:

To serve as a co-ordinating and networking team within the international political advocacy community that can effectively serve evangelicals being persecuted, harassed, and oppressed because of their faith. We do this primarily by responding to and partnering with WEF member bodies.

Ironically, in some countries facing severe repression there is a rapid increase of Christians', points out O'Connell. 'Church statistician David Barrett states that more people have been martyred for their faith in the 20th century than in all previous centuries combined. The greatest growth among evangelical Protestants has been outside the West – now over 70% of evangelicals worldwide. Thirty years ago, that figure was 30%.

RELIGIOUS BACKLASH

The changing situation in Eastern Europe has shown the value of the RLC. When Albania drafted a law that would have discriminated against Protestants by recognizing only Muslim, Catholic, and Orthodox faiths, evangelicals asked the Commission for advice. Concerted representation brought about modifications in the law.

Bulgaria provides another example of how WEF has tried to put its Religious Liberty mandate to work. Formed in 1909, the Bulgarian Evangelical Alliance (BEA) was forced to close down in 1947 when the extremely repressive Communist regime imprisoned its leaders. Restoration of democracy in the early 90s brought new religious liberty, but there was soon a backlash as cults and sects from East and West poured into the spiritual vacuum.

The government, news media, and the quasi-state Eastern Orthodox Church lumped the Protestant minority (1.25% of the population, mostly evangelical) together with the invading cults. A mob of 50 skinheads attacked one congregation, shouting, 'Heretics, dirty Protestants! You will burn in hell!' Bulgaria's largest newspaper praised the attackers' attempt to halt 'the creeping of sects through the Motherland'.

The religious intolerance followed an ordinance requiring all non-denominational religious groups to seek government approval before registering. Operation Mobilization, Youth with a Mission, and a Gideons' International affiliate were among the para-church organizations turned down.

Fragmented by recriminations from the Communist era, Bulgaria's home-grown evangelicals realized the need to work together and seek registration. WEF, through its Regional European Evangelical Alliance, assisted Bulgarian evangelicals to regroup. WEF's David Howard and Peter Kuzmic encouraged them with a visit.

STRENGTH BEYOND NUMBERS

In 1993, Bulgarian evangelical leaders invited Jun Vencer to accompany them in presenting to the office of Bulgaria's President their official request for registration. Although the authorities had lumped evangelicals along with the sects and cults that were invading Bulgaria, they changed their attitude when they heard that Bulgarian evangelicals were part of a worldwide movement of responsible Christian citizens that held to the historic biblical faith. (See chapter 1.)

As Vencer was leaving the Baltic nation, he again met one of the government officials.

'I am not optimistic about your request being approved,' he told Vencer. 'The government recognizes four religions only: Greek Orthodox, Roman Catholic, Jewish, and Muslim. Only they will be allowed to own land.'

'Then what can Bulgarian evangelicals do?' Vencer asked.

'Talk to your people worldwide', the official replied. 'Get them to put pressure on Parliament.'

On the flight out of Bulgaria, Jun Vencer had a fresh realization of the importance of WEF's membership.

'We do not trust in numbers', he later told WEF Council members. 'Our trust is in the Lord, who can work through few or many. But we know that in parliamentary debate, the first question is, "What is your constituency?" I thought of the change in the attitude of the President's advisers when they understood that Bulgarian evangelicals are part of a worldwide family. I could see how important WEF membership is to our brothers and sisters in Bulgaria.

'They may still have difficulty getting registered, but perhaps our visit can help them survive. They were obviously encouraged. Since then the Bulgarian Evangelical Alliance has sponsored a public meeting in Sofia, the capital, to demonstrate evangelical unity and pray for religious liberty. About four thousand evangelicals gathered in the Palace of Culture, where the largest Communist Party meetings used to be held.

'Protecting religious liberty becomes a matter of constituency. In WEF, evangelicals have a grass roots, worldwide constituency on a scale that makes governments sit up and listen.

'So as I flew out of Sofia, I thanked God for raising up WEF', Vencer recalled.

CHAPTER 10

One God, Many Worlds

The powerful relevance of the unchanging Word of God in cultural diversity.

'Agents of the West!' shouted the tall Hindu, snatching the microphone from the Indian evangelist. 'You are preaching a Western religion. Stop!'

Ken Gnanakan and his students from ACTS[1] Institute saw the mood of the villagers change suddenly. They had been enjoying the Indian folk tunes the Christian young people sang, accompanied on typical Indian instruments. Most of the singers wore traditional Indian dress. But as soon as the evangelist opened his Bible and talked about Jesus, one of the listeners strode into the circle and grabbed the microphone. The crowd now looked as if they were ready to stone the little group of Indian Christians.

Gnanakan and the students found this kind of opposition to the gospel wherever they went. His staff and students had been pelted with rotten fruit in Varanasi, Hinduism's holiest pilgrimage site. People accused the group of being paid agents of foreign culture. Gnanakan wondered how the group could show that they were fully Indian while being followers of Jesus Christ.

The young Christians were banned from some villages but slowly won their way back by serving the needs of the community. One hostile village elder was impressed when one of the group, a nurse, came back repeatedly to treat his leg ulcer. He persuaded villagers to allow the group to return. Opposition began to melt as the village realized these young people were not 'paid agents'. They were ordinary Indian carpenters, mechanics, nurses, and clerks who witnessed without being paid by anyone, because they loved their nation and their Saviour.

That was the concept of ACTS – to equip men and women to live

[1]ACTS is the acronym for 'Agriculture, Crafts, Trades, and Studies,' a Christian vocational-Bible institute in Bangalore, India.

as self-supported Christian witnesses within their own culture. 'Mission' meant the involvement of the whole church in society, as in the Book of Acts.

FROM THE BEATLES TO THE BIBLE

Gnanakan himself had travelled a long spiritual pilgrimage. As a university student, he had dropped out of Chemical Engineering for a career in music. He and three other young men formed The Trojans, a Beatles-like rock music group. They played in some of the best hotels and music halls, often to the adulation of screaming teenagers.

Spotlights, throbbing music, wild parties, drugs – they were Gnanakan's life, until the night he found himself in a Youth For Christ service, singing a hymn he remembered from childhood: 'Blessed Assurance, Jesus Is Mine.' Memories of a godly home broke his waywardness, and he cried out to God, 'I am a sinner. Forgive me!' After the service, a youthful evangelist, Ravi Zacharias, helped to affirm his decision to trust in Christ. So did Youth For Christ Director Ray Harrison, in whose home the young people had met.

The Trojans broke up, and Ken turned to journalism. He married Prema ('a very capable Christian', Ken says) and discovered he had the gift of an evangelist. Theological studies took the couple to Australia and Britain, where they made solid friendships with believers in the West.

But as Ken studied the theological debates of the church in Europe, he kept thinking about his own land, which the gospel had reached long before it arrived in Britain. Christianity had become very much part of the culture of Europe, he observed, but in India, after nearly two millennia, it was still looked upon as foreign.

Back in his native India, Ken looked for answers to the contradiction of Christianity and culture. India was famous for its film industry that enchanted movie-goers with traditional music and culture. But whenever a film portrayed a Christian, he or she was always part of a foreign culture. Hollywood stereotypes became synonymous with Christianity.

Then Ken Gnanakan looked around him in church services. The hymns were written by foreigners and the hymn books were printed overseas. His fellow worshippers were formally attired in Western suits and ties. Even the sermon and the preaching style took him back to the cold, stone sanctuaries of Europe – far from the warmth of India's climate and emotions. 'Was there *anything* Indian about the church?' Gnanakan wondered.

India had survived wave after wave of foreign rule – from Persian

Satrap to Muslim Mogul to European Raj. Most Hindus were unaware that the apostle Thomas, according to tradition, had brought the gospel to the subcontinent in the first century. After India gained independence from the British, Mahatma Gandhi instilled a national pride in the people – pride in their culture, in their ability to feed themselves, to manufacture, to govern. Gnanakan, too, was proud of his Indian heritage.

But somehow the church seemed to maintain a colonial mentality: 'Christian' could not be 'Indian'. In the thinking of many Indians, Christianity presumably was from the West. Many of its preachers and other workers had been paid from the West before independence; so the public assumed that they continued to be 'the paid agents of the West'.

REACHING THE SOUL OF INDIA

Ken Gnanakan found Indian Christian leaders and Western missionaries who saw what he saw and who were also keenly concerned about the need for indigenousness. Victor Manogaram, who became head of India's Youth For Christ, was one who listened and encouraged him. Another was New Zealander Bruce Nicholls, teaching at Union Biblical Seminary in Yeotmal.[2]

Gnanakan recalls how, fresh back from theological studies in Britain, he had 'proudly written to Bruce Nicholls of [his] ability to critically evaluate Bultmann and Barth'. Gnanakan, whose name means 'eye of wisdom,' will never forget Nicholls' wise reply: 'We don't need any more teachers of Western Theology. Come back and get to understand the Indian context and teach from what is happening here.' God used that advice, together with other challenges, to awaken the young Indian theologian-evangelist to the spiritual needs of his own soul as well as the soul of India.

Meanwhile, Gnanakan pursued the vision he had received while studying in London: to train Christian men and women in the Bible as well as in vocational skills, for practical Christian witness. Today the result, ACTS Institute, runs an effective programme.[3]

---

[2] Union Biblical Seminary is among the most significant centres for evangelical theological education in India. Initiated by the Evangelical Fellowship of India, it began in Yavatmal (formerly known as Yeotmal) in 1953 and moved to Pune in 1983. Meanwhile the Yavatmal campus is being used essentially as a missionary training institute. There is also a flourishing school for Yavatmal children on the same campus. Correspondence courses are centred in Nagpur.

[3] ACTS Institute was founded by Gnanakan, working closely with International Needs, a wholistic ministry founded by New Zealander Ray Harrison.

But there was an even more basic need to be met, if the church was not to be regarded as part of a foreign culture. Theological students, even if they did not study overseas, used theological textbooks based on the debates of the church in Europe. Those did not prepare them for the conflict of the gospel in the context of idolatrous Hinduism or 'transcendental' Buddhism. Much theology only seemed to reinforce the foreignness of Christianity.

Gnanakan met others of like mind when he became a founding member of the Association of Evangelical Theological Education in India. There he came to the attention of Saphir Athyal, one of the founders of the Asia Theological Association (ATA). Athyal liked Gnanakan's fresh indigenous approach to theological education and invited him to become involved in ATA. The Board elected Gnanakan Chairman, and later General Secretary. All along, he has kept in close association with WEF's Theological Commission.

'Christians in each nation need their own cultural identity', states the rock musician-turned theologian. 'But that does not mean we shun others or stand in isolation. We need interdependence, not independence!'[4]

'THE BIBLE MUST JUDGE EVERY CULTURE'

Christians in other continents have found the same needs. Africa's outstanding evangelical theologian, Byang Kato, discovered that African church leaders in the continent were studying theology developed in Europe and America, not Africa. Although gaining much at evangelical seminaries overseas, nevertheless they returned understanding more about issues in the West than in their own continent. As to the World Council of Churches, it provided scholarships for pastors to study at liberal seminaries overseas, and when they returned to Africa, they interpreted their own culture through theological lenses ground in Geneva or New York. Many returned to their churches well versed in universalism and existentialism.

'What we need is not a white theology or a black theology, but a biblical theology', declared Kato, who became General Secretary of the Association of Evangelicals of Africa. 'The Bible must judge every culture.'[5]

At the time, several government leaders were calling for a return

---

[4]Kenneth R. Gnanakan, *Ken Gnanahan: Still Learning* (Bangalore: ACTS Trust, 1993).

[5]Byang H. Kato, *African Cultural Revolution and the Christian Faith* (Jos: Challenge (SIM), 1975). Kato wrote this booklet for distribution during the Second World Festival of Black and African Arts and Culture, held in Lagos, Nigeria, in 1975.

to ancestral spirit worship as an act of 'authenticity'. Chad's President Ngarta Tombalbaye ordered every male citizen to return to his ancestral village for a traditional initiation ceremony. This involved sacrificing to the spirits, renouncing all previous allegiances, and experiencing a 'new birth' through contact with their ancestors. Many Christians who refused to do so were imprisoned and tortured. Fourteen pastors who rejected the President's order were shot, their bodies dumped in a common grave.

Just after Tombalbaye was finally overthrown, Kato visited Chad. He understood the cultural issues the country was facing, for when he was a child, his parents had dedicated him to serve the ancestral spirits. Now Chad's new leaders, an Army triumvirate, questioned Kato about the Bible's teaching and asked him to return to give seminars on the Christian view of culture. Tragically, the young theologian, not yet 40, drowned before he could return. However, he did leave much in writing.

Kato rejected syncretism outright, but he had seen the importance of the gospel entering and purifying the fabric of culture. 'The attitude of Christians towards cultural renaissance need not be negative', he had written earlier. 'Jesus would not have come to make Africans become American Christians nor to cause Europeans to become Indian Christians. Africans who become Christians should, therefore, remain Africans wherever their culture does not conflict with the Bible. Where a conflict results, the cultural element must give way.'[6]

A Nigerian, Kato was Africa's first doctoral-level evangelical theologian. Conscious that it was necessary for him to take his own doctoral studies overseas, Kato had a vision to develop post-graduate theological schools under the AEA, so that students could study the Scriptures in the context of their own continent.

'Evangelicals came to evangelize Africa', Kato used to say, 'but liberals are coming to teach and train.' He died before his vision was fulfilled through the founding of two graduate schools of theology: one English language (in Nairobi) and one French language (in Bangui).

YESTERDAY'S DREAMS BECOME TODAY'S NIGHTMARES

Theologically, Latin America was a different world, although liberation theology also grew from roots in Europe – in this case from a Marxist hermeneutic. It taught that sin was institutional, and that

[6]Byang H. Kato, *Biblical Christianity in Africa* (Achimota: African Christian Press, 1985).

to find salvation, the poor must destroy current systems or structures – with violence if necessary. Liberation theologians twisted the story of the Hebrew Exodus to imply that the oppressed Israelites rose up and slaughtered the Egyptian first-born in order to make their escape. The Crucifixion became evidence that God condones violence to change society!

Evangelicals had to apply the Scriptures to combat those views, but at the same time they needed to speak to the reality of poverty, and the church's responsibility in society. Their theology also had to deal with the culture's basic spiritism, overlaid with syncretistic Catholicism.

Even Europe, following the collapse of Communism, is now rethinking its theology in the face of current realities. Before the night of Marxist-Leninism descended, the ancient churches had their traditional theologies. These were battered by the materialistic dogma of Communist regimes. However, political freedom has not necessarily brought peace.

'Yesterday's dreams have turned into today's nightmares', says Miroslav Volf of the Evangelical Theological Faculty, Croatia, now teaching at Fuller Theological Seminary, California. He points out that the Orthodox and Roman Catholic church hierarchies assumed that their former position of power would be restored. At the same time, the heavy influx of groups from the West, although very well-intentioned, has caused some cultural-theological confusion. It is important, says Volf, that evangelicals in the former Soviet *bloc* develop theology that addresses the current issues – not one that is imported from cultures inexperienced in those issues.

'When Jesus comes into any culture, he does not come to a strange land but "to what is his own" ', says Volf. 'This holds true even if that culture holds him a stranger, even if only a few receive him and "believe in his name" (John 1:5,9,11,12). Our task is not to import Jesus, like some exotic article from a foreign land. We must proclaim Jesus and, in obedience to his message of salvation, (re)discover the Croatian or Slovakian, Hungarian or Serbian face of Jesus.'

THEOLOGICAL COMMISSION TAKES SHAPE

WEF had early recognized the need for different approaches in different contexts. In 1968 the General Council appointed a Theological Co-ordinator: Bruce Nicholls. He teamed up with someone who shared his concern for theological education, John Langlois. (See chapter 6.)

'Bruce and I noted there was a lot of emphasis on evangelism', Langlois recalls, 'but so often it was shallow, resulting in a ripple lasting only a generation. Because converts were not instructed in the Scriptures, their children could degenerate into theological liberalism. To ensure that evangelical fervour would be biblical in the next generation, churches needed sound teaching in the Scriptures – "reliable men . . . qualified to teach others" '.

Nicholls founded the Theological Assistance Programme (TAP) and launched *Theological News*. Langlois became Administrator and Treasurer. TAP also produced instructive literature, a directory of theologians and schools, and plans for research centres, libraries, and consultations. The only thing lacking was finance to make it all happen.

TAP was obviously filling a niche and helping to unite evangelicals worldwide. The next General Assembly of WEF, held in 1974, turned TAP into the Theological Commission – WEF's first full Commission. Africa's Byang Kato became its first Chairman. Besides editing *Theological News*, Nicholls began editing *Evangelical Review of Theology* – WEF's first regular journal.

'The function of the *Evangelical Review of Theology* is to interpret the Christian faith for contemporary living', stated founding editor Nicholls. 'Our experience of God doesn't take place in a vacuum. Secular materialism and relative religious and ethical values which now pervade every culture mould our theology. They either foster revolution or maintain the status quo in society.'

Now the Theological Commission provides invaluable service to other WEF Commissions, helping to express their theological base. These are reflected in topics covered in the Outreach and Identity Series.[7]

AUTHORS FROM AROUND THE GLOBE

Through the years, WEF has published several major volumes on topics of current theological debate (see Bibliography), reflecting a global cross-section of scholars. Their work provides biblical tools for evangelicals worldwide – whether among lonely Quechua evangelists in the mountains of South America, or a handful of isolated believers in Pakistan, or a crowded seminary classroom in Korea.

WEF's Theological Commission and Lausanne's Theological Working Group, although distinct groups, have jointly sponsored consultations on Evangelism and Social Responsibility, and the Work of the Holy Spirit and Conversion, resulting in books and monographs on these topics.

[7]Outreach and Identity Series, published by WEF Theological Commission, obtainable from WEF offices. See list at front of book.

Other agencies, such as the Overseas Council for Theological Education and Mission (USA) and the Torch Centre (Korea), have helped with strategic funding.

Regional Theological Associations have addressed issues affecting the gospel in their nations. For instance, books produced by the Asia Theological Association[8] demonstrate biblical honesty as well as cultural understanding in confronting major concerns, such as ancestor-worship, poverty, and urbanization. Several of these are collections of papers given at consultations, edited by Korea's Bong Rin Ro, Theological Commission Director from 1989 to 1996.

The Bible and Theology in Asian Contexts, published earlier by ATA, is one of the most significant evangelical contributions to the gospel and culture debate.

Consultation topics dealt with by the TC are obviously basic to evangelicals everywhere, but several hold regional significance. For instance, *The Unique Christ in Our Pluralistic World*, edited by Bruce Nicholls from a consultation held in Manila, addresses concerns of the churches in Asia, pressed by the claims of Buddhism, Hinduism, and Islam.[9]

For churches in Latin America, the evangelical viewpoint on the gospel and poverty holds special significance against the backdrop of liberation theology.[10] In North America and Europe as well as worldwide, continuing debate over biblical inerrancy requires constant attention.[11]

Some theological consultations, such as the one on theological training in China and another focusing on the Islamic world, require keeping a low profile because of religious/political sensitivities. These never appear in headlines but represent careful exploration and prayerful planning.

FRESH INSIGHTS

WEF's Theological Commission stimulates evangelicals in these different theological worlds to speak to the issues affecting their nations. The Commission also provides a channel for sharing

---

[8]The Asian Theological Association is an affiliate of the International Council of Accrediting Agencies for Theological Education, described later in this chapter.

[9]Bruce Nicholls, Ed., *The Unique Christ in Our Pluralist World* (Carlisle: Paternoster Press, Grand Rapids: Baker Book House, 1994).

[10] Bruce J. Nicholls, Ed., *In Word and Deed*. (Carlisle: Paternoster Press, 1985).

[11]Donald A. Carson, *Biblical Interpretation and the Church* (Carlisle: Paternoster Press, 1984).

experience and insights with each other and with the theological world in general.

'While evangelicals in each country develop theologies to guide churches within context, their insights could go unnoticed by the rest of the world', says Peter Kuzmic. 'But WEF gives them a worldwide voice that commands attention.

'For instance, liberal theologians thought they had finally put to rest debates over such doctrines as biblical inerrancy, the uniqueness of Christ, and the resurrection. Evangelicals in the West who still accepted these doctrines were portrayed as "fundamentalists" imposing their narrow views on the rest of the world. But to the surprise of liberals, many young theologians in non-Western nations are defending these basic doctrines. They bring fresh insights that liberals cannot gainsay.'

THE CONTROVERSIAL QUESTION OF CO-OPERATION

There are issues that appear fairly calm on the surface but underneath hide treacherous shoals. The Theological Commission is called upon to provide biblical guidelines for navigating those waters. One of the most controversial issues is ecumenical co-operation. Ecumenical groups accuse evangelicals of refusing to put the unity of the Spirit into practice. Some evangelicals accuse liberal ecumenicals of sacrificing truth for the sake of organizational oneness. Both sides ask, are there any areas in which we can work together?

WEF set up a Task Force on Ecumenical Issues, under the Theological Commission, to draft appropriate guidelines on the question of co-operation not only with Roman Catholics but also with the World Council of Churches. The Task Force was composed of scholars from Latin America as well as from Europe (including the Latin South) and North America. It took into consideration the findings of the Evangelical-Roman Catholic Dialogue on Mission (ERCDOM),[12] and published three significant titles:

Roman Catholicism: a Contemporary Evangelical Perspective
Baptism, Eucharist, and Ministry (a response to the WCC's Lima
    Document of 1982)
Confessing the One Faith (a response to the WCC's Faith and
    Order Document, circa 1992)

---

[12]Basil Meeking and John Stott, Editors, *The Evangelical-Roman Catholic Dialogue on Mission 1977–1984* (Carlisle: The Paternoster Press, 1986). The WEF Task Force was led by Paul Schrotenboer, Christian Reformed Church.

In essence, the Task Force reiterated the principle that there could be no doctrinal compromise for the sake of unity, and pointed out that in spite of superficial changes in attitude, there were still basic doctrinal problems that prevented any theological or evangelistic joint project.

The Task Force did counsel WEF members to show humility and charity, not arrogance and hostility, toward their RC and WCC counterparts. They recognized the presence of individual evangelicals within these bodies. They emphasized the value of making common civic representation to governments in dealing with problems in concerns such as human rights and public immorality. And they recommended that WEF continue communicating with RC and WCC offices to keep evangelical viewpoints before them.[13]

THE ECT DEBATE

These recommendations gave background to the widespread reaction to the document, 'Evangelicals and Catholics Together' (ECT) published by an *ad hoc* committee (not WEF) in 1994. The concept described the areas of concern in which evangelicals and Roman Catholics could be 'co-belligerents', but it also referred to co-operation in evangelism. It was endorsed by a group of 39 scholars and Christian leaders, who signed on an individual, personal basis. Among the co-signers were evangelicals who held fearlessly to biblical fundamentals. To them, the water looked safe on the surface. They were surprised at the reaction of other evangelicals who saw the submerged shoals.

Because of the widespread concern and continuing debate, WEF responded to questions from member bodies with a commentary that referred to the Task Force report accepted by the WEF General Council in 1986.[14]

'The scope of the ECT statement went beyond social activism to evangelism', Vencer pointed out. 'The critical issue really is the doctrinal differences between Evangelicals and Catholics that remain unresolved and must not be denied or underplayed.'

[13] For a significant critique of WCC positions by a non-evangelical, see Ernest Lefever's autobiography, (New York: Simon and Schuster, 1996).

[14] See Appendix H for Dr. Jun Vencer's commentary and a background analysis by the author.

PROVIDING POWERFUL TOOLS

The Theological Commission has special significance to the theological world because its members represent an international cross-section of scholarship. The majority of members are not from Europe or North America – a factor that makes WEF's theological statements even more credible and significant when liberal theologians quote 'Third World' voices to bolster their position. Non-Western evangelical theologians are very clear-cut in their defence of biblical absolutes. In 1983, WEF sponsored the first-ever consultation of theologians from the non-Western world, convened by the Theological Commission in Seoul, Korea.

Besides studying strategic issues, the TC is strong on teaching. Its affiliate, the International Council of Accrediting Agencies for Theological Education (ICAA), formed in 1980, encourages Bible colleges and seminaries to upgrade their standards, faculty, and libraries. It promotes regional accrediting associations, such as the Accrediting Council for Theological Education in Africa (with 197 affiliated institutions and programmes). In 1996, ICAA was renamed the International Council for Evangelical Theological Education (ICETE).

'These regional groups really help evangelical schools network with others', says Roger F. Kemp, an Australian who studied in South Africa and Australia, taught at a Bible school in Zambia, and became ICAA General Secretary. 'It gives them access to materials developed by other countries, and provides credit-transfer possibilities for students.

'As they meet ICAA standards, their credibility with government educators and others goes up. In the past, liberal theologians have excelled in academic standards and have looked down on evangelical institutions. But now evangelicals are proving that they can be both biblically and academically sound.'

Kemp is pleased with the increasing regional co-operation he finds. In 1990 he and Pablo E. Perez (then the Executive Secretary of WEF's Commission on Renewal) made a survey of Latin American countries, in response to a request from Brazil to join ICAA.

'This raised the question of forming a regional theological association,' recalls Kemp. 'We soon learned about the historic divide between Portuguese Brazil and the rest of Latin America, which speaks Spanish.'

To the surprise of Kemp and Perez, Spanish-speaking associations were in favour of a united theological association. Greater was their surprise when Brazil also agreed. In 1992 the Evangelical Association for Theological Education in Latin America was formed.

'Brazil could have stood alone, because they had already developed a strong theological commission', Kemp says. 'Instead, they declared all their own TC positions open, to be filled by anyone voted in, Spanish- or Portuguese-speaking. This desire to work together will have a tremendous impact on the future of theological education in Latin America.'

AFRICAN WORLD VIEW

Isaac Zokoue, an International Council member and Principal of the Bangui Evangelical School of Theology (BEST – the seminary for French-speaking Africa arising from Byang Kato's vision), is an enthusiastic promoter of studying theology in context.

'Our school here in Bangui and the English-language school in Kenya – the Nairobi Evangelical Graduate School of Theology (NEGST) – were established to enable Africans to study the word of God in their own context', comments Zokoue.

The six-foot-tall African Bible scholar once found himself surrounded by appreciative African students after he spoke at a seminary in the USA. All complained that their courses did not apply to the world view of their people back in Africa.

Western theological education tends to treat the body and the spirit as belonging to separate worlds, Zokoue points out. In the West, education deals only with the rational, whereas the African students would be returning to a world of other dimensions, including that of ancestral spirits and demons. They needed to be biblically equipped to interface with that world. They also needed biblical answers to questions raised by tribalism, Islam, and other African issues.

Zokoue studied theology before there was adequate higher-level evangelical theological education in French-speaking Africa. He had to take most of his training, including his doctorate, in France. There he realized that French seminary studies are not as church-related as they are in Africa, nor are they as family-orientated. To Zokoue, these were additional reasons for training future church leaders in their own continent.

'There is a growing urgency for us to train church leaders to understand their context', stresses Zokoue. 'Africa is wide open for good or bad influence. Cults are active. There is an "authenticity" backlash to modernity, but materialism is also moving in. And Islam is increasingly aggressive. Muslim oil countries provide scholarships to study Islam, build mosques all over the countryside, and make loans to businessmen.

'Just as this kind of money is moving in to extend Islam, it seems that Christians in the West are lagging in their financial support of schools like BEST and NEGST. They have heard of thousands of Christian converts and many churches, but they do not realize the strategic need for evangelical leadership-training. Without that, the exciting conversion figures are meaningless.'

ASIAN NETWORK

Bong Rin Ro fully shares Zokoue's concerns, but in a totally different context halfway around the world. Ro has served as Dean of the Asia Graduate School of Theology, an international pro-gramme conducted in four countries, linking 17 seminaries.

'Asians should train in Asia,' states Ro, 'because it is very important for Christian leaders to train in their own context. But in the past the evangelical academic level has sometimes been low. ICAA and the Theological Commission are helping our schools to catch up.

'One major area is in publishing,' says Ro, who has edited a number of theological volumes. 'In the 70s, the World Council of Churches gave massive financial assistance to theological libraries, stocking them with books reflecting liberal theology. Now we are trying to overcome the shortage of evangelical textbooks and study-materials written from an Asian standpoint. These will not only help students but will also put material in the hands of pastors and lay people, to help them withstand the assault of liberal theology.'

Ro is encouraged by the increasing financial responsibility Asian churches are taking for funding theological education, as their national economies improve. The one area where he sees continued help is needed from the West is in endowing theological libraries and in providing scholarship funds for students in still struggling communities.

COMMUNIST DISCOVERS THE TEN COMMANDMENTS

Working with Ro, but from yet another context – Croatia – is Peter Kuzmic, founder of the Evangelical Theological Seminary in Osijek, Croatia – the only evangelical seminary in the former Yugoslavia. His is a fractured, violent world, still reeling from the collapse of the Soviet *bloc* and also of Yugoslavia.

Kuzmic has graphic memories of the hard world of Communism. Under the Communist Yugoslav regime he and other evangelicals courageously witnessed to their faith in the Saviour. The State-controlled press attacked them viciously. Then Communism fell, and with it came a surprise for Kuzmic.

'We want you to write a series of ten articles – one on each of the Ten Commandments', the editor of the largest daily newspaper in Croatia told Kuzmic. 'These will be full-page features, one each weekend.'

'I'm really surprised you are making your newspaper available for religious topics', replied Kuzmic. 'I thought you threw religion out the window a long time ago.'

'That was a mistake', replied the editor. 'We set out to build a new society, but the project failed because it had no foundation. We dare not repeat that mistake!'

The editor explained that he had heard Kuzmic on the radio debating about the importance of religion in morality. Kuzmic had stated that the Ten Commandments were universally applicable and basic to a stable society.

'I asked my aged Catholic mother for a copy of the Ten Commandments', the editor continued. 'She found them in an old prayer book. I read them; you Christians are right! Please do not keep these things locked in your churches and in your theological schools.'

As Yugoslavia disintegrated into warring factions, Croatian friends urged Kuzmic to help mediate peace. He knew that ethnic hatred extended far back to the division of the area by the Romans. Subsequent empires had added to racial and religious strife. Since the 1950s, Communism had suppressed ethnic warfare, but under the surface were the deep-seated animosities of Roman Catholic Croatians, Orthodox Christian Serbians, and Muslim Bosnians, all with their history of atrocities.

BILLY GRAHAM OF EASTERN EUROPE

In this context Kuzmic and his faculty are applying the word of God in training men and women from all over former Yugoslavia and even Russia. In the former Yugoslav region, 80% of current Christian leadership has studied at the Osijek Seminary. Now Kuzmic is also sharing his insights further afield as Distinguished Professor of World Missions and European Studies at Gordon-Conwell Theological Seminary in the USA. But he still plays a strategic role in Croatia, making frequent trips back to that troubled area.

Kuzmic says he himself became a born-again Christian through the prayers of his father. As young Peter gave his testimony, people asked him to preach. He had only his Bible and a hymn book.

'I had never seen another Christian book', recalls Kuzmic. 'I did not even know what a concordance was. The only way I knew to prepare a sermon was on my knees, where I cried out, "O Lord God, they have asked me to preach again! What can I say?" God was faithful. He gave revival.'

As Kuzmic tried to meet the spiritual needs of a nation saturated in atheistic materialism and riven by ethnic hatreds, he realized the need for in-depth study. Yet there was no evangelical theological material written from the standpoint of Croatia and Eastern Europe.

In 1967 Kuzmic became the first Yugoslav to study theology abroad. Not many would have that opportunity, he realized. Also, it was important for them to study their own distinctive issues in their own nation. Upon his return, he founded the Evangelical Theological Faculty and began developing theological study materials.

BACK TO THE SOURCE

'We need to develop in Eastern Europe a whole new base of leadership', says Kuzmic. 'That is why theological education is so important. The Christian faith must be defined at its biblical source. That is the cry of the Reformation: back to the source. Today we face the task of bringing the biblical message to the biblically illiterate, secularized, technological, post-communist age.

'Not only in Croatia and Europe but all over the world, evangelical Christians – authentic biblical Christians – are in a unique position to provide correctives and to be the salt of society', continues Kuzmic, who is now in worldwide demand as a conference speaker. 'In these difficult times, well-trained, dedicated, and well-informed leadership is the key. WEF is committed to helping churches in every nation use that key.'

As WEF observed the 150th anniversary celebrations of the 1846 Evangelical Conference, there was great significance in the theme of the Theological Commission's 1996 Consultation: *Faith and Hope for the Future: Towards a Vital and Coherent Evangelical Theology for the 21st Century*.

That is a strategic aspect of the Evangelical Mandate.

CHAPTER 11

'Our Time Has Come'

Women's crucial role on behalf of communities in pain, whether in Beijing, Berlin, Boston or Buenos Aires.

'What do women mean when they boldly announce, "Our time has come?" Does it mean they are no longer going to cook?'

Judy W. Mbugua posed this rhetorical question at the opening of the Pan-African Christian Women Assembly (PACWA). The President of Kenya, Daniel Arap Moi, was there officially to launch the Assembly – the first of its kind.

Mbugua, PACWA Continental Co-ordinator, went on to explain that whether or not women cooked, evangelicals believed that the time had come for them to face issues affecting society in general and women in particular. That, she declared, was what PACWA was about.

'The urgent issues include AIDS, witchcraft, polygamy, the plight of the widow and her children, poverty and hunger, illiteracy, sexual abuse, social injustices, and battered women,' she explained. 'And in addressing these, the need for evangelism is central.'

EVANGELICAL WOMEN ADDRESS PROBLEMS

While PACWA spoke to issues from an African woman's standpoint, the conference illustrated concerns of women in other continents. Most of all, it pointed up the initiative that evangelical women worldwide are taking in addressing the spiritual and social problems of their nations.

Participating in PACWA, held in Nairobi, Kenya, August 1989, was a broad spectrum of denominations from 36 African nations, with a total of 1650 registered and an overflow of 500 unregistered guests.

A refreshing sense of humour showed through the agenda's heavy subjects – humour often with a serious point. A counselling psychologist, Gladys Mwiti, described Mother Eve as 'the last and the best of God's creation'. 'Eve was blessed with all those wondrous gifts God has given us women', continued Mwiti, herself a wife and mother of four children. 'She was not stupid, but a clever woman, who could even talk politics with the Devil. To do what Eve did needed an analytical woman, who was not content to obey blindly. The Devil knew also that women have the gift of curiosity. The fruit indeed looked lovely, and it would make her wise. You see, she even knew that she needed more wisdom! Then, women also have the tongue, God's great gift of conversation that sets mankind apart from all other creatures. And who talks better than the woman?

'When we are convinced, how fast we can convince others! Many husbands give way just to save themselves from endless discussions which can even turn into nagging. So the Devil knew that he would find Eve with little on her hands, ready to prattle away and ready to quench her curiosity. Man would never have had the patience to argue and talk at such length!'

With her audience laughing at the satire, Mwiti reminded them that women's great gifts are open either to good use or evil abuse.

'It depends on who becomes Lord and Master of our lives – the creative power of the Creator God, or the destructive influence of the evil one. Which will it be for us women of Africa?' she challenged the delegates.

PACWA COVENANT

PACWA took the challenge seriously. Delegates endorsed a seven-point covenant, affirming the equality of men and women, the priority of the home and family, and the need for evangelism and discipleship. PACWA rejected not only social injustice but also the erosion of moral values, as well as 'witchcraft . . . and any form of occultism.'[1]

Critics of the gospel often allege that Christianity destroys culture. Radical African feminists tend to romanticize tradition while calling for radical reforms. But the PACWA delegates would have none of either. They showed an objective realism, commending positive cultural values while rejecting abusive customs. Most of all, they emphasized the transforming effect of the gospel.

'I praise the Lord for Christianity!' declared Nigerian university professor Mary Ogebe, a wife and mother. 'Scripture tells us of the

---

[1]For PACWA Covenant: Judy Mbugua, *Our Time Has Come* (Grand Rapids: Baker Book House, Carlisle: Paternoster Press, 1994), p. 145.

value God places on women. We can compare that with traditional attitudes. In ancient culture, women were seen only as property, equivalent to a field, to produce for men. Even in rural areas today, masquerade festivals reveal the same attitude: women must do all the work preparing food, but may not eat even leftovers, which can be discarded or given to the boys. When the masquerade arrives, women must run and hide or be flogged by the "spirit".

'The Bible tells us that our warfare is not against flesh and blood, so we cannot use carnal methods in overcoming wrongs against women. Joining Women's Lib. is out of the question. Even if the movement were appropriate, where would the poor average woman find funds to operate within the system? We must turn to heavenly logistics!'

SEEKING BIBLICAL SOLUTIONS WORLDWIDE

PACWA is doing what WEF's Commission on Women's Concerns would like to see evangelical women in all continents do – identify their problems and seek constructive solutions. When Beatriz Zapata, a Mexican living in Guatemala, became the first Executive Secretary of the Commission in 1984, she invited an American, an Australian, a Ghanaian, a German, a Haitian, and an Indian woman to form a steering committee to help national fellowships develop their member churches to meet the needs of women.

Zapata had directed Christian Education at the Latin American Evangelical Institute (of which her husband is principal), and is a Bible teacher, counsellor, writer, and radio and conference speaker.

With that kind of experience, Beatriz caught the attention of other organizations, including the World Council of Churches. WCC offered to pay her way to international conferences and urged her to write for their publications.

'But I turned them down', she said. 'My heart could not be in that kind of movement. I must be biblical and true to my conscience and beliefs. But I realized that if we evangelical women do not become active in developing our own ties within the Body of Christ, we are going to be left behind.

'We do not want to become a feminist movement, but we do need to deal with the poor self-image of women. They need to develop the gifts of the Spirit within the Body of Christ. One of the main needs is to help women – especially educated women – grow spiritually mature. Many Christians in the Third World are fed a constant diet of evangelistic preaching but are not getting enough spiritual food.'

Zapata also urges women to put their faith to work in practical

ways. On one occasion, the Guatemala Evangelical Alliance
Women's Commission obtained a bulk shipment of 300,000 pounds
of dried milk to send to refugee camps in El Salvador, Honduras,
and Nicaragua. But how to pack and deliver the milk? Beatriz
appealed for volunteers over two local radio stations, and in no time
had 250,000 one and two-pound bags packed.

'Through our evangelical network, we distributed them to the
refugee camps', says Zapata. 'We even obtained the use of a
helicopter to drop the bags into some difficult-to-reach areas.'

COMMON CONCERNS, DIVERSE PROBLEMS

Zapata quickly realized that although most women face common
societal concerns of marginalization and abuse, problems differ
enormously from one culture to another.

'For example, a women's leader in India wrote to ask my advice
about the problems a 28-year-old woman and her fiancé were facing
in trying to marry', Zapata recalls. 'Although the engaged couple
had been courting for seven years, the pastor refused to perform the
ceremony until the woman's family paid a dowry, which they could
not afford. According to custom, the pastor and the man's family
would each receive half.

'Now, how could I give advice? In Latin America we don't pay
marriage dowries. So I put the Indian leader in touch with people
in India who could help her find a biblical solution within that
culture. But it shows how women need a sounding board for the
problems they run into.'

WEF is very much aware of how widely those problems can differ
from nation to nation. Consider two scenarios:

*MARIA: Maria lives in a nation that provides equal opportunities
for women and men. Girls have access to the same levels of
education and employment. While male attitudes still affect some
aspects of society (including violence and pornography), the law
protects women from discrimination and abuse. Young women
are free to choose the men who will become their husbands.
Women own land and manage business ventures. Their main
debate is over such issues as achieving parity of wages with men,
and government provision of day care for their children. Churches
discuss the role women should play in the church.*

*LILY: Lily's country does not recognize women as equal with
men. Religion and culture teach that women are not only inferior
but also worthless. Female babies are often abandoned. Girls have
their genitals mutilated; parents select their husbands. Rape*

victims are shunned or punished, even put to death. If a man dies, his widow is taken by a relative of the dead man to be his wife. Female adults are confined or segregated from men. Women may not own land, drive cars, or compete for jobs considered to be in the male sector. Churches try to help abused women.

Obviously, women in Nation B are going to face problems different from those in Nation A. Christian women will face different sets of attitudes. In fact, discussions of 'women's concerns' in one nation may seem incomprehensible to another.

CULTURE SHOCK

Ingrid Kern, who chairs WEF's Commission on Women's Concerns (CWC), understands this from personal experience. She was working among women with the Evangelical Alliance of East Germany, long before the Berlin Wall fell.

'In socialist East Germany, my husband and I were cut off from Western society for 21 years', Kern explains. 'When I later visited Western Europe and North America, I went through real culture shock.

'But I had to learn much more about cultural attitudes toward women as I visited non-Western countries. In some of those nations, the agenda of Western women simply does not make sense. It does not seem to have the same priority, because there are so many more basic needs women face.'

Because of this, the Commission does not impose an agenda but encourages churches in each nation to study women's needs and seek effective ways of meeting them.

'We find that a women's group from one developing country is best suited to help a women's group in another country of similar culture,' Kern explained. 'They understand the cultural values, and they find ways of applying the gospel within that culture. In Muslim countries, for instance, only women can minister among women.'

National women's groups are encouraged to teach impoverished women crafts so that they can be self-employed, instead of making a living from prostitution. In one northern Indian village, a Christian community development team supplies piglets to marginalized women, so that they can raise them and use the proceeds to support their families.

Not every project is a success. Community attitudes can cause backlash. For example, Bengali men resented the economic independence of rural women who learned to plant and care for fruit trees.

'WE FEEL LIKE SISTERS'

'I shall never forget the women's consultation we held in Berlin in 1991', explains Dorothy Dahlman of the USA. 'The women were mostly from Eastern Europe and the former USSR. We felt we needed to learn from them. At the end of the consultation, they told us, 'You are the first people who have come without an agenda to tell us what to do. You have listened to us; you prayed with us; you encouraged us. You have done more than if you had a pre-set programme. Thank you. Now we feel like sisters in Christ.'

One woman was from a country where women had worked 18-hour days under the former Communist regime. Now freedom had come, but with it moral licence. 'We need to learn from Christians in other countries how to live for Christ in the new-found freedom that we find so dangerous', she said.

'We've been oppressed for many years, so we are not as courageous and open as women in the West', explained another. 'From childhood, we were harassed for going to church. We lived in fear. Now it is so encouraging to meet women who accept us and say, "We are one in Christ" '.

A Russian woman whose father, a pastor, had died in prison in Siberia, was not allowed to study at university because she was a Christian. Instead she worked in Siberian coal mines. But the elders of her church recognized her spiritual gifts and, faced with a shortage of pastors, they ordained her. God is using her gifts in evangelism and preaching across the Commonwealth of Independent States (formerly the Soviet Union).

Women like that encourage other women as they network through the Women's Commission. Professor Akiko Minato of Tokyo Christian University discovered many women of like mind through the WEF Women's Commission.

'I never realized there was such a group of women worldwide with the same concerns as I have for Japanese women', she said. 'I have found it difficult to reach our women; by working together in WEF, we can help each other.'

Minato is now chairwoman of the Japan Evangelical Association Women's Commission, speaks at conferences, and has written a book on Japanese women's concerns.

In India, Leelavathi Manasseh co-ordinates Women's Ministries for the Evangelical Fellowship of Asia and is a member of the worldwide Commission. She conducts leadership seminars for women under the theme: The Biblical Role of Women in Church, Family, Society, and Mission.

Manasseh edits the WEF Women's Concerns *Newsletter* and has developed television programmes and literacy materials. She and other members on the WEF Women's Commission realize that of the more than one billion illiterates in the world, (98% of Two-Third World adults), nearly two-thirds are women. Yet these women are bringing up the next generation.

'The church needs to meet the basic needs of women by teaching literacy, teaching hygiene, and counselling about family planning,' says Mary Thabit Bassali of the Women's Union of the Evangelical Church in Egypt.

In Myanmar[2], notorious for its denial of human rights, Manasseh conducted a seminar on 'The Biblical Role of Women'. Seventy women courageously took part in the event arranged by Mary Hau Lun Cing, Director of the Women's Commission of the Myanmar Evangelical Christian Fellowship.

FAMILY: STRATEGIC ROLE

While evangelical women in many countries are actively addressing in public societal problems, WEF's Women's Commission also affirms the strategic influence of women in the home – an effective arena for bringing about change. The positive influence of Christian mothers on their families – modelling Christian values and spiritual life – will in turn confront evil in society.

'A very strategic issue for evangelical women today is the family', agrees WEF's Jun Vencer. 'The family is the locus of morality in society. There should be a love relationship between husband and wife, children and parents. This forms the basis for a loving community. This makes us human and humane.'

Eva Sanderson, a Zambian and a member of WEF's International Council, shares that conviction and has seen it make a difference in the home, community, nation, and continent.

For several years deputy mayor of Kitwe, Sanderson says she could never have served publicly without a loving family support base. 'My husband is my number one supporter,' she says. 'Many gifted women are unable to fulfil God's calling on their lives, because their husbands do not share their vision, or feel insecure in their marriage relationship.'

Entering municipal elections at the urging of friends, Sanderson had to face negative church attitudes not only towards women but also towards Christians being involved in politics.

---

[2]Myanmar is the former Burma, where the pioneer missionary, Adoniram Judson, translated the Bible into Burmese. Recently, the courageous human rights stand of Nobel Peace Prize winner Aung San Suu Kyi has brought the nation into the international spotlight.

'When I decided to stand as a candidate for deputy mayor, I told the Lord I was willing to be "salt and light" in the mayor's chambers, if he wanted me there. Often evangelicals react instead of helping to make policy. People of other religions know the value of influencing the nation through politics. Lack of Christian participation has allowed laws, such as those affecting abortion, to be enacted contrary to biblical standards.'

COMMUNITY INVOLVEMENT

As regional representative for the Pan-Africa Christian Women Alliance, and Chair of the PACWA Council, Sanderson has encouraged evangelicals to be involved in the community. In Zambia, the PACWA chapter has helped elderly people and single mothers find shelter and food. They even enabled a blind woman to win child support from the mining employee who had abandoned her. Now government Social Welfare offices refer people to PACWA for advice, including marriage counselling.

Sanderson, a former health officer, became especially concerned for the young people of her nation as she saw the escalating statistics of AIDS. One estimate gives 22% of the urban population as HIV positive. As young people leave the villages they also leave the traditional *mores* of their culture and become prey to the sexual permissiveness of the cities. The hope of the nation, educated youth, are the hardest hit.

Promiscuity spreads the deadly virus among women as well as men, and resultant deaths leave increasing numbers of orphans. One source projects that 600,000 Zambian children will be orphaned because of AIDS by 1997. In Uganda, AIDS is now the leading cause of death, and in Rakai District, one out of every three children has been orphaned by AIDS; in Masaka District, nearly half of all deaths are caused by AIDS.

Figures from other parts of Africa are also serious. Researchers estimate that between 12 and 16% of pregnant women in Cote d'Ivoire harbour AIDS. Africa-wide, south of the Sahara, 11 million people are HIV positive.[3]

Sanderson and her PACWA colleagues decided to do something

[3]Figures are from the World Health Organization and UNICEF, reported in *Together*, Monrovia, Ca: World Vision (July–September 1995). The same issue quotes the *Bangkok Post*: 'South and Southeast Asia will dethrone Africa as the region with the most uncontrollable spread of AIDS within the next two to three years.' By the year 2000, experts predict, 30–40 million people worldwide will become HIV-positive. Ninety percent of them will live in non-industrial countries.

about the scourge. They challenged churches to get involved in the solution, rather than standing aloof.

'Chastity is moral, it is traditional, and it works!' declares Sanderson. "Safe Sex" professes to be moral, but it is permissive, and it does not work. AIDS has given the church an opportunity to emphasize biblical guidelines for sexuality: chastity before marriage and fidelity within marriage. The church must remind the people of God's warning against ungodliness and sin!'

At the same time, the Zambian woman calls on the church to show compassion to AIDS victims and relatives, helping with physical care, day care for the children of patients, and spiritual encouragement.

The PACWA model has caught the attention of evangelical associations in other continents, where similar action-orientated women's groups are being formed.

'The Commission on Women's Concerns motivates the national evangelical associations to deal with women's issues in the home, church, and society,' declares Sanderson. 'It facilitates the sharing of experience and expertise.

'And belonging to WEF amplifies the fact that we are all one in Christ!'

WORLDWIDE PROBLEM: ABUSE OF WOMEN

While some radical feminist groups have captured the spotlight in exposing the abuse of women, South American Sarvia Ortiz of the Commission on Women's Concerns points out that evangelicals should be foremost in facing the problem, as a scriptural mandate. Through the centuries, ambassadors of the gospel in different cultures have sought to restore women to the place of respect designed by the Creator and supported by Scripture.

A sinful world has destroyed that respect. In every society, East or West, North or South, women are discriminated against. Even in cultures that provide for equality, women are victims of community and domestic violence more often than men.

Throughout the world, the sex trade abuses women. The Coalition Against Trafficking in Women highlights several of the worst offenders:[4]

In Japan, the sex industry accounts for an estimated 1% of the country's total goods and services. Added to Japanese prostitutes are 150,000 foreign women.

In India, a quarter of the estimated 2.3 million women prostitutes

[4]*Toronto Star*, (Sept. 5, 1995), p. 14.

are minors – many sold by parents, kidnapped, or lured by fake job offers.

In Thailand, one third of the prostitutes (their number estimated at anywhere from 300,000 to 2.8 million) are children. Each year, more than 5 million men – half a million of them tourists – pay for sex.

However, the problem is worldwide and reflects widespread abuse by men. In San Francisco, 57% of 130 prostitutes interviewed reported that they had been sexually abused as children, and a third said that rape had been their first sexual experience.

Pornography exploiting women is a fast-growth industry. (See Pornography Report in chapter 12 on Youth.)

Mary Bassali reminds her colleagues on the Women's Commission that in some cultures the abuse of females begins at birth and ends only at the time of death. Reports from many sources support her contention. If females have not already been aborted, at birth they may be abandoned or killed because they are not sons[5]; at puberty their genitals may be painfully mutilated; in youth they may be denied schooling; in marriage they face virtual slavery, including beatings; and upon the death of their husbands they become outcasts (a lesser evil than the former fate of being buried or burned alive with the husband's corpse?).

Christian as well as secular women's organizations rightly oppose such maltreatment of women.

NEW THREAT: THE GENDER AGENDA[6]

WEF's Commission on Women's Concerns is facing these issues with cultural sensitivity and scriptural integrity. Many concerns focus on traditional customs and attitudes from the past. However, a new threat to the biblical concept of male and female is emerging, hailed as 'the wave of the future' by radical sociologists. This movement is creeping across the face of the earth like the darkness of an eclipse of the sun.

Called 'The Gender Agenda', it stems chiefly from the humanism of the West. Its philosophy threatens to override the real male -female issues that communities are struggling with, burying them

---

[5]Males now account for 64% of the population in parts of China. Source: 'Pre-natal Tests in China Threat to Girl Babies', *San Francisco Examiner*, (April 24, 1994).

[6]The author realizes that 'gender' is primarily a grammatical term referring to classification of words. However, since 'sex' is increasingly used to mean 'sexual intercourse,' and since 'gender' is increasingly applied to people in terms of being male or female, the author bows to usage, to save confusion.

under perverted concepts of human sexuality. These views could destroy the moral structure of society as we have known it. They deny God's design of sex, family, and humanity. They are openly hostile to biblical spirituality in general and evangelicals in particular. They seek to legitimize and legalize the lifestyle of Sodom and Gomorrah.

The Gender Agenda goes beyond concern about mistreatment of women and seeks to bring about a world in which all distinction between men and women, apart from obvious physical characteristics, would be abolished.

One aspect of this is the abortion issue. This surfaced at the Population Conference held in Cairo in 1994. The world population explosion is undoubtedly a major concern, requiring moral solutions. But radical feminists at the Cairo Conference sought to use it as a platform for promoting 'reproductive rights' (euphemism for 'abortion rights') and safe-sex ideology (euphemism for wanton sex 'protected' by condoms). Only strong opposition, chiefly from the Vatican and Islamic leaders, defeated official acceptance of these agenda items.

The Fourth World Conference on Women, sponsored by the United Nations in Beijing, China, in 1995, produced several declarations that evangelicals could join in commending. Many of the delegates were women with genuine concern for improving the lot of women, defending values that evangelicals could honestly endorse.[7]

Although, regrettably, evangelical women were very few among the delegates, they did try to express biblical views. For instance, Beatrice Zapata of Guatemala's Evangelical Fellowship, personally spoke with her nation's President, to make him aware of the issues. As a result, he included conservatives among the nation's delegation.

WEF's Religious Liberty Commission and the National Association of Evangelicals (USA) combined forces with a Coalition on Women and Society that presented a conservative view. During a pre-Conference forum for Non-Governmental Organizations, World Vision's Linda Tripp moderated a workshop dealing with the issues faced by female children. Evangelicals among the delegates rejoiced at opportunities to share their faith on a personal basis with women from all over the world.

However, radical delegates overwhelmingly pushed the Gender Agenda. The delegates from 170 nations were exposed to a gender

[7]For instance, Prime Minister Benazir Bhutto of Pakistan and other prominent delegates denounced female infanticide, child labour, and prostitution. A few evangelical groups, such as REAL Women, sought to present biblical views during the Non-Governmental Organizations (NGO) parallel conference.

'deconstructionist' ideology that sought to abolish the biblical concept of family, promote lesbian and homosexual relations as normative (and even preferable in some cases), recognize the legitimacy of 'five sexes,' and vilify any opposing religious view.

In the end, delegates from conservative cultures and religions (notably Roman Catholics and Muslims) caused several of the more radical items to be dropped from the final declaration. One African delegate commented: 'This isn't a conference on women. It's a conference on sex.' Another woman complained, 'In my country, women are most concerned about where they can find safe drinking water – not whether lesbians can marry.'

However, proponents of The Gender Agenda will continue to press their views. If they had their way, terminology such as 'wife', 'husband', 'son', 'daughter', 'manhood', 'womanhood' would be replaced by gender-neutral terms, and distinctions between male and female would be discouraged. Even now, in some Western countries, biblical teaching on the dangers of same-sex relations is looked upon as a form of bigotry and hatred.

GREATEST MORAL CHALLENGE YET

The Gender Agenda sounds so far-fetched that evangelicals may be inclined to ignore it. But documented research on this agenda and the philosophy that has led up to it, demands attention.[8] The effects are already filtering into educational systems, government policies, the entertainment industry, and the communication media of the West. With the increasingly global pervasiveness of TV and the Internet, no corner of the world will escape the subtle influence of these concepts.

The Gender Agenda is an issue wider than 'women's concerns.' It concerns all men, women, and children. However, it is being pressed mainly through radical feminism, and evangelical women cannot ignore it. This promises to be one of the greatest moral challenges ever faced by society.

WEF is equipped to take up this mandate, for the sake of the family, the community, the nations, and for the glory of God, the Creator of male and female.

Both Adam and Eve were to be responsible for the rest of God's earthly creation (Gen. 1:27,28). They were People of the Mandate.

[8]Documentation is based on statements made by proponents of The Gender Agenda, as well as by reports of evangelicals who attended. For one summary, see James Dobson, *Focus on the Family*, August 1995 Newsletter; 8605 Explorer Dr., Colorado Springs, CO. 80920 USA.

CHAPTER 12

The Universe of Youth

Hope for a culture of meaninglessness.

'Please speak on Sex and Dating', the youth leader told Paul Borthwick.

It was a long way from Borthwick's church in the United States to Suriname on the northern edge of the Amazon rain forest. Borthwick, an American youth pastor, had taken a group to South America for student ministry. The Suriname youth reflected the multiracial mix of the former Dutch colony: Black, Chinese, Indonesian, Laotian, Hindu, and Amerindian.

Borthwick was accustomed to speaking to youth in suburban Massachusetts, but what would be relevant in Suriname? The reply shocked Borthwick into realizing a fact that has since stood him in good stead as Director of WEF's Youth Commission: *youth all over the world face several common concerns.*

Paul and his wife Christie learned a lot more about the universe of youth when they visited Myanmar in Southeast Asia. The Myanmar Evangelical Fellowship had invited the Borthwicks to lead a conference for teens and youth leaders.

After landing at the airport, Paul and Christie were confronted by a huge advertisement depicting attractive young people smoking a brand of imported cigarettes.

'Smoking is obviously the way to be popular and modern', Christie remarked to Paul. 'And did you notice the brand name?'

'Lexington!' exclaimed Paul. 'Our home town!'

The connection made a conversation opener, as the Borthwicks humorously explained they were not the ones producing Lexington cigarettes. But it also gave them the opportunity to discuss the problems of smoking, drugs, and other urban vices affecting youth. Christie, with a Master's degree in public health, was soon busy giving talks on everything from hygiene to AIDS. Her clinical experience in microbiology and parasitology gave her great credibility in discussing common ills. At home she had known about glue-sniffing and drug addiction; but here a medical doctor de-scribed a Myanmar village in which everyone, apart from young children, was mainlining drugs, and 100% of the villagers were HIV positive.

'WE KNOW ARNOLD'

By way of introducing himself, Paul Borthwick asked what the young people knew about America.

'We know Arnold', they replied through an interpreter.

Arnold? Borthwick suddenly realized the young people had been watching Arnold Schwarzenegger videos – even though most of them could not speak English and knew little of the outside world.

'That was scary to realize', says Borthwick. 'They were viewing films that have little to do with traditional American life, but promote illicit sex, extreme violence, and flagrant materialism as signs of success. We don't want to be defensive about America's image, but we do worry about the effect on youth who tend to idolize anything American.'

A SERPENT IN EDEN

The Borthwicks began to put together a mental picture of what was happening to young people all over the world. Parents were desper-ately trying to hang on to traditional values that had helped to hold families and communities together. Their religion reinforced these values, reacting violently to change. Totalitarian governments sought to protect tradition as a means of political control.

But a beguiling serpent has invaded the world's cultural Edens. In the cities are films and in the markets are videos and audio tapes that corrupt a culture's value system. They by-pass parental, religious, and political authority, seducing the susceptible minds of youth. The serpent croons from radios and cassette players. Some governments, as in India, provide public radio and television sets in even the most remote villages, with all-day programming. For the more affluent who own a television satellite dish, a forked tongue jabs out of from the skies day and night. It may be licentious rock music from the West, or counterpart programming created in Bombay or Hong Kong, but most of it is saturated with sex, violence, and materialism.

India's movie industry, centred in Bombay ('Bollywood'), is the world's most prolific producer of new films. Low-budget and laden with violence and sex, they are popular in other Asian countries as well as in Africa and South America.

'The entertainment media are creating a youth subculture that is quite universal in urban areas, whether in the East or West, North or South', explains Borthwick. 'Teenagers in Athens, Delhi, Hong Kong, Miami, Nairobi, Paris, and Rio de Janeiro may have more in common with each other than with their own parents.' Daniel Offer called this phenomenon "the universal adolescent".'

'The media know no borders', he wrote; 'ideas and events are transmitted to all corners of the globe, defining what is new or desirable, and are assimilated by young minds.'[1]

Youth workers identify music as having the greatest influence. American and European rock music, often on 'pirated' cassette tapes, appears in remote markets almost as soon as it is released in Nashville or London.

Michael Keating reports a conversation with a Fijian from the South Pacific: 'Fijian youth are increasingly rebellious and disrespectful to elders, the crime rate is soaring, and the drug traffic booming.' The man attributed these recent changes in youth attitudes to American music. 'It has captured the youth [with] . . . animal sexuality, rebellion against all authority, violence of every kind, and party, party, party.'[2]

PROSTITUTION AND PORNOGRAPHY

Luis Bush of the AD2000 Movement warns: 'In the cities of the Two-Thirds World, more than 100 million children are growing up on the streets; they have no education, no affection, no adult guidance. Almost a million of them are forced into prostitution.'[3]

Once practised mostly on an individual basis, prostitution has now become a tourist-driven industry in some parts of the Two-Thirds World. Male tour groups descend on cities such as Bangkok, promised cheap sex with children – in the belief that the younger the prostitute, the less likelihood of HIV infection. Tourism prostitution threatens the morality and health of poverty-stricken ethnic groups.

A counterpart of prostitution – and a graphic form of it – is pornography. This used to be limited to movies and magazines, but now rank pornography is readily available on some computer

---

[1]Daniel Offer, *The Teenage World* (New York: Plenum Press, 1988).

[2]Michael Keating, 'The Stolen Generation,' *Pastoral Renewal*, (May 1987), quoted by Paul Borthwick, *Ibid*.

[3]Luis Bush, *Funding Third World Missions* (Singapore: WEF Missions Commission, 1990). *Street Life*, published by Scripture Union, UK, reports the same statistic (100 million worldwide) in 1995.

networks. Instances of teenagers receiving unsolicited pornographic e-mail images have been reported.

Out of concern for the widespread evil of pornography, WEF took part in the Religious Alliance Against Pornography in January 1995. Meeting in Manila, Philippines, 160 religious leaders from 37 countries and 40 faith groups discussed the theme: 'Protecting Our Children's Future.'

THE MANILA DECLARATION

The Manila Declaration on Pornography drafted during the Conference declares: 'We join together out of a broad diversity of faith traditions, believing that unity in action is imperative if we are to protect our children's future – action that offers an increased measure of protection for those harmed by the evil of pornography throughout the world.'

The Manila Declaration reflects a creation theology, referring to sexuality as a gift from God, to be experienced within boundaries designed by God. It includes the following statements:

- Sexually-explicit material which abuses, degrades, or exploits another has destructive consequences for those who consume it or are implicated in its production and distribution.
- No longer strictly an issue of private morality, pornography has become a major economic force with vast communal ethical implications.
- Individual cultures have the right to protection from international commercial enterprises which erode culture through the distribution of degrading, violent, and destructive pornography.
- Pornography has become a multi-billion dollar, international enterprise. . . . Exposure and involvement of children, in particular, have taken on unprecedented global dimensions; sex-related crime is now a global problem.
- International computer networks are increasingly becoming unlimited outlets for the worst and most dangerous forms of pornography. These networks are used as a marketplace by paedophiles to contact children for abuse and to quickly trade pictures of those already abused.
- Pornography distribution is often enmeshed in a larger web of criminal activity.

The Declaration called for 'a new religious initiative, stronger legislation, co-ordinated international action, and recognition by governments of the seriousness of the problem.' The convenors are also planning to hold 'a world congress to end pornography.'

FOCUS: ADOLESCENTS

What should WEF do to help national fellowships and local churches face such problems in their own communities, and penetrate the youth subculture with the gospel? To find out, Borthwick held a discussion with youth leaders, exploring the formation of a Youth Commission under WEF. Providing an international mix were a Colombian, a Ghanaian, an Indian, and a Portuguese. Their goal: to find out what the national fellowships wanted help in doing.

Their first recommendation was to target adolescents – not children, and not post-adolescent youth. There were already excellent agencies working among children and college-age youth. The urgent need was among teens – in many nations a relatively new focus created by the introduction of secondary school.

'In traditional cultures, boys and girls move directly from childhood into adulthood with the onset of puberty', Borthwick points out. 'They work on the family farm or in the family business, and they marry. But secondary schooling has created an in-between group, in which boys and girls are neither children nor adults. Their bodies are filled with adult hormones, but marriage is delayed by education. So they become sexually active outside of marriage. Life may seem meaningless; they take to alcohol and drugs. Some become violent or suicidal.

'And their numbers keep swelling. In some lands, 50% of the population is under 21.[4] So the population explosion along with the subculture created by secondary school education and the entertainment media – these help explain the tensions communities are having with teenagers.'

John Allan, working among youth in Britain, points out that the proportion of teenagers in the world's population increases annually – and that most of them are from places where the church is weakest.[5]

---

[4]Over 60% of Africa's population is under the age of 16, according to the Pan African Christian Leadership Assembly II, November 1994. Worldwide, about one-third of the population is under the age of 15, and 85% of these are in the Two-Thirds World. By the year 2000, over half the world's population will be under the age of 25. (Source, except first sentence: Paul Borthwick, 'Multi-Cultural Challenges Facing Youth Ministry'; WEF Youth Commission, Jan. 3, 1995.)

[5]John Allan, 'New Strategies for Reaching Unreached Youth,' *Evangelical Missions Quarterly*, (April 1988).

HELP FOR FAMILIES

National fellowships told the Youth Commission they need help in ministry to families – how to guide new adolescents, how to curb the use of drugs and alcohol, how to teach biblical principles about sex and marriage. A great need for teenagers as well as their families and churches is culturally relevant literature and videos giving Christian teaching for youth.

'A lot of the material available is written for white and middle-class youth', says Borthwick. 'It is true there are commonalities among youth of all cultures, but we still need to address their concerns in their own ethnic context.

'WEF's approach is to help national fellowships empower their own churches for effective youth ministry. We don't want to bring in a packaged programme that every country has to follow. We want to encourage national fellowships and local churches to discover the best way to help youth in their own context.'

Borthwick found that most para-church agencies are glad to share tools and also to allow local adaptation. Each agency has its strength and contributes to the overall programme.[6]

Borthwick ran into problems in some countries, however. Churches in authoritarian cultures, used to directive leadership, expected him to give them a detailed programme. Some thought that the Youth Commission did not know what to do, because it was not dictating a definite formula. Others did not want the hard work of developing programmes with acceptable local methods. Some simply did not have the finances or trained staff to do so.

Then there was the reaction of the older generation to the topics their young people wanted to discuss. Parents did not realize the sexual permissiveness, drug culture, and violence their children were absorbing on headphones or watching on video. The Youth Commission had to find acceptable ways to discuss these topics without alienating parents.

FROM DONKEY TO JET

'In Colombia, we went from the donkey to the jet in one generation', a pastor told the Borthwicks. It was true. The Borthwicks visited countries where society had jumped in one generation from having

[6]Among the many youth-related agencies with which WEF's Youth Commission works are Campus Crusade, IFES, InterVarsity, Navigators, Operation Mobilization, Scripture Union, Young Life, Youth for Christ, Youth With A Mission.

no telephones to using cellular phones, from having no television to acquiring 40-station capability – and with it a barrage of entertainment from the West.

'With such radical changes taking place, youth are the most vulnerable', Borthwick believes. 'Older folk hang on to the memories and forms of the past. But young people do not have those moorings. To them, modernity with all its trappings is the future – and they don't know how to handle it. They pour into the cities. Some find acceptance in gangs.

'Poverty is another pervasive factor. A malnourished child has difficulty academically. He may grow up to be a non-productive adult. He either cops out of society or strikes back in violence. Even in affluent nations, such as Japan, Germany, the UK, or the USA, young people face uncertainty about the future, unemployment, the national debt, and the spectre of global doom. They feel helpless and hopeless. Some contemplate suicide.'[7]

TEEN CRIME RATES ESCALATE

In the United States alone since 1960, violent crime has increased 560%; illegitimate births by 400%, and teen suicides by 200%. In Canada, murders by teenagers increased 60 % from 1994 to 1995. Some of the murderers were only 13. One was seven years old. Authorities blamed drug addiction and were greatly concerned that the young criminals showed no remorse.[8]

Statistics suggest a pervasive reason for mounting youth crime figures: before completing elementary schooling, the average Canadian child has viewed on television more than 100,000 murders and other acts of violence. 'Often these acts of mayhem are woven into plots that portray immorality and profanity as "normal behaviour" ', comments Brian Stiller of the Evangelical Fellowship of Canada.[9]

John Dilulio of Princeton University predicts a looming major crime wave among youth. The number of male children of 'baby boomers' becoming teenagers, combined with crime statistics (6%

[7] Per 100,000 population, Finland has the highest reported suicide rate (21.1), followed by New Zealand (16.2), Canada (14.4), and the USA (11.9). Japan has just half the rate of the USA. Greece has the lowest (2.5). Very few non-industrialized nations report suicide statistics. The greatest rate-increase has been in countries of the West and Australia-New Zealand: in thirty years, most doubling, several tripling. (Source: *World Health Statistics Annual 1993*. Geneva: World Health Organization, 1994.)

[8] Canadian Broadcasting Corporation Report, August 16, 1995.

[9] 'TV Violence,' Evangelical Fellowship of Canada, Sept. 1995, quoting statistics from the Vanier Institute of the Family, Ottawa.

of young men commit crimes), means there will be 30,000 killers, murderers, and rapists rampant in the USA in the next five years, he estimates.[10]

Youth's fears of becoming victims of violence are not confined to countries known for terrorism. The 1995 *Guinness Book of Records* (p. 484) states that a child in the US is 15 times more likely to be killed by gunfire than one growing up in Ireland.

DRIVEN BY FEAR

From personal experience, Paul Borthwick understands teenage fears and rebelliousness. He himself had been a wayward son, driven by the fear that people might not like him. So he tried to please everyone – capable of giving a 'testimony' at a Christian youth group, but spending the rest of the night with buddies who drank, smoked drugs, and caroused. Friends called him 'The Chameleon'.

One day, out of curiosity, he looked up the word 'fear' in his father's Bible concordance, to see what the Bible could tell him about overcoming his fears. He turned to Isaiah 41:10: 'Do not fear, for I am with you; do not be dismayed, for I am your God. I will strengthen you and help you; I will uphold you with my righteous right hand.'

The Holy Spirit convicted the 17 year old of his need of a saving relationship with Jesus Christ. A church youth leader who helped him grow spiritually so impressed young Paul that he decided youth work was in his future. After university and seminary studies, Borthwick became a youth pastor at Grace Chapel in Lexington, Mass., USA, and is now 'a youth-minded missions pastor' there. Author of books on youth ministries,[11] he strongly believes that ministry to youth should be plugged into churches, not done independently.

'Doing it separately from the church may seem the faster way to get things done', he says; 'but in the end, para-church agencies face the need to disciple youth and form churches. Then they find out what Paul meant by "the care of the churches". They would be better off working through churches in the first place – and many are doing so.

'I believe that the local church is God's instrument to fulfil the

[10]Janet Epp Buckingham, Chair of the Evangelical Fellowship of Canada's Social Action Commission, in *Christian Week*, April 25, 1995.
[11]Paul Borthwick, *Youth and Missions* (Wheaton: Scripture Press, 1988). *Feeding Your Forgotten Soul* (Grand Rapids: Zondervan, 1990).

Great Commission – and that includes reaching youth. National Fellowships and WEF commissions help the churches in their task.'

'LORD, SEND US RAIN!'

The Ghanaian member of the Youth Commission, Kweku Hutchful, devised an acronym to explain the Commission's strategy: RAIN. It stands for the following:

RESOURCES: These vary from country to country, community to community. Resources include people, skills, programmes, materials and finance. WEF's Youth Commission helps to connect resources and needs. Alfredo Abreu, Portuguese member of the Commission, demonstrated the value of resource-sharing in a successful youth programme sponsored by the Portuguese Evangelical Alliance. Campus Crusade for Christ organized training in evangelism, Youth for Christ provided music groups, and InterVarsity Christian Fellowship donated follow-up literature.

AWARENESS: Some cultures do not recognize the potential of young people and do not understand the alienation many are facing because of new forces within society. Youth Commission materials discuss the potential of biblical characters such as Joseph, Daniel, Mary, and Timothy.

INFORMATION: Churches need accurate information on problems facing their communities: the unemployment rate, extent of gangs, crime rates, HIV percentages, demographics, teenage pregnancies, drug addiction, rate of urbanization, public and private programmes available. This information will help evangelicals to plan strategy better. They will also realize that their society is not static – community problems are escalating, and churches had better be prepared.

NETWORKING: The most valuable concept of WEF is people helping people, churches helping churches, nations helping nations. A youth association working in war-torn Lebanon may be able to share its experience with groups in Northern Ireland or Rwanda. A drug addiction programme in Holland may have good suggestions for groups in California. Latin Americans can offer advice on family values to Canadian youth.

Borthwick saw an example of networking during a visit to Namibia, Southern Africa. He introduced the Namibia Youth for Christ (YFC) director to the Evangelical Fellowship co-ordinator of Angola. This resulted in the formation of a YFC branch in Angola.

'Lord, send us RAIN!' cries the exuberant Hutchful. He and others on the Commission have seen RAIN work. In South Africa, Caesar Molebatsi runs the Youth Alive programme in the turbulent township of Soweto. It includes job counselling, retraining, vocational assistance and health care. The programmes help to overcome the despair and oppression of poverty. One of the Christian musical groups summed it up in a song: 'We see a new Africa in the light of the Lord.'

MAJOR OUTREACH RESOURCE

'Young people present the greatest challenge to the church, but they are also the greatest resource it has,' states Borthwick. 'When they come to the Lord and are properly discipled, they can take the gospel to others.'

In Myanmar, Borthwick found that young Christians thought of missionaries as only Westerners. He led Bible studies on the missionary heart of God and spoke about the unevangelized people in Myanmar and neighbouring countries. In response, 70 of the 100 youth in the conference signified their willingness to take the gospel to other peoples. Borthwick later heard that several travelled into China with the goal of planting a church in an unreached village.

'I'm always impressed by the vision and energy of Christian youth,' says Borthwick. 'Take the case of Abubakar, son of a Muslim priest in Indonesia. When an evangelist confronted him with the gospel in 1991, he was wonderfully converted. While studying at Chris Marantika's seminary in Indonesia,[12] he set a goal to win radical Muslims to Christ and form them into a local church. But his long-range vision was to become a missionary to Saudi Arabia – probably the most hard-line Muslim nation in the world!'

CATALYST FOR MOBILIZING YOUTH

Although the Youth Commission was officially launched only in 1992, at the Ninth General Assembly of WEF, it has already encouraged the formation of youth commissions in a number of national fellowships and regional associations. The European Evangelical Alliance, which has a full-time Youth Commission Director in Prague, held a regional consultation in September 1995. The Evangelical Fellowship of Asia is planning a consultation on youth. At GCOWE '95, sponsored by AD2000 in Korea, the WEF Youth Commission was able to serve as a catalyst for leaders dedicated to

[12]Chris Marantika is founder of the Evangelical Theological Seminary of Indonesia, which requires students to plant a church before graduation. His story is told by Ray Wiseman in *I Cannot Dream Less*. (Brampton, ON: Partners International, 1993).

mobilizing youth for world missions reported Borthwick. 'Our commitment is to foster "Networks of Co-operation" '.

Borthwick notes that many church and para-church agencies are seeing increased responsiveness among youth. InterVarsity attracts up to 20,000 students to its Missions Conference held every three years in Urbana, USA. In the Ukraine, InterVarsity staffer Len Andyshak says, 'We are at the edge of something amazing; students are turning to Christ and seeking to win others on campus. They are like the New Testament church.' Navigators, Campus Crusade, and other student ministries are finding a similar response in many nations.

'Young people need leaders who can role-model Jesus for them', states Sri Lanka's Youth For Christ leader Ajith Fernando. 'A bewildered and fractured generation is searching for meaning in life.'[13]

'We need to be agents of hope in a youth culture marked by hopelessness', agrees Borthwick. 'Our mandate is to present Jesus Christ, the hope of the world, the hope for eternity.'

[13]Ajith Fernando, 'Youth: More than Half of the World,' *World Evangelization*, LCWE (Summer 1989).

CHAPTER 13

Renewing the Vision

The basic secrets of evangelical effectiveness.

Half a million Germans praying for spiritual revival? In secular Germany – the land where Nietzsche declared God to be dead? Where scholars methodically tried to destroy the foundations of Christian faith with a flawed 'higher criticism' of the Scriptures?

Why, yes! After all, the praying men and women were of the same spirit as great Germans of faith in earlier centuries – stalwarts such as Luther and Melanchthon. In the 1700s the prayer life of Count Nikolaus Zinzendorf and his Herrnhut Community led to the worldwide missionary outreach of the Moravians.[1] Pietism (concern for personal holiness) spread from the Continent to England and across the Atlantic to the USA, giving impetus to the missionary movement in the 18th and 19th centuries.

Prayer characterized the founding of the Evangelical Alliance in London in 1846. The current nationwide annual day of prayer sponsored by the German Evangelical Fellowship as well as by many Fellowships around the globe, continues in the same spirit.

SPIRITUAL REVIVAL

Praying together in 1846 was more significant than might appear today. The strong separatism of the early Brethren movement (caused by their revulsion at unscriptural practices in the established church of that era), led some evangelicals to oppose joint prayer meetings with anyone else. Other groups, wounded by sectarian battles, were suspicious of any co-operative project – even with fellow evangelicals. And Quakers, reacting against lifeless formality,

---

[1]Stephen Neill, Gerald Anderson, John Goodwin, eds., *Concise Dictionary of the Christian World Mission* (London: United Society for Christian Literature, 1970).

felt they would dishonour the Holy Spirit by taking part in a pre-arranged prayer-time.[2]

Therefore the times of joint prayer before and during the 1846 inaugural conference in Britain were very significant. In themselves, they made an unassailable statement of unity in the Spirit. In 1847, the British Evangelical Alliance inaugurated an annual Week of Prayer held in the first week of the year, including two Sundays. Hearing about the week, missionaries in India requested in 1860 that it be made worldwide. Thereafter (interrupted only by the World Wars) it was called the Universal Week of Prayer and was observed all the way from Paris to Peking and Tokyo to Tiberias.

A letter from Turkey, dated January 10, 1862, described the Week as 'a rich spiritual festival'. A report from Nyasaland (now Malawi), told of concluding the annually observed week with 1,355 believers around 'the Lord's Table'. In China, Cheng Ching Yi described the annual Prayer Week as 'a leading event in the life of the Christian Church of my country'. In London, the Lord Mayor at times led the opening of noon prayer meetings during the Week.[3]

Confession of sin often accompanied prayer meetings, and spiritual revivals broke out. As word of revival spread from one community to another, from one land to another, the Holy Spirit convicted Christians of their coldness. Unsaved men and women turned to the Saviour.[4]

The name of 'Praying Hyde'[5] is especially associated with prayer and revival in India, but in the 1890s there were many other Christians, Indian and expatriate, who were similarly burdened. Revival did break out in several centres, but God chose an unlikely channel for one major breakthrough.

Pandita Ramabai had been a prominent Hindu social reformer before finding Christ as Saviour in 1891. In 1898 she visited the annual Bible convention in Keswick, England, where she challenged attenders to pray for revival in India. In 1905 girls at her Mukti orphanage came under great conviction of sin. As they

---

[2]Ruth Rouse and Stephen Neill, eds., *A History of the Ecumenical Movement* (Geneva: World Council of Churches, 1954).

[3]J.W. Ewing, *Goodly Fellowship* (London: Marshall, Morgan, and Scott, 1946), p. 36–40.

[4]Wesley Duewel describes the spread of significant revivals worldwide, in *Revival Fire* (Grand Rapids: Zondervan, 1993). Duewel, for 25 years a missionary in India with the Oriental Mission Society, has written a number of books on prayer that have touched lives worldwide. Duewel has been a member of WEF's North America Council.

[5]John Hyde, an American Presbyterian missionary, went to India in 1892. He spent long hours in prayer for the conversion of the peoples of India, and challenged missionaries and national Christians to holy living and spiritual revival.

repented and confessed, they experienced unusual manifestations of joy. Groups of them visited other villages to share their testimony. From Mukti, revival spread to many towns across India. About the same time, there were other revival movements in India, from North to South and East to West.

Later, in the 1950s, the Evangelical Fellowship of India grew out of prayer and spiritual renewal. Norman Burns, a missionary serving with the Dohnavur Fellowship (another orphanage), had experienced personal revival through meetings of the East Africa Revival, which he had visited en route to India. In 1951, Joe Church and William Nagenda of the East Africa Revival, along with Victor Manogaram of India's Youth For Christ, were invited by Amy Carmichael, founder of the Dohnavur Fellowship, to speak at Dohnavur. Revival flames ignited there and spread to the conferences that preceded EFI's formation. The revival hymn, 'Search Me, O God', became a favourite in these meetings.[6]

As with earlier prayer movements in other lands, revival produced concern for people who did not have the gospel.

MISSION OUT OF A PRAYER MEETING

'We're not doing right. This is a day of good news and we are keeping it to ourselves', the young high school teacher read from his Bible. N. Emil Jebasingh was one of 125 young men and women at a Bible and prayer conference in a South India village in 1965. A number of them had come to Christ as helpers in vacation Bible schools run by an Indian and an American working with the Church of South India.

In the early 60s, these young Christians met monthly, led by a young Bible teacher from Madras, Samuel Kamaleson. As they studied and prayed, they felt convicted that they were doing nothing to evangelize other parts of India. The 1965 meeting was organized to pray and to discuss what God wanted them to do.

'You remember the story',[7] continued Jebasingh. 'Four starving lepers had found the camp of the Syrian invaders completely deserted. The lepers feasted on abandoned food and helped themselves

---

[6]The revivalist J. Edwin Orr, a regular speaker for EFI, used this hymn extensively. It was written in Swedish in 1885, but years later the English translation was sung to a familiar Maori tune. Harmonization written by a missionary in India and used by EFI impressed Orr so much that he took it back to the USA for his meetings there. Robert J. McMahon, *To God Be the Glory* (New Delhi: Masihi Sahitya Sanstha, 1970), p. 20.

[7]2 Kings 7:8,9

to scattered treasure. But their consciences pricked them; they knew that everyone in the nearby besieged city was starving. They realized they must share the good news of the food with them!

'Today in India we have the Good News of the gospel, but most of our people have not heard. We have to tell them!' Jebasingh urged the young people.

The group took action on the spot by forming the Friends Missionary Prayer Band (FMPB). They would pray all night before public meetings. Every missionary, before being assigned, had to be backed by a prayer group. These groups, most of them in the Church of South India, became catalysts of spiritual revival as well as financial support for the missionaries. FMPB has since sent hundreds of missionaries throughout the subcontinent, and currently lists 600 active.

Jebasingh resigned his teaching job to become the first full-time leader of FMPB. He now heads up Trans-World Radio for India. Another Tamil, insurance broker Patrick Joshua, became FMPB's treasurer, and is now its leader.

One of the board members was the young Bible teacher, Samuel Kamaleson. He had been only a baby when his father died. His mother, as widow of a high-caste Brahmin, found life so intolerable that she decided to drown herself in the sea, near her house. Just as she stepped into the surf, she heard her baby crying. Mother love triumphed over her suicidal depression, and she rushed back to care for her baby in the house.

Shortly afterwards, she heard the gospel and knew that Christ was the one she needed. She renamed her son Samuel and nurtured him with prayer and Scripture. Sam grew up in Madras and began teaching others the word of God.

'WEEP OVER SOULS'

Kamaleson's life was specially touched when he attended the World Congress on Evangelism in Berlin in 1966, sponsored by *Christianity Today*.[8] Evangelist Billy Graham pleaded with the 1200 Christian

[8]Founded in 1956 in the USA, *Christianity Today* was a product of Billy Graham's encouragement, with initial funding through the Billy Graham Evangelistic Association, financed by J. Howard Pew, Christian oil magnate. Carl Henry, a leading member of WEF's Theological Commission, was founding editor of *CT* and Chairman of the Congress. The Congress was the vision of Billy Graham, but to avoid any impression that he was using the Congress to promote his Evangelistic Association, he and Carl Henry agreed that *Christianity Today* should officially sponsor it. Carl F. Henry, *Confessions of a Theologian* (Waco: Word Books, 1986), p. 144, 252.

leaders from more than 100 countries: 'We can get terribly professional. We have to have an experience that will make us weep over souls.'

The young Indian evangelist later recalled, 'I cried as I should have cried a long time before. I wept at the feet of the Lord. There was an awareness of sham and pretence in my private life. I had a time of reckoning with the Lord.'

Kamaleson became known as a gifted Bible speaker in India and overseas. Eventually, he accepted the speaking position of Vice-President-at-large for World Vision, with the understanding that each year he would spend three months ministering in his beloved India – 'my first responsibility,' he still insists.

John Richard was another speaker involved in the Bible studies that led to the founding of FMPB. A radio officer with Indian Airlines, he had trusted in Christ in 1955 through reading Christian literature. The next year he, along with most Christians in India, looked forward to hearing Billy Graham during his evangelistic crusades in India.

'Imagine my excitement when I was assigned as duty officer on the flight that took Dr. Graham into Delhi!' Richard recalls. He seized the opportunity to talk with Graham about finding God's will for service. 'That was the turning point in my spiritual life', he says.

Richard later gave up the financial security of his airline job and in due course became General Secretary for the Evangelical Fellowship of India. He became first General Secretary of the Evangelical Fellowship of Asia, with Jun Vencer as Chairman and Thomas Wang as Vice-Chairman. Later, he chaired WEF's Church Renewal Commission and now assists in the AD2000 movement.

Thomas Daniel was another young man nurtured by FMPB prayer meetings. In the 90s he became principal of Serampore College, founded in West Bengal by William Carey and Joshua Marshman in 1818.[9]

The FMPB emphasis on prayer and spirituality continues as strong as ever. Their July 1995 *Friends Focus* contained a hymn written by Donald Ngoage:

Bend me, O Lord! Rend this callous heart of mine! . . .
Oh, for a heart that knows
Unceasing anguish as an intercessor,
For the five billion souls on Planet Earth!

[9] To this day, all degrees granted in India technically trace their academic validation to the royal charter granted Serampore College by the King of Denmark in 1826.

FACETS OF RENEWAL

India is but one example of spiritual renewal and its results. Mexican Pablo E. Perez, Executive Secretary of WEF's Commission on Church Renewal[10] has seen church leaders and congregations in many lands awaken to 'a closer walk with the Lord. This has also resulted in a keener perception of the Lord's demands for a church's life and witness, fulfilling its God-given task.'

The Commission published a booklet: *The Seven Facets of Renewal.*[11] Commission member David Bryant emphasized the central role of prayer through his Concerts of Prayer.

'Every evangelical alliance should promote prayer and intercession for spiritual renewal in churches', says Jun Vencer. 'This will help to equip believers in spiritual warfare.'

Bill Taylor, Director of WEF's Missions Commission, and his wife Yvonne describe the South Pacific Prayer Assembly they attended in New Zealand in 1995: 'There were no Bible expositions or sermons on prayer, but six days of prayer itself – worship, seeking God, repenting, confessing, challenging. The event was sponsored by the Evangelical Fellowship of the South Pacific and attended by some 250 people from eight island nations. There was an incredible generational, racial, cultural, and church diversity.'

Peter Kuzmic of Croatia, who became a Christian through the prayers of his father, emphasizes the role that prayer played in preserving the church under Communism.

'The church had been stripped of all earthly power and even outlawed in some countries', Kuzmic explains. 'At best, Christians were barely tolerated, and at worst, brutally persecuted. But God heard their prayers and brought down the oppressive enemy of the church.'

In contrast with the small prayer groups in Eastern Europe that often had to meet secretly, 'history's largest prayer meeting' took place on June 25, 1994. 'It involved 12 million people in 177 countries,' reported Luis Bush, International Director of AD2000 (the organizing body). 'What a blessing to be among 700,000 gathered for prayer at the Yoido Plaza in Seoul, Korea!' The historic globe-encircling prayer chain prepared the way for the Global Consultation on World Evangelism II held in May 1995 in Seoul.

---

[10]Pablo Perez retired in 1994. The work of the Commission is now part of Prayer and Renewal Ministries.

[11]D. John Richard, *The Seven Facets of Renewal* (Singapore: WEF, 1993).

PERSONAL HOLY LIVING

WEF believes that prayer should result in personal holy living, as
well as arise from it. At the Ninth General Assembly, held in Manila
in 1992, Ajith Fernando, Honorary President of the Evangelical
Alliance of Sri Lanka, preached powerful messages on holy living.

'Those who walk in the light are committed to walk transparently
before God and his people', Fernando said, preaching on 'The
Seriousness of Sin in a Believer'. He pointed out the way back to
God; he also emphasized the accountability to fellow believers that
can help keep Christian workers honest.

In the 1980s, Christians worldwide had become increasingly
concerned about the number of prominent evangelicals being en-
snared by sin. Their public confessions shook their communities.
What could be done to help strengthen Christian leaders against
temptation, of whatever nature? Did these lapses into sin indicate
wrong priorities in many a busy leader's life?

According to Charles R. Swindoll, American radio preacher and
author, the rash of moral failures during the 80s had one common
element: those who fell into sin did not have any serious kind of
accountable relationship. WEF wondered what could be done to
strengthen moral and spiritual accountability.

Bill Taylor, Missions Commission Director, in reading a *Time*
magazine cover story on Billy Graham, noted reference to 'The
Modesto Manifesto'. It outlined a covenant that Graham and his
team had made with one another in the early days of their evangelistic crusades. Graham and his organization had never been involved
in a scandal. Taylor wrote for a copy of the Manifesto and drafted
a similar covenant for WEF.

WEF International Director Jun Vencer asked Taylor to present
his draft for discussion and development at the 1994 Staff meetings
in Singapore.

THE SINGAPORE COVENANT

The result was the Singapore Covenant.[12] It commits WEF personnel
in seven specific areas of life:

1. Personal purity.
2. Spiritual discipline.
3. Family responsibility.
4. Local church involvement.

[12]See Appendix I for The Singapore Covenant in full.

5. Financial integrity.
6. Respect for other Christian organizations.
7. Honest communication.

'Lord, if you see that I am about to dishonour you, please take me home!' prayed Chairman Tokunboh Adeyemo, reflecting the attitude of all the International Council and Staff as they accepted the Covenant.

ENGAGING SOCIETY

The evangelical emphasis on personal ethics should make an impact on society itself. The history of the spiritual revivals of the 18th and 19th centuries documents this effect (see chapter 2, footnote 5, regarding the revolutionary impact of John Wesley's preaching).

'Praying together has always been the basis for the existence of the European Evangelical Alliance', states EEA General Secretary Stuart McAllister.

'However, praying together must not become a kind of "safe haven" – an end in itself – for evangelical unity', continues the former pub bouncer. 'That has always been the danger of the monastery. True prayer should result not in withdrawal from society, but in engagement with it, as the people of God.'

One example of involvement took place in the Caribbean island of St. Kitts. After a problem-filled national general election in 1992, the St. Kitts Evangelical Association (SKEA) worked with the Christian Council to develop and monitor a Code of Conduct for the next election, in 1995. The difference was like 'a wind of change', stated SKEA.

WEF believes that evangelicals have a revolutionary example to set, in a world that has largely rejected biblical ethics.

'People are tired of bankrupt philosophies', points out WEF Treasurer John Langlois, who, as a Member of the Guernsey Parliament and an international lawyer, has a world perspective on ethics. 'Some churches have been ambivalent on many ethical issues. On the other hand, there are evangelical churches that have gone overboard in extremely strict interpretations. But there is a large middle ground of Christians who hold Scripture to be the inspired word of God and seek to live by it. WEF has a network of such Christians, able to make a major impact in applying biblical standards to today's world.'

Jun Vencer quotes a letter from an Estonian schoolgirl, written a few years after the collapse of Communism:

> It has been made impossible for us youth to find our way in which is true and what is false. Teachers beg pardon and claim they have

been forced to lie. Parents confess they have brought us up with wrong principles. Everyone can disclaim his own words. But we have noticed that the churches still preach what they have preached in earlier times. Their message has been unchanging. We want to try the churches.

IMPROMPTU EUCHARIST

Once between flights, Jun Vencer and Reg Reimer found themselves together in a Hong Kong hotel room. Both were physically fatigued and emotionally drained. Vencer had just met with national fellow-ship leaders in several countries, each group with its own burdens. The needs of WEF as a whole weighed heavily on him. He was also concerned for his wife and children, having to cope so often without him.

Reimer was on his way home after meeting with pastors and members in South East Asia. Several had told him of the harassment and persecution they faced. The 'care of the churches', as the apostle Paul put it, rested heavily upon him.

'Jun shared with me his deep concern for one of his children who was struggling personally', Reg recalls. 'I could relate to that, because, like most parents, my wife and I had once faced similar concerns within our family.'

'Reg and I shed a few tears together', adds Jun.

It was late at night, but Reimer quietly slipped out and found a place where he could purchase a bottle of juice and a loaf of bread. Back in the hotel room, the two men prayed together and read the Scripture account of the Last Supper. Then they served each other the bread and juice in commemoration of the Lord's body and blood given for them.

'The burdens lifted as we remembered what Jesus Christ had borne for us,' the two men recall. 'The Holy Spirit refreshed our hearts as we ministered to each other at this impromptu Commu-nion service. Our communication with each other was changed into communion in the Spirit. In the name of our risen Saviour and Lord we could go on with the tasks God had given us – in his power and strength.'

* * * * *

'Then the two told what had happened on the way, and how Jesus was recognized by them when he broke the bread' (Luke 24:35).

CHAPTER 14: EPILOGUE

Filling a Strategic Niche

Why Evangelicals are called 'the growing edge' in every country.

Obviously there is no end of need, opportunity, and challenge for the World Evangelical Fellowship and its member bodies. As we approach the 21st century, there is also a new reality: evangelicals are now recognized as the growing edge of Christianity. That applies to the evangelical element in all kinds of denominations.[1]

British theologian Alister McGrath, principal of Wycliffe Hall, Oxford University, UK, and lecturer at Regent College, Canada, goes so far as to state: 'Evangelicalism thus provides global Christianity with a firm theological foundation and motivation for evangelism. It is no exaggeration to suggest that the future of Christianity will depend on this continuing motivation.'[2]

WHO ARE THESE IRREPRESSIBLE EVANGELICALS?

These evangelicals who keep popping up in every generation and nearly every church denomination and in every continent are – to put it simply – really just disciples of Jesus Christ. They believe the same core truths as the early disciples did. These are the truths that the 1846 Evangelical Alliance stated, and that WEF adopted in its Statement of Faith in 1951.[3]

---

[1] This was stated by the General Secretary of a mainline, worldwide denomination at an ecumenical gathering in Geneva in 1995, in the presence of the author. Researchers David Barrett and Patrick Johnstone support this view. Patrick Johnstone, *Operation World* (Carlisle: OM Publishing. 1993).

[2] Alister McGrath, *Evangelicalism and the Future of Christianity* (Downers Grove: InterVarsity Press; London: Hodder and Stoughton, 1995), p. 165.

[3] For the complete WEF Statement of Faith, see Appendix C. For a thorough treatment of evangelical beliefs, see Carl Henry and Kenneth Kantzer, Eds., *Evangelical Affirmations* (Grand Rapids: Zondervan, 1990). See also Alister McGrath, op. cit., p. 55, 56.

Understandably, evangelical beliefs are going to clash with the views of non-evangelical Christians and followers of other faiths. Preaching the cross of Christ is in itself an affront to human pride, because it asserts that men and women are sinners in need of salvation. Moreover, it states that Jesus Christ is the only way of salvation.

Little wonder, then, that reactions to evangelicals can range from benign disregard to fierce hostility. Evangelical essential truths must be expressed in love and not in arrogance. Although God uses human agencies to announce the good news of salvation, ultimately it is the work of the Holy Spirit to 'convict the world of guilt in regard to sin and righteousness and judgment' (John 16:8).

Charles Colson, President of Prison Ministries, understood the tension involved in declaring the gospel when he gave the Templeton Address for 1993.[4] At the University of Chicago, with many delegates from the pluralistic Parliament of World Religions present, he boldly stated: 'I speak as one transformed by Jesus Christ, the living God. He is the Way, the Truth, and the Life. . . . That is a claim to truth. It is a claim that may contradict your own.'

Colson then continued with appropriate logic: 'Yet on this we must agree: the right to do what I've just done – to state my faith without fear – is the first human right.'

TRUTH AND LOVE

In stating their faith, evangelicals seek to combine truth with love. 'Truth and love' became the rallying motto for the conference of 1846, at which the Evangelical Alliance was formed. That harked right back to the apostle Paul's quaint phrase, 'truthing in love'.[5]

Paul prayed for the Philippian believers, 'that your love may abound more and more in knowledge and depth of insight' (Phil. 1:9). He knew that love flowing outside the guiding channel of truth could soon lose its way in the marshes of error. A biblical

---

[4]'The Enduring Revolution,' *Sources* (Washington DC: The Wilberforce Forum) 1993. The Templeton Prize for Progress in Religion was established by philanthropist Sir John Marks Templeton, to be awarded annually to a person who has shown 'extraordinary originality in advancing humankind's understanding of God.' The recipient is invited to give the annual Templeton Address. (Charles Colson became convicted of his own need to receive Jesus Christ as Saviour while serving time for politically-motivated crimes in the USA. He has since devoted his life to sharing the gospel with prisoners worldwide.)

[5]An awkward phrase in English, but perhaps the nearest equivalent for the Greek employed by Paul in Ephesians 4:15.

world-view should lead to gracious tolerance toward people of other views. This has largely characterized Protestant society. However, tolerance, when it has taken priority over truth, has also led to harmful compromise.

Evangelicals look to the Scriptures for truth, the same truth that guided the early church. John Stott, who drafted the Lausanne Covenant, states: 'The evangelical faith is not some eccentric deviation from historic Christianity. On the contrary, in our conviction, it *is* Christianity in its purest and most primitive form.'

WHY A CHANGE IN WORLD-VIEW?

Why do evangelicals find themselves faced with unique opportunities today, when at other times they have been declared passé, if not dying out? There are numerous factors, but three are of special note:

1. The bankruptcy of secularism in a post-modern world.

Many philosophers and scientists spent the 19th century expelling God from the Garden of Humanity. For most of the 20th century much scholarship tried to make God in mankind's own image. Now, as they approach a new century, many existentialists are confused.

The philosophy of the Enlightenment, the theology of Higher Criticism, and the materialism of secularism have failed society.

The Age of Reason turned out to be the Era of Illusion. Atheistic dialectics of social revolution turned the Garden into a dust bowl. Humanism, once standing proud and impregnable, collapsed like the Berlin Wall.

Disillusioned, many thinkers of the post-modern era have come to believe that there is neither God nor Garden – there is no such thing as objective truth or meaning. Because the human soul is designed to worship in a filial relationship with God, many disillusioned people search for spirituality in any form. One indicator of this is the wide circulation of New Age literature in North America and Europe. Post-Communist Russia provides another example, as even scientists and business people turn to the occult in their quest for meaning and success in life.

The void resulting from secularism and liberalism provides an opportunity for the evangel to fill it with truth and meaning. But it will never be done by a sterile Christianity which discards truth for relativism and meaning for illusion. Absolute truth, once labelled as arrogance, now has an appealing ring to many struggling to make sense of a bankrupt world.

2. Self-destructive forces in society.

Decent communities have been shocked into realizing that humanity possesses an innate self-destructive bent. Even in nations that once felt they were on the way to becoming the Promised Land, the escalation of corruption and violence, the tyranny of unbridled power, hatred fomented by nationalism and racism, threats of nuclear terrorism – these have gripped populations with fear.

Adding to the global coronary thrombosis are the population explosion, poverty and hunger, deadly epidemics, the drug trade, environmental deterioration, and threatening economic collapse.[6]

In Europe and North America, national leaders are re-examining social philosophies that have excluded moral values. Evangelicals have preserved biblical values and constantly affirmed, through their own lives, that those values are as applicable today as they were in Moses' day.

3. The spiritual vitality of non-Western Christianity.

In the West, popular Christianity has at times become weary in defending truth or has been diverted into other pursuits, including a prosperity gospel, experiential hedonism, humanistic causes, and lust for political power.

Meanwhile, in lands once considered by the West to be 'heathen', the gospel has taken root and is flourishing. Believers are witnessing to their own people; theological scholars are enunciating eternal biblical truths, and doing so within their own cultures. Most of all, the vitality of non-Western Christianity has made the tired West sit up and listen afresh to the evangel.

Clearly, the gospel is not the product of a defunct Western imperialism; it is the timeless message of the eternal God in a changing world.

PARADIGM SHIFT

These are among the identifiable factors that have brought about a paradigm shift in world-view. Never have the factors of impending

---

[6]'Future world conflicts are likely to occur at the points of contradiction between our increasing economic and technological interdependence and our enduring religious and cultural differences', states Os Guinness, an expert on the post-modern world. From 'The Crisis of the Mandate of Heaven', *Occasional Paper* of the National Association of Evangelicals, (Wheaton, IL. Dec. 1993). See also 'The Coming Anarchy' by Robert D. Kaplan, *Atlantic Monthly*, (Feb. 1994), pp. 44–76.

social disaster and ideological bankruptcy combined to threaten humanity with potential apocalypse on such a global scale. However, 'where sin increased, grace increased all the more' (Rom. 5:20). In a world in crisis, evangelicals have a strategic niche to fill.

The Church of Jesus Christ has always possessed the powerful resources of the word of God and of prayer. But now, as never before, churches are joined in a partnership that can utilize those resources to bless the nations. There are believers among almost all cultures, constituting a network of experience and expertise. And God's people are making use of new communication tools to evangelize and disciple men, women, and children.

As the apostle Paul reminded the Ephesians, God has given spiritual gifts in the unity of the Spirit, 'to prepare God's people for works of service, so that the body of Christ may be built up until we all reach unity in the faith and in the knowledge of the Son of God . . .' (Ephesians 4:12,13).

TEMPTATIONS EVANGELICALS FACE

This is no time for triumphal celebration, however. Evangelicals, being human, face the same temptations that all men and women face: temptations presented by that notorious triad: the world, the flesh, and the Devil.

These are temptations that could sap the energy, divert the focus, damage the witness, and detract from the effectiveness of evangelicals in their moment of greatest opportunity:

POWER: Dependence on power is always a temptation. Satan even tried to tempt Jesus with an offer of power. But Jesus triumphed over Satan through the supreme act of weakness – the cross.

This is not to imply that evangelicals should remain fragmented and ineffective. That would be a twisted interpretation of the principle of the cross. The issue is one of ultimate dependence – not on human devices, people, and programmes, but on the cross of Christ. The world looks upon the preaching of the cross as foolishness (1 Cor. 1:18), but when we apply his cross to our lives and our witness, we discover the power of the Spirit.

Cuba provides a contemporary example. Fidel Castro stripped the institutional church of its power. Evangelicals had no political power to begin with, but were further marginalized by the Communist regime. Pastors were imprisoned, believers were sometimes denied employment, churches were unable to obtain permits to repair or rebuild their places of worship. But evangelicals quietly continued witnessing and practising their faith. They proved by their integrity and industry that they were trustworthy citizens –

to the point where Castro eventually urged Communist youth to emulate the work ethic of Christian youth.[7] Meanwhile, evangelical churches grew under persecution. They were made strong in weakness.

God has given WEF great strengths to use to his glory, but as soon as members rely on their own strength to gain power in society, they will fall into temptation. Instead, they must take their place at the foot of the cross, among 'the weak things of the world to shame the strong' (1 Cor.1:27,28).

PRIDE: Human pride is so subtle, we can become proud that we are humble. While rejecting the spiritual emptiness they have perceived in some forms of institutional Christendom, evangelicals can unfortunately develop a sense of spiritual elitism. Thankfulness for being among 'the called-out ones' must be accompanied by a great sense of humility. Paul, who rejoiced in his position in Christ, nevertheless reminded his converts that he had no merit in himself – only in the righteousness of Christ.

Holy living – a scriptural truth – becomes hollow hypocrisy if it is the source of pride. As the 16th century preacher John Bradford said upon seeing a criminal led to execution, 'There, but for the grace of God, goes John Bradford.'

Any tendency to take pride in our methods and means for world evangelism should be tempered by the realization that through the centuries the Holy Spirit has raised up powerful messengers of the gospel and given them prophetic ministries for their day.

CONTENTIOUSNESS: While Paul exhorted Timothy to 'fight the good fight of the faith', he also told the young pastor that 'the Lord's servant must not quarrel; instead he must be kind to everyone, able to teach, not resentful.' He was to 'pursue righteousness, godliness, faith, love, endurance, and gentleness' (1 Tim. 6:12; 2 Tim. 2:24; 1 Tim. 6:11). In facing error, God's people need to show charity, not arrogance. They also need to avoid contention over secondary matters that would sap their strength and divert their energies from the major issues of the kingdom of God.

COMPLACENCY: Evangelicals can quickly become complacent. Although many find themselves in the disadvantaged brackets of society, their emphasis on honesty, industry, and frugality tends to make them 'upwardly mobile.' (Persecution of the Huguenots arose as much from resentment of their mercantile success as from their evangelical faith.) Today there are large evangelical memberships which make little impact on their society or on a world in need, because materialism, misguided goals, and self-centred comforts have immobilized them.

[7] W. Harold Fuller, *Tie Down the Sun* (Scarborough: SIM, 1990), p. 280.

EVANGELICAL LEGALISM: Ironically, evangelicals can become as legalistic as the systems they eschew. This tendency may arise from concern for truth, but truth that is encased in narrow tradition or culture can become hardened legalism.

'What is the essence of the Christian life?' asks Henry Brglez.[8] 'Is it something we simply do for God? Calvin called that "legal worship". Or is the Christian life a gift to us to participate in the Son's communion with the Father? Unless we carefully work out what our relationship as believers to Christ is, we can very easily fall victim to a man-centred Christianity, promoting self-justification and exclusivity because we base everything on our response, not on God's initiative.'

Evangelicals must constantly resist all such temptations and tendencies, for the believer's only *raison d'etre* is Christ himself. The author of *Hebrews* warned his readers that 'we must pay more careful attention, therefore, to what we have heard, so that we do not drift away' (Heb. 2:1).

FOCUSING ON THE ESSENTIALS

Although evangelicals can trace their roots back to the disciples of Jesus Christ (and farther back to the Old Testament men and women of faith), they find themselves in a very different world. That makes the Mandate even more of a challenge: declaring age-old truths in a contemporary context. The Psalmist David, we read, 'served God's purpose in his own generation' (Acts 13:36). We must do this in our generation, as we seek to fulfil our mandates:

1. Mandate of the Word of God

Evangelicals are utilizing many communication tools available today, but they must never lose the emphasis on the word of God itself.

The apostle Paul faced privation and imprisonment, but he reminded believers that 'God's word is not chained' (2 Tim. 2:9). He asked them to pray that 'the message of the Lord may spread rapidly and be honoured' (2 Thess. 3:1).

In the British Isles, the gospel did spread rapidly after John Wycliffe and William Tyndale translated the Scriptures into the

---

[8]Brglez explores this topic in his unpublished dissertation, 'Saving Union with Christ, in the Theology of John Calvin: A Critical Study.' (University of Aberdeen, 1994).

language of the people. During Tyndale's time (1494–1536), the Chancellor of Gloucester declared that he would 'sooner have the Pope's word than God's.' Tyndale responded: 'If God spare my life, ere many years I will cause a boy that drives the plough to know more of Scripture than thou dost.'[9]

'We evangelicals are Bible people', states Stott. 'We believe that God has spoken fully and finally in his son, Jesus Christ, and in the biblical witness to Christ. We believe that Scripture is precisely the written speech of God, and that because it is God's word it has supreme authority over the church.

'The supremacy of Scripture has always been and always will be the first hallmark of an evangelical. We deplore the cavalier and sometimes even arrogant attitudes to Holy Scripture which are flaunted in the church today. We see these as derogatory to the Lord Jesus Christ, whose attitude was one of humble, reverent submission to Scripture.'[10]

2. Mandate to Proclaim the Cross of Jesus Christ

Evangelicals must recognize that they live in a pluralistic world, in which Christianity has no privileged position. However, the popular view that all religions lead to the same end is not only erroneous, but it is also presumptuous fiction to think that such a view would make Christianity more palatable to other faiths.

Even Hinduism, which is so eclectic, believes that it alone holds ultimate truth. Buddhism regards Jesus as a worthy role model, but insists that the Buddha's way (the pursuit of soullessness) is the only right way.

Rather than being intimidated by accusations of arrogance for declaring that Jesus is the only Saviour, evangelicals need to share clearly his claim: 'I am the way, and the truth, and the life. No one comes to the Father except through me' (John 14:6). This needs to be stated with conviction, not apology; but in humility, not arrogance; in love, not hostility.

---

[9]Tyndale's translation transformed the church, lay Christianity, society, and the English language. But he paid with his life for the crime of translating the Scriptures into the language of the people. He was strangled and burned in Belgium in 1536. (Four hundred years earlier, Peter Waldo had translated Scripture portions into French and Spanish dialects. His followers, the Waldensians, were brutally persecuted.)

[10]Rev. Dr. John Stott, quoted in *Who do Evangelicals think they are?* (London: Evangelical Alliance, 1993).

3. Mandate to Practise Holiness of Life

A superficial evangelicalism that does not reflect 'Christ in you, the hope of glory' (Col. 1:27), will remain weak and dishonouring to God. The gospel must demonstrate that the indwelling of the Holy Spirit is able to transform sinful human nature.

In order to keep their vitality, evangelicals must constantly seek Christ himself, and the renewal which takes place in him through the power of his Holy Spirit.

After a personal spiritual experience, the Presbyterian minister, Albert B. Simpson,[11] emphasized use of the spiritual gifts. Later he came to recognize the subtlety of the fallen nature even in the pursuit of spirituality. He summed this up in the words of a hymn:

Once it was the blessing, now it is the Lord;
Once it was the feeling, now it is his Word;
Once his gift I wanted, now the Giver own;
Once I sought for healing, now himself alone.

4. Mandate to Reach Out to the Whole World

Christ died for the world; yet most of the world's population has not understood or even heard this truth.

Evangelicals can effectively fulfil Christ's Great Commission only as they show forth their Lord and Saviour, who went about not only teaching but also touching people where they were hurting. The inborn joy of Christ's life in present-day disciples should overflow in witness and service, in word and deed. Christ's life will give evangelicals genuine concern for the problems of their world. His disciples are not disembodied spirits; they are men and women who live where others live, who sit where they sit, who suffer along with a suffering world. But they do so with a message of hope. They show forth Christ himself.

One of the most encouraging aspects of missions today is the realization that the task belongs to the church worldwide. As Aisake Kunanitu of Fiji says, 'When Jesus was on earth, we were "the ends of the earth". We are as far as you can get from Jerusalem. Now we in Fiji also want to help send the gospel to "the uttermost parts". That may mean sending missionaries to London or Jerusalem.'

[11] Albert B. Simpson, 1844-1919, was born in Canada, ministered in both Canada and the USA, and founded a missionary movement which became a church denomination: the Christian and Missionary Alliance. He was greatly influenced by the 1873 Evangelical Alliance convention in New York.

5. Mandate to Express the Unity of the Spirit

Evangelicals sometimes find themselves pressured between two
extremes: (1) Liberals,[12] who give highest priority to visible unity,
and accuse evangelicals of fostering disunity; (2) separatists, who
give highest priority to purity, and accuse non-separatist evangelicals of compromise.

Evangelicals believe it is possible – and necessary – to preserve
both unity and purity. They deplore sectarian disunity among
believers, and they recognize their oneness with all who are born
again of the Spirit – regardless of organizational labels. They are
held together not by a conciliar structure, but by the essentials of
their faith. Their spiritual unity transcends politics, geography, and
culture. In fact, their oneness in the Spirit could be called a biblical
'ecumenism.'[13]

The British revival historian, J. Edwin Orr, expressed it this way:
'The Evangelical Alliance view of Christian unity (namely that as
soon as a sinner accepts Christ as Saviour, he becomes one with all
the members of the body of Christ throughout the earth) was so
widely adopted that it led to a practice of fraternal fellowship having
the force of a major doctrine.'[14]

Mark Ellingsen, lecturer at the Institute for Ecumenical Research,
Strasbourg, France notes: 'These Christians sense themselves to have
a special kind of fellowship with others who identify themselves as
evangelical – a fellowship more intimate than evangelicals have with

[12]'Liberalism,' as used in this book, refers to theological liberalism, sometimes called
'modernism' (again, in a theological sense). Although it varies in different contexts,
its main distinctives are (a) a low view of Scripture and its authority, (b) divine
immanence (therefore little or no distinction between the natural and supernatural),
(c) willingness to adapt scriptural truths to contemporary culture, and (d) humanistic
optimism (the world will increasingly improve until it becomes in fact the kingdom
of God). Many theological liberals regard Jesus as a role model but not the unique
Son of God and Saviour of mankind. For a more complete definition, see Walter A.
Elwell, Ed., *Evangelical Dictionary of Theology* (Carlisle, UK: Paternoster Press,
Grand Rapids: Baker Book House, 1984.)

[13]Ecumenical: from Greek, 'belonging to the whole inhabited world.' The word is
neutral in itself, as is the word 'catholic' (universal). However, to many evangelicals,
both words have taken on negative connotations. Actually, the compromising
ecumenism promoted by liberal theology should be called 'liberal ecumenism' and the
worldwide oneness experienced in the Body of Christ should be called 'biblical
ecumenism.' For a study on the topic of biblical unity, see Ian M. Hay, *Unity and
Purity* (Scarborough: SIM, 1983).

[14]J. Edwin Orr, *The Second Evangelical Awakening* (London: Evangelical Alliance,
1955), p. 126.

those in their own denomination who do not identify themselves as fellow evangelicals.'[15]

International educator Ted Ward points out: 'WEF attempts to reach across the peculiarities that distinguish the many denominations and agencies, and to reach across parochial affiliations – all within a Bible-centred theological framework.'[16]

In practising such basic oneness, evangelicals have had to accept with charity each other's secondary differences. Two centuries before the formation of the Evangelical Alliance in 1846, Richard Baxter (a Church of England cleric and Puritan preacher) expressed the classic guidelines for Christian unity:

In essentials, unity;
In non-essentials, liberty;
In all things, charity.[17]

BACK TO THE CORE MANDATE

'My vision for WEF is the same one given to the church two thousand years ago – that the nations of the world should be discipled', declares Jun Vencer. 'Unfortunately, some Christians have shifted from theology to therapy, from transformation to techniques, from the absolute to the relative. The greatest need of the church is to hear once again the clear and authoritative word of God, calling her to missions. We need to recover the authority of "Thus says the Lord" and believe in the power of his word as the Spirit's sword. We must not selectively study Scripture and see only the grace of God, but also his awful judgment against sin.

'In the midst of a world in crisis, confused by religious pluralism and modernity, the church can feel overwhelmed. But I think of the Chinese character for "crisis" – it stands for problems and opportunities. Our spiritual eye must not be blinded by crisis nor be out of focus in vision for God and the lost.

[15]Mark Ellingsen, *The Evangelical Movement* (Minneapolis: Augsburg Publishing House, 1988).

[16]Ted Ward in a note to the author. Ward has been a professor at Michigan State University and Trinity Evangelical Divinity School, Deerfield, IL., USA. He has travelled widely and is known for developing the concept of Theological Education by Extension.

[17]N.H. Keeble and Geoffrey F. Nuttal, eds., *Calendar of the Correspondence of Richard Baxter, Volume I, 1638–1660* (Oxford: Clarendon Press, 1991), p. 226. Baxter borrowed his couplet from Rupertus Meldinius, a Lutheran. Both may have had in mind a similar statement made by St. Augustine: '*In veritate, unitas; In dubiis, libertas; In omnibus, caritas.*'

'Jesus said, "I will build my church and the gates of Hades shall not prevail against it." We must commit ourselves to two fundamental duties: to say YES to our true and living God alone, and to say NO to anything else. God is looking for such disciples.'[18]

INTO THE 21ST CENTURY

Evangelicals are alive and well today, not because of an organization or a creed, but because of the Spirit of Christ, who indwells them. They are interconnected in the unity of the Spirit to an extent never before realized, sharing strengths with each other, planning together, communicating. Increasingly they are equipping themselves to evangelize and disciple the nations.

In 1846 the Evangelical Alliance fulfilled the need to experience and express the unity of the Spirit. Since then, many evangelicals have been actively involved in fulfilling the mandates of Scripture. But for some, 'fellowship' has meant a comfort zone rather than front-line engagement in world evangelization, discipling, and making an impact for good on their nations.

When the apostle Paul told the Philippians that he thanked God for their 'fellowship in the gospel' (Phil. 1:5 AV), he used a word that connotes 'a joint participation in a common interest and activity.' The World Evangelical Fellowship seeks to be both unity-orientated and task-orientated. More than ever, it has moved from simply connecting Christians in fellowship, into pro-active participation in a global task.

As evangelicals enter the 21st century, they face the greatest opportunity the church has ever had to fulfil Christ's mandate to evangelize and disciple our world.

On the 150th anniversary of the vision of 1846, this is the task for the

PEOPLE OF THE MANDATE.

---

[18] For the WEF International Director's vision for WEF, see Appendix J, 'On the Vision of WEF,' August 25, 1995.

APPENDIX A

WEF Addresses

WEF International Office
141 Middle Road, 05-05 GSM Bldg.
Singapore 0718

International Director
Rev Dr Augustin (Jun) Vencer
PO Box 1294-1152
Quezon City, 1100, Philippines

Treasurer: Mr. John Langlois,
Emrais de Bas, Castel,
Guernsey, GY5 7YF UK

REGIONAL OFFICES:

Association of Evangelicals in Africa
Dr Tokunboh Adeyemo
PO Box 49332
Nairobi, Kenya

Evangelical Fellowship of Asia
Rev Francis Sunderaraj
4-1-826 JN Road
Hyderabad 500 001, India

Evangelical Fellowship of the Caribbean
Rev Gerry Seale
41 Elizabeth Park 2
Worthing, Barbados

European Evangelical Alliance
Mr Stuart McAllister
Postfach 23, A-1037
Wien, Austria

Confraternidad Evangelica Latinoamericana
Dr Ruben Poiretti
PO Box 96, Sucursal 31
1431 Buenos Aires, Argentina

Evangelical Fellowship of South Pacific
Rev Michael Maeliau
PO Box 670
Honiara, Solomon Islands

North America Office
Mr Dwight Gibson, Director,
PO Box WEF
Wheaton, IL 60189-9963

APPENDIX B

Countries with Member Organizations

AFRICA
Angola
Benin
Botswana
Burundi
Burkina Faso
Cameroun
Central African Republic
Chad
Cote d'Ivoire
Egypt
Eritrea
Ethiopia
Gambia
Ghana
Guinea
Guinea-Bissau
Kenya
Liberia
Malawi
Mali
Namibia
Nigeria
Rwanda
Senegal
Sierra Leone
South Africa
Swaziland
Tanzania
Zaire
Zambia
Zimbabwe

ASIA
Bangladesh
Cambodia
India
Indonesia
Israel
Japan
Korea
Malaysia
Myanmar
Nepal
Pakistan
Philippines
Singapore
Sri Lanka
Taiwan
Thailand

CARIBBEAN
Antigua and Barbuda
Barbados
Guyana
Grenadines and St. Vincent
Haiti
Jamaica
St. Lucia
St. Kitts
Trinidad and Tobago

EUROPE
Albania
Austria

Belgium
Bulgaria
Croatia
Cyprus
Czechoslovakia
Denmark
Estonia
Flanders
France
Germany
Greece
Hungary
Italy
Netherlands
Norway
Portugal
Romania
Serbia
Slovakia
Spain
Sweden
Switzerland
United Kingdom

LATIN AMERICA
Argentina
Bolivia
Brazil

Chile
Colombia
Costa Rica
Dominican Republic
Ecuador
El Salvador
Guatemala
Honduras
Mexico
Nicaragua
Panama
Paraguay
Peru
Puerto Rico
Uruguay
Venezuela

NORTH AMERICA
Canada
USA

SOUTH PACIFIC
Australia
Fiji
New Zealand
Papua New Guinea
Solomon Islands
Tonga

APPENDIX C

Statement of Faith of World Evangelical Fellowship

We believe in

The Holy Scriptures as originally given by God, divinely inspired, infallible, entirely trustworthy; and the supreme authority in all matters of faith and conduct;

One God, eternally existent in three persons: Father, Son, and Holy Spirit;

Our Lord Jesus Christ, God manifest in the flesh, His virgin birth, His sinless human life, His divine miracles, His vicarious and atoning death, His bodily resurrection, His ascension, His mediatorial work, and His personal return in power and glory;

The Salvation of the lost and sinful man through the shed blood of the Lord Jesus Christ by faith apart from works, and regeneration by the Holy Spirit;

The Holy Spirit, by whose indwelling the believer is enabled to live a holy life, to witness and work for the Lord Jesus Christ;

The Unity of the Spirit of all true believers, the Church, the **Body** of Christ;

The Resurrection of both the saved and the lost; they that are saved unto the resurrection of life, they that are lost unto the resurrection of damnation.

What We Are Called to Do

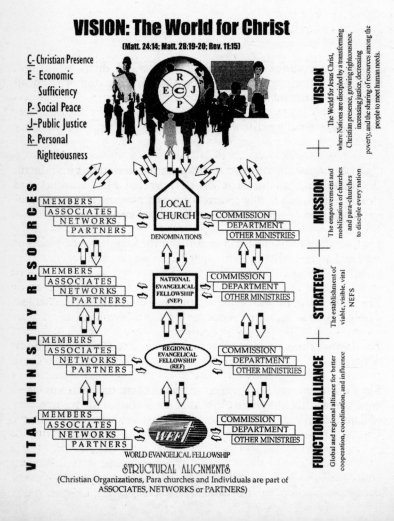

VISION: The World for Christ
(Matt. 24:14; Matt. 28:19-20; Rev. 11:15)

C- Christian Presence
E- Economic Sufficiency
P- Social Peace
J- Public Justice
R- Personal Righteousness

VISION
The World for Jesus Christ, where Nations are discipled by a transforming Christian presence, growing righteousness, increasing justice, decreasing poverty, and the sharing of resources among the people to meet human needs.

MISSION
The empowerment and mobilization of churches and para-churches to disciple every nation

STRATEGY
The establishment of viable, visible, vital NEFS

FUNCTIONAL ALLIANCE
Global and regional alliance for better cooperation, coordination, and influence

VITAL MINISTRY RESOURCES

MEMBERS
ASSOCIATES
NETWORKS
PARTNERS

LOCAL CHURCH
DENOMINATIONS

COMMISSION
DEPARTMENT
OTHER MINISTRIES

MEMBERS
ASSOCIATES
NETWORKS
PARTNERS

NATIONAL EVANGELICAL FELLOWSHIP (NEF)

COMMISSION
DEPARTMENT
OTHER MINISTRIES

MEMBERS
ASSOCIATES
NETWORKS
PARTNERS

REGIONAL EVANGELICAL FELLOWSHIP (REF)

COMMISSION
DEPARTMENT
OTHER MINISTRIES

MEMBERS
ASSOCIATES
NETWORKS
PARTNERS

WEF
WORLD EVANGELICAL FELLOWSHIP

COMMISSION
DEPARTMENT
OTHER MINISTRIES

STRUCTURAL ALIGNMENTS
(Christian Organizations, Para churches and Individuals are part of ASSOCIATES, NETWORKS or PARTNERS)

APPENDIX E

The Gospel Truth in Context

Guest editorial in The Independent, *London, England.*
August 25, 1995

The abuse of power by one Anglican priest in Sheffield no more invalidates contemporary attempts by the Church to communicate to those beyond its doors than the abuse of power by a young man at Barings Bank negates the crucial workings of the entire City of London.

Shock waves from the scandal surrounding the Nine O'Clock Service will be felt within the Church for some time. I join the Archbishop of Canterbury in praying for the victims of a tragedy that should never have been allowed to happen. But it would be a mistake to dismiss as worthless all 'alternative youth services' with their drama, video and modern music. They illustrate a centuries-old tradition in the Church of representing to each generation the unchanging message of salvation through Jesus Christ – without distorting its content.

In fact, Christianity would never have survived had it not engaged with different cultures in a way that made its message easily understood by those outside its own sub-cultural ghetto. William Booth and the Salvation Army utilized military uniforms and brass bands, John Wesley took gospel preaching into the open air; Robert Raikes and Hannah More founded the Sunday School movement. Their names are now venerated but their innovations were all fiercely attacked at the time. And let's not forget that the sound of a piano in a church service was once considered to be irreverent; an organ was positively carnal.

The evangelical movement is the fastest growing section of the Church. This is precisely because of its acknowledged ability to present the message of Christ in a way that people can clearly understand. Family services, contemporary worship and modern translations of the Bible are among developments that help support the presentation of the age-old gospel message. Of course there are dangers. Youth services and other forms of evangelism, in their attempts to be culturally appropriate, must never fall into the trap of distorting Christian teaching or of being compromised into justifying double standards.

It appears that Sheffield's Nine O'Clock Service lacked accountability. It became locked into its own ghetto, with little interface with the wider Church, while absorbing ingredients from New Age culture and the controversial Creation Spirituality that could be regarded as incompatible with the New Testament.

The problem is not one of style but content. We should employ contemporary methods to proclaim age-old truths. But we need to avoid the temptation of baptising our culture. For Christian truth has not changed. If the Church were to sacrifice its integrity and the consistency of its message, the shockwaves generated would eclipse the collapse of a thousand Barings Banks.

Rev Clive Calver,
Director General of Evangelical Alliance, UK

APPENDIX F

Letter of Apology from the Japan Evangelical Association

TO: THE EVANGELICAL FELLOWSHIP OF ASIA, OUR FRIENDS IN CHRIST

'For behold, the darkness shall cover the earth, and gross darkness the people; but the Lord shall arise upon thee, and his glory shall be seen upon thee. And the Gentiles shall come to thy light, and the kings to the brightness of thy rising' (Isa. 60:2,3AV).

The Japan Evangelical Association (JEA) today unanimously passed a resolution to apply for membership in the Evangelical Fellowship of Asia. We who are part of the Body of Christ deeply thank our Lord for the privilege of this opportunity to have a part in attesting to the unity of the Church. At the same time we are keenly aware of the fact that inviting us to join you in the common task is possible only because of the mercy of our Lord Jesus Christ and the long-suffering of the Church of Asia.

Our record as a nation in Asia in days gone by is not without blemish toward other countries of Asia. We who are members of the Church in Japan are reminded of the blame that is ours. We especially regret that in the face of national aggression and devastation of other countries, the Church of Japan was powerless and can only beg your forgiveness anew.

We who are members of God's people and part of the fellowship of the Church of our Lord Jesus Christ want to do our share in promoting the spiritual renewal of the Church and the advancement of the gospel beyond national boundaries and racial differences.

Today we cannot deny that trend in Japan is continuing which, were it not for the grace of God, could again easily cause harm to the nations of Asia quite different from that of the past.

Join in prayer that the Church in Japan may be faithful to its primary call, the proclamation of the gospel within and beyond Japan and that in so doing it may fulfill its role. This we ask in the bonds of Christ.

Japan Evangelical Association
signed by Joshua Tadashi Tsutada
June 10th, 1987.

APPENDIX G

A Simple Lifestyle: How?

Broadly speaking, Indian evangelicals, if possible, so far as it depends on them, will need to observe the following principles:

1. To evaluate all things from God's point of view;
2. To make ourselves available to anyone in need, whether material, physical or spiritual;
3. To speak up for truth and righteousness in any quarter whenever these become casualties;
4. To cause committed Christians to get involved in our country's politics and thus be heard in decision-making bodies such as State Legislatures, the Lok Sabha, etc.
5. To cause committed Christians to penetrate all strata of society, including government and commercial agencies;
6. To pay back good for evil at all times;
7. To suffer, if need be, rather than encourage social evils like dowry, bribery and corruption;
8. To engage in the ministry of encouragement and restoration;
9. To cease criticising others destructively;
10. To cease spending money on non-essentials;
11. To cut down on intake of food;
12. To practise hospitality ungrudgingly;
13. To be an example to our children in all matters that make up our lifestyle;
14. To learn to live within our means; and
15. To give faithfully to the Lord and thereby make available funds for the total work of the Church in India.

D. John Richard, All India Conference Evangelical Social Action, October 1979.

APPENDIX H

Co-operation between Evangelicals and Roman Catholics

THE BACKGROUND TO THE ECT DEBATE
– W. Harold Fuller

The document, 'Evangelicals and Catholics Together,' published by an *ad hoc* committee (not WEF) in 1994, has produced a lot of discussion – much of it helpful, some of it questionable. The statement (popularly known as ECT) was drafted and signed by individuals, not by the organizations they represent. The signers are sincere men and women, and the protesters against the document are equally sincere. The following brief analysis seeks to provide some context to the debate, and promote understanding of the positions. It does not speak to the theological concerns, which have been well addressed by others.

DIFFERING GEOGRAPHIC VIEWPOINTS

In North America, in particular, Protestants and Roman Catholics show a lot of tolerance for each other. Many Protestant leaders know Roman Catholics who are 'born again' believers and who join with Protestants in Bible studies.

Faced with public immorality and deteriorating family values in the nation, many evangelicals recognize that there are areas of community action in which they have common cause with people of other faiths. For instance, Jews, Roman Catholics, Protestants, and Muslims have taken part in protesting against community violence, pornography, and the abuse of women. Doing so together involves commonly held moral values, not doctrinal compromise.

From this irenic standpoint, some North Americans and Northern Europeans find it difficult to understand the strong reaction in other parts of the world, to proposals for evangelical-Catholic co-operation.

For instance, the Italian and Spanish Evangelical Fellowships reacted strongly when Roman Catholic observers at the WEF General Assembly in 1980 were asked by someone, unauthorized, to bring greetings. As a result, the Italians withdrew from membership of WEF for several years. This led to WEF's commissioning a task force to draft biblical guidelines on co-operation.

Similarly, Latin American delegates to the Global Consultation on World Evangelism (not WEF sponsored) held in Singapore in 1989 threatened to walk out when Roman Catholics were welcomed to participate in discussions.

Some conference convenors, especially those from North America, found their reaction difficult to understand. They argued that these Roman Catholics were evangelical individuals. It seemed petulant not to welcome them. But Latin American delegates saw them as part of a powerful, hostile system with which they could not collaborate without compromising their churches at home.

'We recognize the work of the Holy Spirit in the life of non-protestant/non-evangelical people and churches', they stated. 'However, we cannot co-operate with the structures they represent. In our Ibero-American continent, the religious-political force of the Catholic Church is the most fierce opponent to all evangelistic efforts on our part.

'To the present day, Ibero-American Catholicism is incompatible with our evangelistic vision. Mary more than ever holds the first place in the faith, tradition supersedes the Bible, salvation by works is placed over the finished work of the Lord Jesus Christ on Calvary. . . .'

At the same conference, Filipino evangelicals had similar reactions. They knew that a Roman Catholic bishop had recently viciously attacked 'born-again fundamentalists' in a pastoral letter widely quoted in the Filipino press.

THE WIDER IMPLICATIONS

Some critics of the ECT document felt that although the co-signers had the best of motives, several had lost sight of wider implications. Most evangelicals have no problem in fellowshipping with born-again Roman Catholics on a personal basis. However, they point out that official Roman Catholic dogma has not changed in several key areas, preventing joint evangelism.

The increasing incidence of individual Roman Catholics becoming evangelicals – 'born again' believers – is partly due to the decreasing authoritative control of Roman Catholic dogma over many of its members. Difficult though it may be for some Protestant evangelicals to understand, individual Roman Catholics who experience salvation through personal faith in Jesus Christ, may choose to stay within the Roman church as a cultural community. How can they do that without contradicting their new biblical faith? They simply disregard unbiblical church dogmas.

In fact, this 'cafeteria approach' to religion (selecting aspects that appeal, while rejecting others) seems to be a phenomenon of Western society. It affects Protestants as well as Roman Catholics, and no doubt contributes to shallowness of faith.

As British theologian Alister McGrath explains, 'Many Roman Catholics, especially in the United States, remain outwardly and publicly loyal to their church, while inwardly and privately they embrace the leading ideas of evangelicalism.'

Veteran theologian Carl F. H. Henry recognizes the large number of Catholics, including some priests, who are 'embracing justification through grace alone, by faith alone', but he points out that this is done privately and that 'Rome views her dogmatic formulations as infallible'.

'In the light of the contemporary pressures for Christian traditions to form a united front against the encroaching anarchy of moral relativism, certain fundamental questions must be considered long and hard: Is unity more important than doctrinal fidelity on an issue [Justification – Ed.] that appeared neither in the classic ecumenical creeds nor in the "five points" of American fundamentalism? . . . Dare we disregard the apostle Paul's warning to the Galatians?'

Some critics of the ECT statement feel it was signed from the idealistic and comfortable viewpoint of North America, where leaders of various faiths frequently work together on community projects. North America's tolerance is far removed from the hostility of nations where Catholics and Protestants are engaged in pitched battles – actual or figurative.

Evangelicals who are struggling to survive in the face of hostile Catholicism may look upon the ECT concept as some kind of North American arrogance. 'Co-belligerency' (joint action, including evangelism, by evangelicals and Catholics) may seem like a North American luxury.

A DIFFERENT CATHOLICISM

Latin American evangelicals felt the pain when Catholic priests circulated copies of the ECT statement to convince villagers that Catholics and evangelicals really are one. But people who understand history are keenly aware that Catholicism in South America is far different from Roman Catholicism in North America.

An indication of this difference is found in the fact that traditional South American Catholics do not call themselves 'Roman.' They are Iberian Catholics – a Catholicism that was imported from the Iberian Peninsula (Spain and Portugal). It had not benefited from the moderating effect of the Reformation which influenced Roman Catholics in Northern Europe. Instead, it was shaped by the moribund fatalism and cruel intolerance of the Muslim invasion of Iberia.

This was the 'Christian' faith that Spanish and Portuguese Catholic priests took to South America five hundred years ago. The indigenous peoples of the continent were subjected not only to the violent greed of the Conquistadors, but also to the brutality of the Spanish Inquisition. Protestants were considered enemies of the Iberian Catholic Church and were banished, imprisoned, or killed. Until the early part of this century, preaching by evangelicals was punishable by death. Even today, Catholic priests, where they retain power, harass Latin evangelicals in an attempt to suppress them.

Latin American believers felt that this suppression was encouraged as recently as Pope John Paul II's tour of Latin America in 1994. The Pontiff warned about the 'rapacious wolves' of 'sects' – a term used in Latin America to include evangelicals.

This gives background to the reaction, especially in the Two-Thirds World, to the document, 'Evangelicals and Catholics Together.' The commentary issued by Dr. A. Jun Vencer on behalf of WEF keeps the theological and practical concerns in mind.

– W. Harold Fuller

'Commentary on Evangelicals and Catholics Together'

Dr. Jun Vencer, WEF, January 31, 1995

I was speaking at an Alliance men's breakfast in Manila when, during the open forum, someone asked about WEF's position on the 'Evangelicals and Catholics Together: The Christian Mission in the Third Millennium' (ECT). Earlier than that some colleagues in North America asked me the same question. Let me share my observations.

It is tragic when evangelicals begin to aim their 'polemical rifles' at each other rather than the enemy. In this instance, let it be said that the target is not the persons but the issues. The issues raised by the ECT have resulted in division and tension among evangelicals in the United States and even beyond. The presence of respected and renowned evangelicals who signed and endorsed the Agreement carried weight and gave a wider coverage than may have been intended. The use of the generic term 'evangelicals' presumed a consensus beyond the signatories or their organizations. Since they did not represent the other evangelical denominations, churches and organizations, the reactions become understandable.

I agree that evangelicals should re-engage society. The evangelicals can engage in critical collaboration with other religious faiths to make a common stand on socio-political issues such as religious liberty, injustice and oppression, abortion, women and child abuse, pornography, and homosexuality. Isolationism is not an evangelical option. These collaborations are being done by many national evangelical fellowships whether they be in North America, in the United Kingdom, in Malaysia or the Philippines. These united actions against evils that undermine Christian values in society or deny human dignity are even desired especially in countries where the evangelicals are in the minority, are marginalized by their governments, or persecuted by majority groups. Such evangelical collaboration must not in any way compromise doctrines or surrender biblical positions to the rule of the majority in such a coalition. The freedom to dissent must be safeguarded.

The context of the ECT is too culture-specific, i.e. Roman Catholicism in North America. The assumption that the attitudes and practices of the Catholic participants are also that of most Catholics in the United States or in other parts of the world is certainly unwarranted. Is the example of a few also the experience of the many? Catholic relationships with evangelicals vary from country to country. It can range from cordiality to persecution.

The scope of the Agreement, moreover, went beyond social activism to evangelism. This is where much of the negative criticisms come from. This is also the most sensitive because reality admits exceptions. But, in general, if culture wars can allow 'ecumenism on the trenches' does it justify evangelicals and Catholics doing evangelism and missions together? The critical issue really is the doctrinal differences between the two that remain unresolved and must not be denied or underplayed. The use of a common religious language does not mean that the meanings are the same. There are reasons to believe that they are not and have not changed since the Reformation. Can the two partner in missions together if they don't have the same authority and message of salvation? Care must be done so that the pragmatics of united action in socio-ethical issues should not obscure the theological differences or confuse our constituencies. Let the theologians continue the process of discussions towards a vision of a common doctrinal orthodoxy, if it is possible.

Until then, I voted for the approval by the WEF 1986 General Assembly of the report of the Ecumenical Issues Task Force of the Theological Commission concluding, 'We are constrained by the commission of our Lord (2 Cor. 5:18–20) and by the love of Christ (2 Cor. 5:14) to proclaim the gospel to all people, including those who are Roman Catholic.'

– Agustin (Jun) Vencer, January 31, 1995

The Singapore Covenant

World Evangelical Fellowship

WEF MISSION STATEMENT:

The World Evangelical Fellowship and member organizations exist to establish and help regional and national evangelical alliances empower and mobilize local churches and Christian organizations to disciple the nations for Christ.

In dependence upon the Holy Spirit, fully identified with World Evangelical Fellowship, supporting its mission statement, and in sincere inter-dependent partnership with each other as vital members of the WEF family, we the staff members solemnly affirm these commitments before the Triune God.

1. We commit ourselves to personal purity. We affirm the need for vital personal growth in Christ, with transparency before God and our colleagues. Integrity, holiness must mark our personal walk with God. These are intimate matters, but at the same time we can and must submit them to scrutiny by loving and honest colleagues. We will establish a personal team of fellow servants who will call us to authentic accountability in our private, family and public worlds. When necessary we will submit to and support restorative discipline.

2. We commit ourselves to the spiritual disciplines. We confess that as Christian leaders we have given too little time to prayer and the Word, and we ask God's forgiveness for this inconsistency. We as WEF staff desire that our ministry be marked by personal godliness, not only by competency, strategic thinking, and effective programmes. We pledge to encourage and challenge each other, by sharing articles and books that have impacted us directly, by praying for each other and by informing each other that we do so pray.

3. We commit ourselves to our family. We affirm that parents and/or spouse and children are our initial responsibility. May our

ministry not be at their expense, producing bitterness, but rather resulting in love and respect. We will seek to maintain a balance between family and ministry to others. We shall submit our travel schedules to our spouses as well as to our accountability team.

4. We commit ourselves to a local church. We will seek opportunities for witness and service according to our gifts and time. We will model in our local churches what we in WEF desire to see built in the worldwide Body of Christ.

5. We commit ourselves to financial integrity. We accept our responsibility as stewards of God's resources, and will act with honesty as we raise, use and account for funds. We will open our personal financial records to trusted colleagues. Our corporate financial books can be evaluated by those who have valid need to do so.

6. We commit ourselves to respect other Christian organizations and leaders. We seek to build up the Body of Christ! We confess that too easily we can belittle others. We wish to be characterized as a movement that genuinely affirms other leaders and the ministries they serve. Where there is error, however, we will speak the truth in love.

7. We commit ourselves to honest communication. We will report stories and statistics accurately, without embellishment. We shall give credit to the individuals and organizations involved.

We covenant that our lives and ministry will by God's grace exemplify Scripture: 'You are witnesses, and so is God, of how holy, righteous and blameless we were among you who believed' (1 Thess 2:10).

To the greater glory of our God and in anticipation of that magnificent, ongoing worship scene in heaven.

Signed in Singapore, July 5, 1994.
Endorsed by WEF International Council

APPENDIX J

On The Vision of WEF

Dr A. Jun Vencer, WEF, August 25, 1995

The *vision* of WEF is to see the world reached for Christ. It is to disciple every nation where there is a vital Christian witness, justice for all, diminishing poverty among the poor, and where lasting peace is enjoyed by people.

The *mission* of WEF is the total mobilization of churches and Christian organizations to work together and to share resources in discipling every nation for Jesus Christ. This *bayanihan* is consistent with the Lord's prayer that 'they all may be one . . . that the world may believe.'

The *strategy* of WEF is the national evangelical fellowship that is controlled by the national churches and organizations themselves. Our task is to assist, wherever possible, in the development of a viable, visible and vital fellowship that will provide a national vision and voice for God's people.

WEF provides the global egalitarian network for all evangelical churches and organizations particularly through their regional and national evangelical fellowships to proclaim the whole gospel to the whole man to the whole community in every nation in the world. Our goal is to establish 237 viable and vital national evangelical fellowships in the world. Does this mean simply the development of structures? Certainly not! If we can stretch our imagination, think in terms of 237 national missions associations, 237 national church growth strategies, 237 national prayer and renewal networks, 237 theological associations, 237 national relief and development agencies, 237 leadership and institutional development institutes, 237 national religious liberty commissions, 237 specialized ministries – women, youth, retired citizens, family, etc. – all working in concert and as a global network for Christ! I believe that WEF is going to be a critical force to transform nations for Christ. It is worth living for.

– A. Jun Vencer, 1995

Select Bibliography

ADEYEMO, Tokunboh. *The Making of a Servant of God*. (Nairobi: Christian Learning Materials Centre, 1993).

ALLAN, J.D., ed. *The Evangelicals*. (Carlisle, UK: Paternoster Press. Grand Rapids: Baker Book House, 1989).

ALLAN, J.D. *Who do Evangelicals think they are?* (London: Evangelical Alliance, 1993).

ANDERSON, Gerald H., COOTE, Robert T., HORNER, Norman H., PHILLIPS, James M. eds. *Mission Legacies*. (Maryknoll: Orbis Books, 1994).

ANDERSON, Ken. *Bold as a Lamb*. (Grand Rapids: Zondervan Publishing House, 1991).

BEYER, Werner. *Einheit in der Vielfalt*. (R. Brockhaus Verlag Wuppertal, 1995).

BIRD, John L., *England a Mission Field*. (London: Evangelical Alliance, 1963).

BOCKMUEHL, Klaus. *Evangelicals and Social Ethics*. (Downers Grove: InterVarsity Press, 1975).

BORTHWICK, Paul. *Youth and Missions*. (Wheaton: Scripture Press, 1988).

BORTHWICK, Paul. *Feeding Your Forgotten Soul*. (Grand Rapids: Zondervan, 1990).

BOSCH, David J., *Transforming Mission*. (Maryknoll: Orbiss Books, 1991).

BRADSHAW, Bruce. *Bridging the Gap*. (Monrovia, CA: MARC, 1993).

BRIGHT, Bill. *A Movement of Miracles*. (San Bernardino, CA: Campus Crusade for Christ International, 1977).

BRYANT, David. *A Call for Concerts of Prayer*. (Madison, Wis: Inter-Varsity Missions. 1984).

BURKHARDT, Helmut. *The Biblical Doctrine of Regeneration*. (Downers Grove: InterVarsity Press, 1974).

BUSH, Luis. *Funding Third World Missions*. (Singapore: World Evangelical Fellowship Missions Commission, 1990).

BUTTERFIELD, Herbert. *Writings on Christianity & History*. (New York: Oxford Press, 1979).

CAMERON, Nigel M. de S., ed. *The Challenge of Evangelical Theology*. (Edinburgh: Rutherford House Books, 1987).

CARSON, D.A., ed. *Biblical Interpretation and the Church: Text and Context*. (Carlisle, UK: Paternoster Press, Grand Rapids: Baker Book House, 1984).

CARSON, D.A., ed. *The Church in the Bible and the World*. (Carlisle, UK: Paternoster Press, Grand Rapids: Baker Book House, 1987).

CARSON, D.A., ed. *Teach Us to Pray*. (Carlisle, UK: Paternoster Press, Grand Rapids: Baker Book House, 1990).

CARSON, D.A. *The Gagging of God*. (Grand Rapids: Wm. B. Eerdmans Publishing, 1996).

CHAO, Jonathan, ed. *The China Mission Handbook*. (Hong Kong: Chinese Church Research Center, 1989).

CHERRY, W.H. *Outstretched Hands*. (London: Ceylon and India General Mission, 1960).

CHESTERTON, G.K. *Orthodoxy*. (Garden City, NY: Image Books, 1959).

CHILTON, David. *Productive Christians in an Age of Guilt Manipulators*. (Tyler, TX: Institute for Christian Economics, 1981).

CHO, David J., ed. *The Third Force*. (Seoul: East-West Center for Missions, 1976).

CUNNINGHAM, William. *The Reformers and the Theology of the Reformation*. (Edinburgh: Banner of Truth Trust, 1862).

DOUGLAS, J.D., ed. *Let the Earth Hear His Voice*. (Minneapolis: World Wide Publications, 1975).

DOWLEY, Tim, ed. *The History of Christianity*. (Grand Rapids: Wm. B. Eerdmans Publishing Co., 1977).

DRAKE, Michael, ed. *Time, Family and Community*. (Oxford: Blackwell Publishers, 1994).

DUEWEL, Wesley L. *Mighty Prevailing Prayer*. (Grand Rapids: Francis Asbury Press, 1990).

DUEWEL, Wesley. *Revival Fire*. (Grand Rapids: Zondervan Publishing House, 1993).

EDWARDS, David L., *Evangelical Essentials*. (Downers Grove: InterVarsity Press, 1988).

EGERTON, George, ed. *Anglican Essentials*. (Toronto: Anglican Book Centre, 1995).

ELLINGSEN, Mark. *The Evangelical Movement*. (Minneapolis: Augsburg Publishing House, 1988).

ELWELL, Walter A., ed, *Evangelical Dictionary of Theology*, (Carlisle, UK: Paternoster Press, Grand Rapids: Baker Book House, 1984).

ESHLEMAN, Paul. *I Just Saw Jesus*. (San Bernardino, CA: Campus Crusade for Christ, 1985).

EWING, John W. *Goodly Fellowship*. (London: Marshall, Morgan & Scott, Ltd., 1946).

FIEDLER, Klaus. *The Story of Faith Missions*. (Oxford: Regnum Books, 1994).

FRIZEN, Jr., Edwin L. *75 Years of IFMA 1917–1992). (Pasadena: William Carey Library, 1992).

FULLER, W. Harold. *Mission-Church Dynamics*. (Pasadena: William Carey Library, 1980).

FULLER, W. Harold. *Tie Down the Sun*. (Scarborough: SIM International Media, 1990).

GILLARD. *In the Name of Charity*. (London: Chatto and Windus, 1987).

GNANAKAN, Ken. *Ken Gnanakan: Still Learning*. (Bangalore: ACTS Trust, 1993).

GUINNESS, Os. *Fit Bodies Fat Minds*. (Carlisle, UK: Paternoster Press, Grand Rapids: Baker Books, 1994).

GUNDRY, Stanley N., JOHNSON, Alan F. eds. *Tensions in Contemporary Theology*. (Chicago: Moody Press, 1976).

HARLEY, David. *Preparing to Serve*. (Pasadena: William Carey Library, 1995).

HAY, Ian M. *Unity and Purity: Keeping the Balance*. (Scarborough: SIM, 1983).

HEFLEY, James and Marti. *By Their Blood*. (Milford, MI: Mott Media, 1979).

HENRY, Carl F.H. *God, Revelation, and Authority*. (Waco: Word Books. 1976–1983).

HENRY, Carl F. H. *Confessions of a Theologian*. (Waco: Word Books, 1986).

HENRY, Carl F.H. *Carl Henry at His Best*. (Portland: Multnomah Press, 1989).

HENRY, Carl F.H. and KANTZER, Kenneth, eds. *Evangelical Affirmations*. (Grand Rapids: Zondervan, 1990).

HOUSTON, Tom. *Scenario 2000*. (Monrovia, CA: MARC, 1992).

HOWARD, David M. *The Dream That Would Not Die*. (Carlisle, UK: Paternoster Press, Grand Rapids: Baker Book House, 1986).

HOWARD, David M. *The Elusive Dream*. (Carlisle, UK: Paternoster Press, Grand Rapids, Baker Book House, 1989).

HUGHES, Philip E. *Christian Ethics in Secular Society*. (Carlisle, UK: Paternoster Press, Grand Rapids: Baker Book House, 1983).

JOHNSTON, Arthur. *The Battle for World Evangelism*. (Wheaton: Tyndale House Publishers, Inc. 1978).

JOHNSTONE, Patrick. *Operation World*. (Carlisle: OM Publishing, Grand Rapids: Zondervan Publishing House. 1993).

KATO, Byang H. *Theological Pitfalls in Africa.* (Kisumu, Kenya: Evangel Publishing House, 1975).

KATO, Byang H. *African Cultural Revolution and the Christian Faith.* (Jos: Challenge (SIM), 1975).

KATO, Byang H. *Biblical Christianity in Africa.* (Achimota: African Christian Press, 1985).

KEATING, M. 'The Stolen Generation' in *Pastoral Renewal.* (May 1987.

KEEBLE, N.H., NUTTAL, G.F., eds., *Calendar of the Correspondence of Richard Baxter, Vol. 1, 1638–1660.* (Oxford: Clarendon Press, 1991).

KENDALL, Elliott. *The End of an Era.* (London: SPCK, 1978).

KESSLER, J.B.A. *A Study of the Evangelical Alliance in Great Britain.* (Netherlands: Oosterbaan & Le Cointre N.V., 1968).

KIRBY, Gilbert W. *Why All These Denominations?* (Eastbourne, UK: Kingsway Publications, 1988).

KIRK, J. Andrew. *Theology & the Third World.* (Downers Grove: InterVarsity Press, 1983).

KRAAKEVIK, James H., WELLIVER, Dotsey, eds. *Partners in the Gospel.* (Wheaton: Billy Graham Center, 1994).

LAMBERT, Tony. *The Resurrection of the Chinese Church.* (Wheaton: Harold Shaw Publishers, 1994).

LATOURETTE, Kenneth Scott. *A History of Christianity*, Vol. I and II. (New York: Harper & Row, Publishers, 1975).

LEFEVER, Ernest. *An Autobiography.* (New York: Simon and Schuster, 1996).

LEWIS, Jonathan, ed. *Working Your Way to the Nations: A Guide to Effective Tentmaking.* (Pasadena: William Carey Library, 1993).

LEWIS, Norm. *Priority One.* (Orange, CA: Promise Publishing Co., 1988).

MANGALWADI, Vishal. Missionary Conspiracy – Letters to a Postmodern Hindu. (Mussoorie: Nivedit Good Books, 1996).

MATTHEWS, Arthur H. *Standing Up, Standing Together.* (Carol Stream: National Association of Evangelicals, 1992).

MBUGUA, Judy, ed. *Our Time Has Come.* (Carlisle, UK: Paternoster Press, Grand Rapids: Baker Book House, 1994).

McGRATH, Alister. *Evangelicalism & the Future of Christianity.* (Downers Grove: InterVarsity Press, 1995).

McMAHON, Robert J. *To God Be The Glory.* (New Delhi: Masihi Sahitya Sanstha, 1970).

MEEKING, Basil, and STOTT, John, eds. *The Evangelical-Roman Catholic Dialogue on Mission 1977–1984.* (Carlisle, UK: Paternoster Press, 1986).

METCALFE, John. *The Church, What is it?* (Penn Buckinghamshire, UK: John Metcalfe Publishing Trust, 1990).

MOFFETT, Samuel Hugh. *A History of Christianity in Asia.* (San Francisco: Harper, 1992).

MOORE, James R., ed. *Religion in Victorian Britain, III Sources.* (Manchester: Manchester University Press, 1988).

MOTZ, Arnell, ed. *Reclaiming a Nation.* (Richmond: Church Leadership Library, 1990).

MULLIN, Redmond. *The Wealth of Christians.* (Carlisle, UK: Paternoster Press, 1983).

MYERS, Bryant L. *The Changing Shape of World Mission.* (Monrovia: MARC, 1993).

NEILL, Stephen. *A History of Christian Missions.* (Hammondsworth, UK: Penguin Books, 1982).

NEILL, Stephen, ANDERSON, Gerald, GOODWIN, John, eds. *Concise Dictionary of the Christian World Mission.* (London: United Society for Christian Literature, 1970).

NEWBIGIN, Lesslie. *The Open Secret.* (Grand Rapids: Wm. B. Eerdmans Publishing Co., 1978).

NICHOLLS, Bruce J., ed. *Church and Nationhood.* (New Delhi: Statesman Press, 1978).

NICHOLLS, Bruce J. *Contextualization: A Theology of Gospel and Culture.* (Downers Grove: InterVarsity Press, 1979).

NICHOLLS, Bruce J. *In Word & Deed.* (Carlisle, UK: Paternoster Press, 1985).

NICHOLLS, Bruce J. *The Unique Christ in our Pluralist World.* (Carlisle, UK: Paternoster Press, Grand Rapids: Baker Book House, 1994).

NICHOLLS, Bruce J., WOOD, B., eds., *Sharing the Good News with the Poor.* (Carlisle, UK: Paternoster Press, 1996).

NOELLISTE, Dieumeme. *Toward a Theology of Theological Education.* (Seoul: WEF Theological Commission, 1993).

OFFER, Daniel. *The Teenage World.* (New York: Plenum Press, 1988).

ORR, J. Edwin. *The Flaming Tongue.* (Chicago: Moody Press, 1973).

ORR, J. Edwin. *The Fervent Prayer.* (Chicago: Moody Press, 1974).

ORR, J. Edwin. *The Fervent Feet.* (Chicago: Moody Press, 1975).

ORR, J. Edwin. *The Second Evangelical Awakening.* (London: Evangelical Alliance, 1955).

PACKER, J.I. *'Fundamentalism' and the Word of God.* (Grand Rapids: Wm. B. Eerdmans Publishing Co., 1958, 1985).

PALAU, Luis. *Calling America and the Nations to Christ.* (Nashville: Thomas Nelson Publishers, 1994).

PARRINDER, Geoffrey, ed. *World Religions From Ancient History to the Present.* (New York: Facts on File Publications, 1971).

PHILLIPS, James M., COOTE, Robert T. *Toward the 21st Century*

Christian Mission. (Grand Rapids: Wm. B. Eerdmans Publishing, 1993).

PRANGE, Gordon W. *God's Samurai.* (Washington: Brassey's (US) Inc., 1990).

RAWLYCK, George. *Is Jesus Your Personal Saviour?* (Kingston: Queens University Press, 1996).

REID, Daniel G. *Dictionary of Christianity in America.* (Downers Grove: InterVarsity Press, 1990).

RICHARD, John D. *The Seven Facets of Renewal.* (Singapore: WEF, 1993).

RO, Bong Rin, ed. *Christian Alternatives to Ancestor Practices.* (Taiwan: Asia Theological Association, 1985).

RO, Bong Rin, ed. *Christian Suffering in Asia.* (Taiwan: Asia Theological Association, 1989).

RO, Bong Rin, ed. *Evangelical Christianity and the Environment.* (Seoul: WEF Theological Commission, 1993).

RO, Bong Rin, ed. *An Evangelical Response to Confessing the One Faith.* (Seoul: WEF Theological Commission, 1993).

RO, Bong Rin, ALBRECHT, Mark C., eds. *God In Asian Contexts.* (Taiwan: Asia Theological Association, 1988).

RO, Bong Rin, ESHENAUR, Ruth, eds. *The Bible & Theology in Asian Contexts.* (Taiwan: Asia Theological Association, 1984).

ROBINSON, John A.T., *Christian Freedom in a Permissive Society.* (London: SCM Press, 1970).

ROUSE, Ruth, NEILL, Stephen, eds. *A History of the Ecumenical Movement.* (Geneva: World Council of Churches, 1954).

SAMUEL, Vinay, SUGDEN, Chris, eds. *The Church in Response to Human Need.* (Grand Rapids: Wm. B. Eerdmans Publishing Company, 1987).

SCHLOSSBERG, Herbert. *Idols for Destruction.* (Nashville: Thomas Nelson Publishers, 1983).

SCHROTENBOER, Paul G., ed. *Roman Catholicism, A Contemporary Evangelical Perspective.* (Grand Rapids: Baker Book House, 1987).

SCOTT, Waldron, ed. *Serving Our Generation.* (Colorado Springs: WEF, 1980).

SCOTT, Waldron. *Bring Forth Justice.* (Grand Rapids: Wm. B. Eerdmans Publishing Co., 1980).

SIDER, Ronald J., ed. *Lifestyle in the Eighties.* (Philadelphia: The Westminster Press, 1982).

SIDER, Ronald J. *Rich Christians in an Age of Hunger.* (Downers Grove: InterVarsity Press, 1978).

SIGSWORTH, John Wilkins. *World Changers.* (Stirling, ON: Easingwold Publications, 1982).

SINE, Tom, ed. *The Church in Response to Human Need*. (Monrovia, CA: MARC, 1983).

SOOKHDEO, Patrick, ed. *New Frontiers in Mission*. (Carlisle, UK: Paternoster Press, 1987).

STACKHOUSE Jr., John G. *Canadian Evangelicalism in the Twentieth Century*. (Toronto: University of Toronto Press, 1993).

STILLER, Brian. *A Generation Under Siege*. (Wheaton: Victor Books, 1983).

STILLER, Brian C. *Critical Options for Evangelicals*. (Markham: Faith Today Publications, Evangelical Fellowship of Canada, 1991).

STILLER, Brian C. *From the Tower of Babel to Parliament Hill*. (Toronto: HarperCollins, 1996).

STOTT, John R.W. *God's New Society*. (Downers Grove: Inter-Varsity Press, 1979).

STOWELL, Joseph M. *Shepherding the Church into the 21st Century*. (USA: Victor Books, 1994).

TAN, Kim-Sai. *The Great Digression*. (Malaysia: Malaysia Bible Seminary, 1981).

TAYLOR, William D., ed. *Kingdom Partnerships for Synergy in Missions*. (Pasadena: William Carey Library, 1994).

VAN GEEST, William. *God's Earthkeepers*. (Canada: EFC, 1995).

VARGHESE, Abraham. *The Intellectuals Speak out about God*. (Dallas: Lewis and Stanley, 1984).

VENCER, Jun. *Your Gifts From God*. (Leadership Development Institute, 1986).

VENCER, Jun., ALLAN, J.D. *Poor is No Excuse*. (Carlisle, UK: Paternoster Press, 1989).

VENCER, Jun. *The World for Jesus Christ: A Primer for Leaders of National Evangelical Fellowships*. (Singapore: WEF, 1994)

WAGNER, C. Peter. *Church Growth and the Whole Gospel*. (San Francisco: Harper & Row, Pub. 1981).

WAGNER, C. Peter. *On the Crest of the Wave*. (Ventura, CA: Regal Books, 1983).

WALLSTROM, Timothy C. *The Creation of a Student Movement to Evangelize the World*. (Pasadena: William Carey International University Press, 1980).

WAYMIRE, Bob, WAGNER, C. Peter. *The Church Growth Survey Handbook*. (Santa Clara, CA: OC Ministries, Inc., 1980).

WEF. *Focus on Frontier. Evangelism – Our Theology and Practice*. (New Delhi: Evangelical Theological Commission of the Evangelical Fellowship of India, 1966).

WEF. *An Evangelical Agenda – 1984 and Beyond*. (Pasadena, William Carey Library, 1979).

WEF. *Student Mission Power*. (Pasadena: William Carey Library, 1979).

WILLIAMS, Theodore, ed. *World Missions – Building Bridges or Barriers*. (Bangalore: WEF, 1979).

WILSON, J. Christy, Jr. *Today's Tentmakers*. (Wheaton: Tyndale House, 1979).

WISEMAN, Ray. *I Cannot Dream Less*. (Brampton: Partners International, 1993).

WOLFFE, John, 'The Evangelical Alliance in the 1840s: An Attempt to Institutionalise Christian Unity,' in *Voluntary Religion*; (London: The Ecclesiastical History Society, 1986), pp. 333–346).

WRAITH, Ronald, SIMPKINS, Edgar. *Corruption in Developing Countries*. (London: George Allen & Unwin Ltd, 1963).

YAMAMORI, Tetsunao, *God's New Envoys*. (Portland: Multnomah Press, 1987).

YANCEY, Philip. *Praying with the KGB*. (Portland: Multnomah Press, 1992).

Index

GOSHEN COLLEGE - GOOD LIBRARY

3 9310 01008700 3

DATE DUE

		WITHDRAWN	

GAYLORD   PRINTED IN U.S.A.